A Tale of Two Worlds:
Why Contemporary Western Culture Contends against Christian Faith

J. Andrew Kirk

Kingdom Publishers

Copyright© J. Andrew Kirk 2023

All rights reserved. No part of this book may be reproduced in any form by photocopying or any electronic or mechanical means, including information storage or retrieval systems, without permission in writing from both the copyright owner and the publisher of the book. The right of J. Andrew Kirk to be identified as the author of this work has been asserted by him in accordance with the Copyright, Designs and Patents Act 1988 and any subsequent amendments thereto.

A catalogue record for this book is available from the British Library.

All Scripture Quotations have been taken either from the New Revised Standard Version or from the New International Version of the Bible.

ISBN: 978-1-911697-99-2

1st Edition 2023 by Kingdom Publishers, London, UK.

You can purchase copies of this book from any leading bookstore or email **contact@kingdompublishers.co.uk**

Endorsements

■ J. Andrew Kirk - *A Tale of Two Worlds: Why Contemporary Western Culture Contends against Christian Faith*

Professor J. Andrew Kirk is a well-respected Christian theologian and missiologist who has written a series of important books on how Christians should understand and engage with contemporary culture. His new book *A Tale of Two Worlds* focusses on the contrast between the beliefs and values prevalent in the contemporary world, as exemplified by the three issues of abortion, same-sex relationships and transgender, and the message about the coming new world proclaimed by Jesus and witnessed to by Scripture. Kirk emphasises that the difference between the two results from having a human centred or a God centred view of the world and that the three issues on which he focusses make clear that a human centred view of the world has failed to deliverer the liberty and justice promised by the advocates of a post-Christian society in the second half of the twentieth century. This is a very valuable study that will be extremely helpful to anyone seeking to understand the three contemporary issues Kirk highlights from a Christian perspective, and to anyone who wants to understand how Jesus' message about the coming of the new world offers a compelling alternative to the values of modern secular society.

Martin Davie,
Dr Martin Davie is a theological consultant to the Church of England Evangelical Council (CEEC). From 2000-2013 he was the Theological Secretary to the Church of England for Christian Unity, Theological Consultant Council for Christian Unity, Theological Consultant to the house of Bishops, and Secretary of the Faith and Order Commission.

■ This is an eye-opening, heart-lifting and hugely helpful book. J. Andrew Kirk has given us a masterclass into how to approach three of the most contentious issues in Western societies, underpinning it with a deft presentation of the core beliefs of both the prevailing world-view and of biblical Christian faith. The result is a methodology for understanding and responding both to particular issues as they arise and to the culture as a whole. Fair-minded, non-polemical, and tightly argued, he has sought to set aside his presuppositions, whilst acknowledging them, and looked four-square at the scientific data that has been used to support abortion, transgenderism and, for example, the existence of a gay-gene. This combined with his astute analysis of the language used by activists reveal just how far from objective evidence and rationality the debate has departed. How then shall Christians live? There too Andrew offers us a way forward. I was left shocked, grateful for having my own false presuppositions exposed, and immensely encouraged by being offered a way forward.

Mark Greene,
Former Director and now Mission Champion, The London Institute for Contemporary Christianity

■ Do NOT read this firecracker of a book unless you are willing to think logically and clearly, and to confront the easy assumptions of most of the western media and academy about the nature (and meaninglessness) of human life defined by a totalitarian ideology which deliberately disregards the intrinsic value of all human beings, undermines the basis of family life, and regards all dissent as offensive. The highly contentious issues of abortion, homosexuality and transgenderism represent a fundamental upending (attack) on the Christian explanation of human identity.

Canon Dr Chris Sugden,
A former member of the Church of England Synod

■ With characteristic clarity of insight, reasoned argument, and thorough research and documentation, Andrew Kirk courageously exposes the extent to which the world of biblical understanding of human existence, with its profound influence on western culture over past centuries, has been supplanted by a radically different and fundamentally idolatrous ideology of human selfhood. And, like all idolatry, the cost to human lives, health and well-being is immense. With its critique of so much contemporary "received wisdom", the book echoes Paul's verdict in Romans 1, that human rejection of God and his created order turns the claim to be wise into folly, with calamitous social outcomes.

Revd. Dr. Chris Wright,
Global Ambassador, Langham Partnership

Contents

Acknowledgements	15
Foreword	17
Preface	21
PART I	27
THE WISDOM OF THIS WORLD MADE FOOLISH	27
CHAPTER 1	29
Abortion: an act of bereavement	29
Abortion and the law	29
Abortion and the COVID-19 Pandemic	32
A Thorough Change of Direction	35
The Causes of the Change	36
Only two starting points	36
Abortion and being human: personhood, as determined by humans	38
Abortion and being human: personhood, as determined by God	40
The right to life: who decides?	41
"My body, my choice?"	42
The mother's rights?	43
Infanticide	47
A future like ours?	50
Abortion, the law and moral virtue	53
CHAPTER 2	56
Human Sexuality (Part I): Truths and Illusions	56
Why this subject?	56
The Importance of Sexuality	57
A sea-change in views of human sexuality	57
Approaches to the verification of truths about human sexuality	59
Sexual orientation	61
The value of scientific findings	61

Is sexual orientation a helpful, explanatory category? 62
Born that way? 64
Same-sex attraction and possible abuse in childhood 66
Sexuality, Mental Health Outcomes and Social Stress 70
An explanation for higher adverse health outcomes in the homosexual population compared to the heterosexual. 72
Gender identity and transgenderism 75
A Timely Warning 81
CHAPTER 3 82

Human Sexuality (Part II): Real and False Conclusions 82
The opposing world-views 82
Ex-gay? Post-gay? 86
Sexuality and marriage 91
The definition 91
Discrimination? 94
What should children be taught about sexuality? 95
Department of Education Briefing Paper (Relationships and Sex Education in Schools (England)) 102
A Timely Warning 104
Postscript 105
Chapter 4 109

'In Praise of Folly?' 109
Preface 109
Erasmus's essay 110
The Case of Abortion 112
Confusing the language 112
The Case of Sexuality 117
How important is sexuality? 117
Sex is binary 118
Sexuality converted into a political project 119
Sexuality and human rights? 121
No gay gene 123

The Case of Gender	126
The physical, mental, emotional and moral development of children	126
'Gender affirmation'	129
'Gender affirmation' as a therapeutic practice	130
The folly of 'gender affirmation'	131
Possible causes of the desire to live as someone of a different gender	135
The ideological origin of transgender belief	137
Conclusion	139
PART II	141
CHAPTER 5	143
Why Listen to God's Word?	143
The meaning of divinely-inspired	144
The phenomenon of the Bible	145
The Nature of Scripture	145
The purpose of Scripture	147
Interpretation	147
Scripture alone (sola Scriptura)	148
Tradition	149
Reason	150
Explanation	152
Conclusions	153
CHAPTER 6	157
The Announcement of a New World in the midst of the Old	157
A new regime is declared	157
The substance of the good news	158
The engagement with Satan	159
The conversation with Nicodemus	160
Jesus before Pilate: a mini-discourse on political power	162
CHAPTER 7	165
A New Order is in Place	165
The beginnings of a new community	165
The new order in the teaching of Jesus	167

The Sermon on the Mount	167
The Beatitudes	167
What comes out from a person defiles	170
What will it profit to gain the whole world and forfeit one's life?	172
"The seed that dies"	173
"The truth will make you free"	174
"For this reason I was born"	175
Contrast with the old order	178
A literal sense	178
A metaphorical sense	179
The world in defiance of God and the ones he has sent	180
The world as the object of God's love	183
The nature of Jesus' kingship	184
CHAPTER 8	187
The Contours of the New World	187
The new community grows and expands	187
The ordering of the new community	188
Breaking free from the old world	190
Between two worlds	193
A vision of the new world	196
CHAPTER 9	200
A New Heaven and a New Earth: the Home of Righteousness	200
A comprehensive vision of the future	200
Three images of resurrection	204
Pictures of the new world	206
Interpreting the symbolic language	206
The final instalment of God's creative action	208
PART III	215
CHAPTER 10	217
News Items and Observations	217
Introduction	217
Abortion	220

Sexual Orientation	224
Sex-orientation therapy	226
Transgenderism	228
Its origin	228
'There is only one gender..."	232
The Meaning of Gender	233
"Facts not ideology determine reality"	234
Puberty Blockers and Cross-sex hormones	237
Self-creation is not freedom	238
Conclusion	239
Abortion	240
Sexual orientation	240
Transgenderism	241
Chapter 11	244
The end of folly and re-gaining good sense?	244
The existence of two worlds	244
The parting of two ways	244
Current ambiguity towards Christian moral standards	246
The prophetic mission of Christian communities	249
The destructive impulse	251
Abortion: folly and good sense	253
Sexuality: folly and good sense	254
Institutional acceptance of homosexuality	254
Counselling for those experiencing unwanted homosexual attraction	256
Transgenderism: folly and good sense	258
Sex-assigned at birth?	261
Conclusion	265
APPENDIX A	268
Personhood and Human Rights of the Unborn Child in International Law	
	268
Preface	268
The basis of human rights in the modern world	268

Subsequent International Conventions and Covenants concerning Human Rights Law 271
Human rights philosophy reinterpreted 274
APPENDIX B 279

Transgender identity and its ideological roots 279
    Introduction 279
    The theoretical origins of transgenderism in post-modern philosophy 280
    The second stage of transgender ideology 281
    The third stage of transgender ideology 286
    The theoretical origins of transgenderism in redesigning the self 289
Conclusion 291
Bibliography 293
Index 301
About the Author 305

Acknowledgements

Most authors are indebted to a whole range of people and institutions that have contributed to their understanding of the material they have written. I would like to name just a few that have helped me to keep up to date with issues around abortion, sexuality, marriage and transgenderism. Some of these are taken as examples of a world estranged from the God who has revealed himself in his written word and his living word, Jesus Christ. I am particularly grateful for those matters that touch on changes in law both enacted and hinted at for the future.

The Christian Institute, Christian Concern, Citizen Go and ADF International are in the forefront of organisations that have successfully defended people wrongly arrested or dismissed from their jobs or voluntary posts for speaking in favour of their Christian beliefs, and even for praying. Voice for Justice, UK, Life Institute, Right to Life, and Coalition for Marriage, have been tireless in promoting beliefs and policies that safeguard the convictions of those pursued by groups campaigning for more laws to restrict freedom of speech, religious faith and traditional values of an open society. I have found the Family Watch Newswire Published by Family Watch International invaluable in bringing a host of news items, concerning the lives of the pre-born, the family as a cornerstone of civilised life, lifelong marriage of two people of the opposite sex, and the binary nature of sex, to the attention of the general public.

I would like to thank those who have most generously endorsed my book, Martin Davie, Mark Greene, Chris Sugden and Chris Wright and Craig Bartholomew who has written the Foreword. They have been wholehearted in their tribute to what I have attempted to achieve – more than I deserve. I am honoured to know them as friends and colleagues.

Finally, I would like to show my appreciation to all the people at Kingdom Publishers who have been involved in the publication of this book. In particular I owe a debt of gratitude to Maria, who agreed to have the text published and began the process and to Andy Yiangou who has seen it to completion. They have been incredibly helpful, efficient, cordial, and patient, always quick to respond to all my questions. Thank you so much for making this publication possible.

J. Andrew Kirk

Foreword

As I write this foreword to Andrew's courageous, stimulating, and civil book, the backdrop remains the first war on European soil since World, War II, namely Russia's unprovoked and brutal invasion of Ukraine. Understandably, Ukraine looks to the West as the entity of which it wants to be a part. Compared with authoritarian, oppressive countries the West certainly has a great deal going for it. The Enlightenment has yielded in this regard many good developments for which we ought to be grateful.

However, it would be misguided to think that all is well in the West. In the 1980s postmodernism caught on like wild fire in the academic world, challenging many of the presuppositions of the Enlightenment world-view but retaining the Enlightenment commitment to human autonomy. Many regard the 20th century as the most brutal in history and by the end of it the Enlightenment traditions underlying modernity were left tattered and floundering. If postmodernism is now in demise, it has left in its wake uncertainty about the foundations of Western culture and an absence of a constructive and compelling vision for moving forward. I have no desire simply to denigrate postmodernism. In my view it brought many, important insights but turned out to be largely deconstructive rather than constructive. I see it as an important symbol of the unravelling of the inherent tensions in modernity.

The modern West is an uneasy amalgam of the Judeo-Christian World-view and that of the Enlightenment. Jonathan Israel argues compellingly that the radical Enlightenment with its opposition to religion and tradition became dominant as the Enlightenment developed,[1] and it is ironic, instructive, and

---

[1] Jonathan I. Israel, The Radical Enlightenment: Philosophy and the Making of Modernity 1650-1750 (Oxford: OUP, 2002).

disturbing to see how this tradition is now unravelling. In his *An Essay Concerning Human Understanding* (1690), John Locke (1632-1704) identifies human nature as the citadel that needs to be stormed if we are to achieve true understanding in the academic disciplines. Whatever we may think of it, it is surely ironic that 333 years later *the* question that many politicians want to avoid at all costs is "What is a woman?" Whatever our view of this question, it would seem that the Enlightenment tradition has unravelled to point where we are at sea when it comes to the question of what it means to be a human being.

The brutality of the 20th century and postmodernism - as a symbol of the Enlightenment's unravelling -, have undermined our trust in reason and science, for better and for worse. Worse, in the sense that once reason is gone all one is left with is power, and it is not hard to find example after example in our cultures today of a rejection of reasoned discourse and simple assertions of power. One simply aligns oneself with the right or left of contemporary culture and then closes down – cancelling if possible - any opponent, as Andrew documents in this book.

Ironically, even as a hard, Western secularism turns against Christianity in many ways, well documented by Andrew, while being deeply indebted to it, we are witnessing a major renaissance of Christianity in the majority world, a phenomenon that Philip Jenkins has documented in several, important books.[2] A result is, as Andrew argues, that we live increasingly amidst two antagonistic worlds.

Andrew's argument reminded me forcefully of Mark Lilla's *The Stillborn God*. Lilla observes of the Enlightenment that,

> By attacking Christian political theology and denying its legitimacy, the new philosophy simultaneously challenged the

---

[2] Philip Jenkins, The Next Christendom: The Coming of Global Christianity, 3rd. ed. (Oxford: Oxford University Press, 2011); The New Faces of Christianity: Believing the Bible in the Global South (New York and Oxford: Oxford University Press, 2006).

basic principles on which authority had been justified in most societies in history. That was the decisive break. The ambition of the new philosophy was to develop habits of thinking and talking about politics exclusively in human terms, without appeal to divine revelation or cosmological speculation. The hope was to wean Western societies from all political theology and cross to the other shore. What began as a thought experiment became an experiment in living that we inherited. Now the long tradition of Christian political theology is forgotten, and with it memory of the age-old quest to bring the whole of human life under God's authority.[3]

Now however, as Lilla recognises, we are amidst a major resurgence of religion so that any triumph of secularism and predicted demise of religion has, at the very least, been "postponed."[4] The result, according to Lilla:

> The story reconstructed here should remind us that the actual choice contemporary societies face is not between past and present, or between the West and "the rest." It is between two grand traditions of thought, two ways of envisaging the human condition. We must be clear about these alternatives, choose between them, and live with the consequences of our choice. That is the human condition.[5]

It is not hard to see the parallels between Lilla and Andrew's argument. Of course the clash between these two worlds always manifests itself in particular areas, and Andrew courageously attends to two of these, namely abortion and human sexuality. Readers may wonder if Andrew's Part II is really needed. Once note Lilla's point about the fact that the Christian tradition has been forgotten, and you will see just how important is the articulation of the contours of the biblical, Christian tradition, if we are to

---

[3] Mark Lilla, The Stillborn God: Religion, Politics, and the Modern West (New York: Vintage, 2007, 2008), 5.
[4] Lilla, The Stillborn God, 3.
[5] Lilla, Stillborn God, 13.

have any hope of negotiating our ways through our contemporary cultural challenges.

Nowadays it takes courage to address issues such as abortion and sexuality and gender. Alas, we seem to have drifted a long way from Voltaire's commitment, quoted by Andrew, "I disapprove of what you say, but I will defend to the death your right to say it". It is therefore important to note the civil, courteous and yet strong, ways in which Andrew explores these issues. In relation to Lilla, we might say that Andrew carefully and courteously invites his readers to a discussion of these issues in relation to the two worlds of our day. He rightly appeals to reason, argument and science but without expecting them to deliver more than they can, one of the better contributions of postmodernism.

Andrew is one of our best missiologists, and in the great tradition of thinkers like Lesslie Newbigin, he attends not only to the hot button issues of our day but penetrates behind them to place them in their illuminating larger context. He also shows us just how much is at stake in these debates, reminding us that quick, pragmatic decisions and knee-jerk reactions will serve no one's interests.

For the foreseeable future these two worlds will coexist alongside each other in our western societies, and thus it is important that they find ways to do so peacefully but without hiding their deep differences and consequences. Andrew's calm, civil and clear discussion of these emotive issues is a model of the sort of dialogue we urgently need to recover in the West. It will be a mark of hope if readers who agree and disagree with Andrew's thesis are able to engage with it strongly, thoughtfully, respectfully and openly.

Dr. Craig G. Bartholomew
Director, Kirby Laing Centre for Public Theology in Cambridge,
October 2023.

Preface

The main purpose of this study is to respond, from a Christian perspective, to the way in which the Christian faith is currently being treated in the Western world. During the last sixty years, for the first time in many centuries, Western nations, speaking generally, are systematically spurning their long Christian heritage. To an outsider this may seem surprising, since it has been the bedrock that has moulded them spiritually, culturally and morally for many centuries, and been the main focus of the way in which they have understood their corporate identity. In its place, an amorphous secular humanism has taken centre stage as the key alternative interpretation of human existence. The latter's belief system now dominates contemporary cultural, social, legal and political discourse. The conflicting narratives may be understood as two contrasting worlds, existing side by side, engaged in a serious conflict about the content of what is ultimately true. This supposition will be tested in the following chapters.

The last six decades, then, has witnessed profound social changes that have succeeded in wrenching these nations, in their collective world view, thought-processes, ethical decision-making, legislation, understanding of key concepts (like tolerance, equality, discrimination, human rights, extremism and the exercise of power in public life), from their hitherto Christian moorings. There are many factors that have combined to cause this immense cultural shift. Much has been written about it. I will not attempt to summarise all these influences, for this is not my purpose in writing this book.[6] I will take for granted that, by the beginning of the third decade of the 21st century, a sea-change in the relationship between the

---

[6] I have written elsewhere about my interpretation of the immense and continuing changes, that have taken place, see The Future of Reason, Science and Faith: Following Modernity and Post-Modernity (Aldershot: Ashgate Publishing, 2007); Civilisations in Conflict? Islam, the West and Christian Faith (Oxford: Regnum Books International, 2011); The Church and the World: Understanding the Relevance of Mission (Milton Keynes: Paternoster, 2014) Being Human: An Historical Inquiry Into Who Who We Are (Eugene, OR: Wipf and Stock, 2019), and The Abuse of Language and the Language of Abuse (Tolworth: Grosvenor House Publishing, 2019).

Christian faith and society has taken place. Although this association will continue to change in the future, social life is too complex to be able to predict with any confidence how this may develop.

My intention, then, is to propose a coherent understanding of the current situation of Western societies in their connection with the Christian faith and suggest, from a Christian standpoint, the reasons why the considerable changes have taken place. So, the work, although it will allude to prominent social matters, and engage with non-Christian thinking, will not attempt a systematic, socio-cultural analysis. Its main source of reflection will be theological, that is a survey of Christianity's core beliefs, deducible from its Scriptures, as a means of discerning the light they may shed on the profound historical shift that is now taking place.

I hope to be able to demonstrate, from an understanding of the message and practical life of the first Christian communities, that what is happening in the Western world, is not, after all, particularly surprising. What should be more remarkable is the way the Christian church, in its many manifestations, has developed its power relationship to political authority from the time of the emperor Constantine until modern times.

The opposite movement by the state towards the church's intrusion in the affairs of governance is part of the same story.[7] The current tendency within the church to speak about Western nations as being 'post-Christian' can be construed, according to different perspectives, either negatively or positively or, perhaps, both at the same time. What is clear is that the long-established Church-State relationship of preceding centuries has been conclusively shattered.[8] It is hard to defend the notion that any Western nation is any longer 'Christian' in any meaningful sense.[9]

---

[7] A fascinating account of this monumental interaction has recently been published; see, Tom Holland, Dominion: The Making of the Western Mind (London: Little, Brown, 2019).
[8] Not, perhaps, in a formal sense, for in some Western nations state churches still exist. However, in real, everyday life the former status of the church within the cultural, social and political ethos of Western nations has considerably diminished in recent years.
[9] I suppose that, in the case of European nations, Poland and Hungary at the present time might be counted as exceptions, because they are still adhering to their Christian traditions; although only in part.

Within the Christian community in the Western world there are plenty of people who are despondent about the direction the culture they live in appears to be heading. This may be due in part to their age. The advancement of years tends to bring on a kind of wistfulness for times in the past when life seemed less complex, more socially integrated, founded more on common-sense judgements and moral absolutes, more in keeping with well-tried and proven social traditions than exist today. Older people tend to be increasingly bewildered by the speed of change. They are inclined to subscribe to the notion that change should be resisted, just because it is change.

So, many people, when facing the evolution of certain social realities that make a negative impact on them, tend to become increasingly discouraged by the current state of society. Many different examples could be mentioned. By way of illustrating the sense of growing unease, one could refer, in no particular order, to the apparently cataclysmic state of the environment, the failure of multiple attempts to alleviate poverty across the globe, the increase in mental and emotional distress that is affecting a growing body of people (especially the younger generation), the increased investment by super-powers in research projects connected to technological warfare and by criminals to electronic crime, cross-border trafficking of minors for the sex-industry or domestic servile labour, and the rise in sexually-transmitted diseases. Above all, the surge in threatening attitudes to the opinions of others, leading to curtailment of free-speech and personal victimisation, is causing alarm in societies once esteemed for their genuine toleration.

Behind much of this latter manifestation there seems to be a considerable lessening of civility towards those who hold divergent opinions, particularly manifested in direct derisive diatribes posted on social media. Tolerance has been reinterpreted from its original meaning of being willing to accept the right of people freely to expound their views, which others find thoroughly offensive,[10] to being prepared only to tolerate opinions approved by minority, militant sectors of society. Language is abused and the use of abusive language is much more frequent than in former generations.[11] In interpersonal relations deliberately hurtful statements, false accusations and innuendos, against not only a person's beliefs and actions, but their personal integrity, appear to be on the increase. These often spill over into threats of violence against the targeted people and their families.

When it comes to what society is now willing to permit, that a couple of generations ago it would have strongly resisted, numerous examples could be given. As the book argues that there are two quite distinct 'worlds' in operation on the one planet, I will refer to two of those that are now being defended most pugnaciously in the West by one 'world' and repelled by the other. For the first group, a permissive society, albeit one that carefully selects the objects it affirms, is a sure sign of progress. Within the second group there are people (not just Christians) distressed by the way that Western societies have, in recent years, either deliberately or by default, replaced the principles and virtues of the Christian moral code with a free-wheeling moral attitude to choices and behaviour.

In the first part of the study, I will attempt to present an overview of some of these changes and the consequences they have brought that, from a Christian standpoint, are both disturbing and destructive. Some of them are deeply emotive and controversial. For these reasons they are often approached in a highly-charged atmosphere that does not make a sane discussion easy. My intention is to follow judicious, reasonable argumentation. I will, therefore, endeavour to eliminate unfruitful rhetoric as much as possible, whilst acknowledging that reason is not always best promoted, when most dispassionate.

I will describe something of the widening gulf that is occurring between the

---

[10] This is expressed forcefully in a quote, attributed to Voltaire, the 18th century French philosopher and author: "I disapprove of what you say, but I will defend to the death your right to say it" (see S.G. Tallentyre (a pseudonym of Evelyn Beatrice Hall), The Friends of Voltaire (London: G.P. Putnam's Sons, 1907), 199, (an updated edition of her book has been published by the Pacific University Press, Eugene, Oregon, 2003).
[11] I have surveyed the words that are most commonly corrupted or used most insultingly in my book, The Abuse of Language.

current shaping of world-views, moral beliefs, political discourse and legislation in the West and basic Christian convictions. I will not do this at any great length as I have already attempted to produce a fair representation of the core tenets of secular humanism, as this has emerged out of particular intellectual convictions of the last two and a half centuries.[12] Alongside this, I have appealed to five leading theologians of the 20th century, all of whom have born witness, within a secular age, to mainstream Christian teaching on human identity.[13]

Although some of my interpretations may well be challenged, I believe that my basic understanding of both these 'grand narratives' is accurate enough to demonstrate that two worlds exist in contention.[14] Within the following discussion, therefore, I will return to the basic differences of opinion between them as they both seek to explain what 'being human' really means.

In the first four chapters, I will lay out arguments, using two particular case-studies that illustrate the rift between the two discourses concerning current moral convictions. Both claim universal validity for their beliefs and values. They also both denounce and defend vigorously the most important consequences produced, not only for societies moulded by the history of the West, but across the globe. In the case of Christianity, I will not attempt to exonerate the thoroughly malignant outcomes down the ages of certain misplaced Christian teachings. Their effects have often been harmful and sometimes destructive. What I will do, however, is to show that they do not represent the core teaching of Jesus and his original disciples. This aspect of the book's principal argument will be deferred until the second part of the study.

The first part of the study, then, will analyse two significant examples of the ways in which the effects of the secular humanist narrative have failed to

---

[12] Being Human, chapter 10.
[13] Being Human, chapter 11.
[14] Philip Rieff in his trilogy, Sacred Order/Social Order (Charlottesville: University of Virginia Press, 2006-2008) also speaks of different 'worlds'. He categorises them as pagan, sacred and non-transcendent. Although small groups of people in the West are guided by pagan beliefs and practice pagan rituals, my interest will focus exclusively on the conflict between the sacred world in its Christian expression and the non-transcendent or imminent world of secular imagination.

bring the liberty and justice so ambitiously and pretentiously promised during the second half of the twentieth century. The examples chosen touch deeply on one of the most crucial issues of our times, namely the question of human identity.[15]

The legalisation of abortion and the decriminalisation of homosexual practices, both in the 1960s, have opened a 'Pandora's box' of moral, spiritual, legal, political, social and cultural conflicts that have escalated during the last two decades. They are not just about certain practices, previously forbidden by moral conscience and legal systems, but then approved as lawful, thus eliminating fear of a conviction for contravening accepted moral codes or legal statutes. They are also indicators of what is perverse about new ways of regulating certain human relationships in community. At the same time, by virtue of highlighting the nature of the conflicting views, they point to what is right and wholesome in human behaviour.

I am setting the debate, then, within the reality of two contending worlds, whose differences have now been exposed by practices, formerly concealed and obscured, but now openly championed. The existence of two worlds, co-terminus with the whole of humanity, encompasses one of the most central themes of Christianity's foundation document, the Bible's Old and New Testaments.

In order to do justice to the debate, it is necessary to consider both the practices and the stated and unstated reasons used to justify them. The actions and beliefs highlighted in this study, considered detrimental by most Christians, but defended by those who oppose the Christian world-view, will certainly be part of the controversy between adherents of the two worlds. My wish is that, in the ongoing disputes, all participants will use a civilised conversation to support their views, based on objective evidence and credible arguments, rather than on specious rhetoric or personal sentiments. In any case, the truth about them will eventually be exposed by either their constructive or destructive fruits.

---

[15] This study was started some time before the Covid-19 viral pandemic spread throughout the world. However, one of its consequences has been to press isolated people to mull over deep questions about their existence and self-perception.

PART I

THE WISDOM OF THIS WORLD MADE FOOLISH

CHAPTER 1
Abortion: an act of bereavement

"A voice was heard in Ramah, wailing and loud lamentation, Rachel weeping for her children; she refused to be consoled, because they are no more".[16]

"It makes no difference whether one takes away life once born or destroys it as it comes to birth. He is a man, who is to be a man, the fruit is always in the seed".[17]

Abortion and the law

Close to the top of the list of potent and significant changes in the moral landscape of Western societies would be the legalisation of abortion. In Britain it followed previous rulings passed in the 19th and early 20th centuries making abortion illegal:

The Offences Against the Person Act 1861 (OAPA) protected children in-utero by making abortion a criminal offence in England, Wales and Northern Ireland. The following sections spell out the terms of the law's violations:

Section 58 - A woman is guilty of an offence if she unlawfully procures her own miscarriage;

---

[16] Matthew 2:18.
[17] Tertullian, Apologeticus, (197 A.D.).

Section 59 - Anyone who supplies drugs or instruments to be unlawfully used to procure abortion is guilty of an offence;

Section 60 - Anyone who secretly disposes of a child who died before, at, or after birth is guilty of an offence.

The Infant Life (Preservation) Act 1929 makes it illegal intentionally to 'destroy the life of a child capable of being born alive' (fetal viability was set at 28 weeks).

The Abortion Act 1967, however, states: 'a person shall not be guilty of an offence under the law relating to abortion' [i.e. sections 58 and 59 of the OAPA 1861] if the following conditions are satisfied:

Up to 28 weeks: 'to reduce the risk of harm to the physical/mental health of the mother or any of her existing children';

Up to birth: 'to prevent grave harm to the mental/physical health of the mother; to reduce the risk to the mother's life; if the baby will be 'seriously handicapped''.

Since the passing of the Abortion Act, the only major legal change in the law in Britain was an amendment included in The Human Fertilisation and Embryology Act 1990 that lowered the legality of an abortion from 28 to 24 weeks of gestation, a point at which the unborn child was considered able to survive outside the mother's womb.

In practice, however, it is now rare for a mother's request for abortion to be rejected on any ground. In something like 95% of cases the ground for procedure is 'to reduce the risk of harm to the mental/physical health of the mother or any of her existing children'. Such a reason is so broad in its scope that authorisation of an abortion is being based almost entirely on the request of the mother (i.e. abortion on demand). Frequently the justification given is "unwanted pregnancy."[18]

In the last few years a groundswell for decriminalising abortion altogether up to the date of birth has arisen. It is now being suggested by abortion agencies, and by a number of medical professions, that the stated conditions for clearing both the mother and those who carry out abortions from committing a crime have become irrelevant. In other words, abortions should no longer be considered a matter for the law to adjudicate. The state should no longer be involved in the personal wish of the mother[19] to be rid of the living being that she is carrying in her body. Abortion is to be classed simply as a medical procedure. Therefore, like any other medical intervention, it is considered just a health issue.

Institutions promoting abortion, such as the World Health Organisation (WHO), euphemistically use the language of 'health and reproductive rights' to conceal the reality of what an abortion entails. Those who promote this language have failed to answer satisfactorily three crucial questions. Firstly, what international authority has unanimously agreed that abortion is to be constituted an inviolable right to be upheld, whenever a woman desires to end her pregnancy? If the answer is none, how then can it be designated a reproductive right? Secondly, on what grounds can it be maintained that the ending of the life of a healthy fetus is a health issue? Thirdly, how can a woman's supposed right to end the life of a living human being she is carrying be separated from the right of that being to be protected from an act of brutality? The WHO is more than a little hypocritical to define

---

[18] Harm to the mother, particularly if in an erratic, unmarried relationship with her partner, might well be the inability to continue in her employment and pursue a career requiring a full-time commitment. Another cause might be the mother's perceived inability to care for another child, when already the mother of several others, or when it is diagnosed as likely to be born seriously disabled. In the latter case, children with Down's Syndrome are considered to fit into this category, even though many born with this impairment have been able to live useful and fulfilling lives. In the UK 90% of pre-born babies diagnosed as having Down's Syndrome are aborted. In light of the fact that disability is a protected characteristic in Equality Law, the fact that abortion regulations allow the abortion of any child, over the 24 week period of gestation, deemed to suffer from a disability is astonishingly hypocritical.
[19] In a number of cases, the cause is psychological pressure from the mother's family or partner.

reproductive rights 'to include the right of all to make decisions concerning reproduction free of discrimination, coercion and violence'. Thus, it approves of abortion, as part of that right, although it is a destructive act of eradication against a helpless, and usually healthy, living human. It is also discriminatory in the case of making the choice of the sex of the child a sufficient cause for eliminating any deemed to be the 'wrong' sex. In consequence, it is doubly deceitful in what it approves.

There are, moreover, initial signs (particularly in the USA) that the deliberate ending of the life of a child can, in some circumstances, be carried beyond birth. For example, a bill fairly recently presented to the US legislature to safeguard the life of pre-born children who have survived an abortion has been rejected in the Senate. In other words, it has knowingly approved infanticide as an option beyond the censure of the law. The extent of the right to end a life, for example if the baby will be 'seriously handicapped' (Abortion Act, 1967), is now being advocated for those who have taken their first breath outside the womb. Historically speaking, this would signify a reversion to the practice of pagan Europe and other parts of the world. Such is the logic of the demands of the abortion lobby.

Abortion and the COVID-19 Pandemic

The emergence of the virus at the end of 2019 threatened continuing access to abortion offered by those organisations whose existence depends on ensuring its business remained uninterrupted. The fact that it risks appropriating medical resources vital for treating those suffering from the virus is not considered relevant. It has given pro-abortionists the opportunity to press governments strongly to allow mothers to undertake abortions themselves at home alone by means of two pills sent through the post. This is a new phase in the pressure to liberalise abortion to such an extent that it is no longer regulated by law.

This new venture has been named 'tele-medicine' or more euphemistically

'DIY' abortion. The purpose behind this unprecedented move is to allow women to self-administer abortion without having to go in person to a clinic. The consequence is that the pills are dispensed after a cursory telephone call with a medical professional (who does not have to be a doctor), without undergoing an ultrasound that can pinpoint the length of the pregnancy and detect whether it is ectopic (located outside the womb).

A survey from Finland has showed that women are four times more likely to suffer severe complications as a result of a chemical abortion in comparison with that done surgically.[20] In- person consultation is clearly needed. A phone or video call to someone at home who may not have the ability to speak in complete confidence may cause important information to be hidden (e.g. coercion by a partner to abort). The introduction of home abortions is a policy that is more likely than not to depart from the essential tenets of a medical duty of care. These should be based on proper clinical assessment and post-abortion vigilance, to avoid the risk of serious injury and harm being done to women self-administering Mifepristone and Misoprostol at home.

The panic that arose amongst abortion-providers, when governments announced that non-essential, elective surgery would no longer be undertaken, has underlined the false reasoning behind abortion in the first place. Elective abortions are not an essential component of comprehensive women's health care, for they do not treat any disease process. Essential health care would include routine pap-smears, mammograms and pelvic examinations. These, however, were postponed during the pandemic to reduce risk of exposure to the virus and to conserve scarce resources.

In the midst of the whole-hearted dedication given by the medical

---

[20] 'Immediate Complications after Medical compared with Surgical Termination of Abortion', Obstetrics and Gynecology, March 2010; see, www.researchgate.net/publication/41532599. The complications listed are haemorrhage; post-abortal infections; incomplete abortion; injuries requiring surgical operations; embolism and thrombosis; psychiatric morbidity (depression, intoxication and psychoses), and death. All the risks are also present in surgical abortions. However, in the latter case they are statistically less likely, and happen in a place where medical treatment is immediately available.

profession to saving the lives of those affected by the COVID-19 virus, an enormous storm of protest arose at the callous killing by a white policeman of an unarmed black man in Minneapolis. The fully-justified outrage was the culmination of a string of similar cases, across the USA, where black people were the victims of unlawful police brutality. The slogan, 'Black lives matter', was adopted to highlight a systemic failure on the part of authorities to bring the perpetrators to justice and to ensure that such cases were never repeated again. The cause of all racist beliefs and actions has been laid by some media outlets squarely at the door of a white supremacist ideology.

At the same time, few if any of the demonstrators thought to point out that a large percentage of abortions in the USA have been carried out on black pre-born babies.[21] Comparing the number of unarmed black people killed unlawfully by the police per annum with black babies killed in the womb the figure is 9 to 90,000. Though the cold, indifferent killing of just one black person is a horrific crime, what about the 90,000? In light of the claim by Planned Parenthood (the chief entity in the USA involved in the abortion industry) that pro-life campaigners represent a white supremacist attack[22] on black women's 'reproductive rights', is it not legitimate to ask whether the abortion providers, in the case of the black community, have not surreptitiously adopted the unspoken catchphrase, 'Black lives are matter'. Is it not warranted, therefore, to ask, in the latter case, which other institutions can also be declared 'white supremacist'?

Pregnancy as such is not a medical condition, unless there are complications affecting the life of either the mother or child. Real health care does not sell abortions. Above all it addresses women's underlying care needs, something that the abortion institutions fail to do. They are, apparently, uninterested in

---

[21] Calculated to be, on average 247 per day (90,155 per annum). According to census figures, the black population represents 13% of the whole in the USA; its abortion rate, however, amounts to 40%.

[22] It should, of course, be noted that many members of black communities across the USA are also pro-life, appalled at the rate of the destruction of pre-born black human beings that is being carried out.

providing alternative solutions to the predicament women face when an unplanned pregnancy is confirmed. It means protecting, extending and improving lives. Pro-life charities have saved thousands of lives, precisely by attending to the mother's whole-life circumstances.[23] An abortion may, at most, be a quick fix for an immediate predicament. By and large, abortion clinics are not interested in checking the personal, human consequences of the physical and emotional outcomes of terminating a human life in-utero.

A Thorough Change of Direction

In comparing the wording of the three Acts, mentioned above, that have regulated the practice of abortion since 1861 in Britain, two outstanding differences may be noted. Firstly, the language used of the living being conceived in the woman's womb has changed strikingly. In 1861 and again in 1929, this living being was called a child, presumably from conception. In 1967, the pre-born being was called a baby, but only with reference to the gestation period from 28 weeks to birth. Since abortion in practice has been widened far beyond the initial conditions for it to be counted legal, it has usually been known as a fetus, embryo or, even more impersonally, 'the product of conception'.

Secondly, in the first two Acts the emphasis was on preserving the life of the child in-utero, although in 1929 this appeared to be applied only to one capable of surviving ex-utero (from 28 weeks onwards, amended in 1990 to 24 weeks). In the 1967 Act, however, attention was focused primarily on the physical and mental health of the mother and her ability to care for the baby, given the social circumstances of her life.

Between the first and third Acts a monumental shift of understanding of the relationship between the child in gestation and the mother carrying it

---

[23] Even so, it is calculated, on the basis of the law of averages, that between March and June, 2020, there were 10.5 million abortions world-wide. Each one of these represents the death of a unique, valuable human life that can never be replaced.

took place: in 1861 carrying out an abortion was illegal, notwithstanding the circumstances, but in 1967 it became legal under certain circumstances. The fundamental changes concerned the status of the new living being and the rights and responsibilities of the mother. In 1861, the baby, from conception, was deemed to be a living human person in the first stage of its development. In 1967, the mother was considered to have rights in law that overruled, in certain circumstances, the right of the infant to be carried to the end of the pregnancy.

The Causes of the Change

In weighing up the moral justification for the shift in the balance of prerogatives between baby and mother, that presumably informed the change in the law relating to abortion, it is necessary to argue on the basis of a well-grounded, rational appreciation of human reality. In other words, moral reasoning and decisions, indeed all properly rational thought, need to rest upon a set of coherent and true claims about human life in the world. It is a fact that all ethical systems, promoted at different historical periods, have had to answer the fundamental human identity question: how does one explain comprehensively, consistently and cogently what it means to be human?

Only two starting points

By the end of the second millennium of the present era, in the Western world, only two answers, proposed as having sufficient qualifications to unravel the enigma of human existence, were left standing. In historical sequence, the first answer has been informed by the long-standing affirmation, based on the Judaeo-Christian religion and supported by Islamic belief, that behind the material universe exists one eternally, self-subsisting, supreme, personal being who is the creator and sustainer of all that exists. This being has made itself known to the whole human race. This conviction has permeated all Western societies and many others across the world, gradually superseding a variety of religious, philosophical and pagan beliefs in existence.

The second answer has been informed by a denial of this conviction (e.g. by atheists, sceptics, and pantheists). In its place, a materialistic creed has been promoted that maintains that nothing exists outside of the physical, the concrete and the tangible.[24] In the first case, the universe (and the planet earth within it) owes its origin to the acts of a one and only existing deity. In the second case, what exists today is the result of an impersonal, lengthy process of change and development that has been self-generating from the beginning. It has no particular purpose beyond what humans themselves consider worthy to be believed. In spite of the intellectual commitment to a pure materialism, there are signs amongst its adherents, not least in a renewed search for a lost spirituality, that such a creed does not satisfy. However, materialists are locked in by their philosophy to seek an ephemeral satisfaction beyond the material within the confined space of their own limited experience.

The first answer advances the belief that humans are unique, special and irreplaceable, worthy of special care because created as individuals in the image of the one, living God. The second answer believes that humans have evolved purely by chance; their arrival has, accidentally, just happened this way. Their worth can only be determined by other humans, who constitute the most advanced living beings yet detected in the universe. On the one hand, the significance and value of humans is determined independently, from outside the human race. On the other hand, their worth is resolved purely by humans, those who have managed to persuade or coerce others to accept their beliefs.

---

[24] There is a further category of belief, polytheism. This, however, does not qualify as either monotheistic or materialistic.

Abortion and being human: personhood, as determined by humans

In the context of abortion, the second way of understanding humanness means that a fundamental distinction can be drawn between a foetus, considered solely from a biological perspective, and a person. Until a certain point has been reached in the development of the foetus, or until birth, the living being in the womb can only be contemplated as a human, because it possesses faculties that eventually will evolve into a person, qualitatively distinct from all other sentient beings. One might summarise these in terms of spiritual, mental, emotional, social and moral capacities wholly unique to the human species. Not surprisingly, those campaigning for the lifting of all restrictions in law on abortions up to birth do not use the term person of the pre-born infant.[25]

The problem with this argument is that it is impossible, on this understanding of personhood, to define a moment when it actually occurs. According to one set of definitions, the characteristics central to personhood consist in sentience (a particular set of responses to physical and emotional feelings), the experience of an emotional life, the ability to reason and communicate through language, self-awareness, and moral agency. Consistent with this set of criteria, an independent living entity, still existing in the womb, could not be counted as a person. It is also doubtful that a new born baby could be counted as a person either. For example, babies are not moral agents. And if not, at what age are they deemed to be morally responsible for their actions? On the basis of this set of personhood tests, it might well be logical to argue that no biologically-determined human reaches the status of person until they are considered to be adult (at the age of 18 according to the law, but even later, perhaps around 25, if one judges that the maturation of the brain happens around this age).

If the argument states that a post-natal baby is potentially a moral agent,

---

[25] Further considerations on the personhood of the pre-born baby from conception, and the legal implications of accepting or denying such a status are addressed in Appendix A.

and therefore a person, why would this not be equally true for a pre-natal baby? What is the objective logic in setting 24 weeks of gestation as the limit up to which an abortion is legally permissible? The difference between that date and birth is only a matter of a few weeks. Is a pre-born baby suddenly transformed into a person during the remaining 16 weeks of pregnancy? It seems to be based on the fact that a baby can survive outside the womb, being still alive at 24 weeks. Does that mean that achieving personhood is dependent on the ability to survive? If that were the case, personhood would be determined by the existence of sophisticated medical resources necessary to keep the premature baby alive. By inference it would also mean that where those resources were not available the baby, who could not survive without them, and therefore would die, would have to be counted as a non-person. The whole idea is ludicrous.

Some people have argued, on the basis of a built-in ambiguity about recognising a biological member of the human species as a person, that even a late-term foetus (having lived beyond 24 weeks) has no more right to life than do a certain class of large-brained mammals (i.e. apes, belonging to the classification of Simiidae, namely gorillas, chimpanzees, orang-outans and gibbons, monkeys of various species, generally classified as Simiiformes or Simians, marine mammals, belonging to various species of Cetacea, such as whales, dolphins and porpoises; elephants and dogs might also be included).

On the other side of the argument, some people have argued that foetuses should be counted as persons from conception, using 'potentiality' as the reason for allowing them this status. This means they should be considered persons, based on a comparison with a fully-fledged adult into which they will grow one day. They are, therefore, to be counted as 'one like us.'

There is, nevertheless, a fundamental flaw in all arguments that attempt to determine personhood on the basis of certain qualities that are added to their biological constitution. The fallacy lies both in the subjective nature of the personhood criteria used and in the stage of human growth when the norms can be applied with a measure of universally-agreed objectivity. The distinction between humanness and personhood was used in the famous US Supreme Court ruling (1973) in the case of Wade vs. Roe that allowed abortion to take place legally in certain circumstances in the USA.

There is, however, a cogent argument that the distinction is irrelevant, since the overriding reason for valuing pre-born babies is that they are humans, and therefore persons, from conception.[26] Adding the qualification of personhood to humanness at some stage of gestation is, therefore, a counter-productive strategy for abortionists, for it suggests criteria can be applied as to when abortion is no longer morally justified.

Abortion and being human: personhood, as determined by God

Meanwhile, the one universal standard that completely transcends idiosyncrasies based on arbitrary human classifications has been waiting in the wings ever since God made himself known to human beings:

"Then God said, "Let us make humankind in our image, in our likeness...So God created humankind in his own image...He created them male and female" (Genesis 1:26-27).

The designation of a human's status as a person is removed completely from human speculations; it is centred, instead, on the reality of divine creation. The consequence of this principle is to remove all doubt about the question whether certain classes of people can be considered fully human: e.g. races, castes, people with severe physical or mental disabilities, women, and infants. The doctrine of imago Dei signifies that different levels of personhood do not exist. Every living being, conceived by the sexual union of a male and female human, has equal standing, honour and respect.

---

[26] A good scientific definition of a human would be that a human female's egg fertilised by a human male's semen, complete with its unique and distinct DNA, is from the moment of conception a human being. Moreover, most Thesauruses in the English language make human and person interchangeable. What right, then, do pro-abortionists have unilaterally to change the language?

Moreover, the concept of creation is extended right back to the time that the mother's ovum is fertilised by the father's sperm:

"You (God) knit me together in my mother's womb...My frame was not hidden from you when I was made in secret...Your eyes beheld my unformed substance" (Psalm 139: 13, 15-16).

Here, the Psalmist identifies himself with the zygote formed by the fusion between the oocyte and the spermatozoon.

The right to life: who decides?

From a Christian perspective, the absolute right of the foetus to have its life protected during the whole of pregnancy is not a matter for humans to decide. It is prescribed by its human nature in relationship to the one who created this means of bringing a new person into the world. In other words, the physical integrity of the foetus is protected by an authority above that of any human agency to change. The pre-born baby is protected, therefore, from the vagaries of the mother's decision either to carry the baby to the end of pregnancy or to end its incipient life.

Clearly, this contention is based on a belief that the world, and all human life within it, is ordered in a particular way for the maximum flourishing of God's special creatures. Those who do not believe in the existence of a supreme Being, to whom everyone is accountable, who has structured life in a particular way, such that when the structure is fractured painful consequences follow, hold that the mother is the final arbiter of the decision to continue or to terminate the pregnancy. When, therefore, an individual state agrees to legislate in favour of abortion, it implicitly arrogates to itself the place of God. If this latter premise is continued to its logical conclusion, there should be no time limit on abortion. The mother alone has the right to dictate, right up to birth, whether to continue or end the pregnancy. Once God is removed from the argument, this conclusion is indisputable; the mother constitutes the supreme authority in making the decision; the state merely acquiesces.

"My body, my choice?"

This conclusion, that a mother has the absolute right to request the ending of the life of the foetus, based on her situation at the time of the pregnancy, is based on a bizarre, false assumption. It is stated, as a matter of fact, that the foetus is part of the mother's body. It stands to reason, therefore, that as part of her physical constitution, she can decide how the situation of this new arrival should be handled. Hence the routine slogan proclaimed by pro-abortionists: "my body, my choice." This alleged right is based on an interpretation of the privacy principle. The assumption is that no-one, external to the one carrying this living being, has a warrant to interfere in the woman's sole prerogative to choose what future course of action to follow. The logical conclusion of this way of arguing is that the woman, demanding to exercise the sovereign control of 'her own body', decides whether the living entity is to be called a baby or is merely a conglomeration of tissues that can be disposed of according to her will.

The assumption is false, because, as a matter of biological fact, the foetus growing inside her, is not part of her body in the sense that one of the organs with which she was born is part of her physical make-up. Prior to the sexual act her body was completely devoid of this entity. The new organism is there, because one of her eggs has been fertilised by the intervention of a male. That is the simple reality of reproduction. It is amazing, therefore, that any argument based on another slogan, "I have the right to control my own body," was ever promoted as a convincing reason to approve the mother's decision to procure an abortion.

The slogan, "my body, my choice" cannot, in any case, be universalised, for there are instances in which people do not have an unlimited option as to how they control their bodies. A person, for example, who resists arrest for a suspected crime cannot demand that the police "keep their hands off my body."

The mother's rights?

The question of whether the mother has any rights in the matter remains. Here, we are not talking about a legal right, for that already exists. The law admits, under certain circumstances, the legitimacy of the forced termination of a pregnancy. Legality, however, does not eliminate the need for a moral justification to end a human life, however under-formed it may be in the first few weeks of gestation. What it is legal to do may well not be morally right to carry out.

The main line of reasoning adopted is that, because the foetus is not yet assumed to be a person, its moral rights cannot be respected in practice, because they would severely undercut the moral rights of those who clearly are. Therefore, assuming that the pregnancy was not planned, but happened accidentally, the woman should not be obliged to undergo the many inconveniences of offering her body for nine months to this unwanted intrusion into her life and, later, the huge responsibilities involved in nurturing the child into adulthood.

The reasons given, then, for terminating a pregnancy are, more or less, entirely pragmatic. The sex act, presumably, was not properly protected by a contraceptive device, or the contraceptive precaution failed to work. The mother, however, is not in a psychological frame of mind to care properly for the baby. The baby, therefore, is likely to be born into circumstances that are highly disadvantageous to its well-being: for example, the mother does not possess the economic means to provide adequately for the new-born; or, the mother is already attempting to cope with a number of other children and one more will simply tip the balance away from her physical and emotional stability; or, pregnancy will seriously curtail her ability to prepare for a career or maintain and progress in the one she presently enjoys.

Even those who approve of abortion have to admit that only on the basis of a consequentialist moral theory can "abortion be justified as a means of avoiding undesirable consequences."[27] Some pregnancies may be the result of rape or incest, but most result from presumed consensual sexual behaviour. The fundamental moral question then is whether the normal prolongation of the life of a pre-born baby can ever be overruled by the adverse consequences of having to bear the sacrifices of an unwanted pregnancy.

It is often argued by those who defend the mother's right to secure an abortion that, where the pregnancy has not been planned the result amounts to an invasion of the integrity of the woman's body. Whereas, neither the woman nor the man, when they came together, had any intention of bringing a new being into the world, now the situation has been dramatically changed, with far-reaching repercussions. Therefore, the best way of dealing with the dilemma is to eradicate the cause of their potentially disrupted life: get rid of the uninvited intrusion.

A little reflection, however, will show that the reasoning is deceptive. It amounts to a defence of abortion as a belated means of contraception.[28] Surely, the other side of the argument is that, assuming that the couple did not take sufficient precautions against an unwanted pregnancy, before their act of sexual intercourse, the woman, by implication, has given the foetus the right to use her body for sustenance and shelter for nine months; the man, too, has also involved himself in the consequences of their folly and should share the responsibility for the event. It could also be contended that the pre-born baby, having not participated in the decision to be created, and being totally vulnerable and wholly dependent on the woman for continued existence, has a moral right on the mother (and father) for its survival.

---

[27] Mary Anne Warren, 'Abortion' in Peter Singer (ed.), A Companion to Ethics (Oxford: Blackwell Publishers, 1993), 305.
[28] Of course, abortion is no such thing, for conception has already occurred. The most that could be said is that an abortion follows a failed or lack of an attempt to prevent conception. The idea that it is just another means of contraception is to commit a linguistic deceit, designed to cover over the reality that the living being conceived is a human being.

One response to what appears to be a harsh contention might be to say that the sexual act was not planned but happened by seduction or, much worse, as the result of a man's forced penetration of the woman (rape). In the case of seduction, where consent was apparently forthcoming, even though not properly considered, the couple allowed their combined physical and emotional intensity to overcome all their inhibitions. In such circumstances, the possible result of their sexual act was swept aside. The woman might defend herself on the grounds that the events that led to unprotected intercourse were beyond her powers to resist. Although ultimately she acquiesced (i.e., she was not physically forced to submit), she should be exonerated from the guilt of a failure to be responsible for her actions. The man is equally accountable for what transpired, or quite possibly even more so.

Even in the case of rape, certain precautions can be taken prior to the incident happening. For example, it is surely plain foolishness to walk alone late at night in unfrequented places, after enjoying a night out in venues where lots of unknown people congregate, without taking with her an alarm system or other form of defence to ward off unwanted attention. An even greater folly would be to accompany a male, whom she hardly knows, into a place where the two are alone together (e.g. in his residence), or to allow herself to lose control of her ability to act clear-headedly through over-drinking.[29] The lack of observing such obvious safeguards does not imply that the woman is in any way responsible for being raped.[30] That would be a totally indefensible conclusion.

Such advice may seem easy to give in the cold light of day. However, in the reality of a situation where emotions can easily overpower rational thinking and a disciplined will, many people would find themselves in a very vulnerable situation. Moreover, it is not fair that the woman is the one expected to manage the precautions. The man, unjustifiably, is likely to

---

[29] The woman, of course, is hardly responsible in the event that her drink has been spiked by someone intending to render her defenceless against resistance to unwanted sex.
[30] There will be occasions, when a rape is committed, when the woman has no reason for thinking that she needs to take special precautions. Such situations raise the fundamental question of the law and policing being adequate to protect women from wholly unprovoked and undesired violence to their bodies.

blame the woman for the mess they have arrived at in the event of a pregnancy happening. Men can act very casually and callously, refusing to admit their responsibility for what has occurred. Nevertheless, in a society, where relaxed attitudes to non-committed relationships are widespread, the reality of the consequences are also well known.

The outcome of this discussion is that excuses for unwanted pregnancies are much more flimsy than pro-abortionists are prepared to admit. The alleged rights of the woman, in the face of the undoubted claims of a new, living human being are much less convincing than 21st century 'liberal' cultures suppose. There is, incidentally, nothing liberal about killing a 'something' in the woman's womb that is deemed to have arrived there by misjudged circumstances. Rosalind Hursthouse has summed up the situation precisely and honestly:

> "Pregnancy is not just one among many other physical conditions; and hence that anyone who believes that an abortion is comparable to a haircut or appendectomy is mistaken. The fact that the premature termination of a pregnancy is, in some sense, the cutting off of a new human life, and thereby connects with our thoughts about the procreation of a new human life, and about death, parenthood and family relationships, must make it a serious matter. To disregard this fact, to think of abortion as nothing but the killing of something that does not matter, or as nothing but the exercise of some right one has, or as the incidental means to some desirable state of affairs is to do something callous and light-minded, the sort of thing no virtuous and wise person would do. It is to have the wrong attitude not only to fetuses, but more generally to human life and death, parenthood and family relationships."[31]

---

[31] 'Virtue Theory and Abortion' in Hugh LaFollette (ed.), Ethics in Practice: An Anthology (Oxford: Blackwell Publishers, 2002/2), 99.

Infanticide

Infanticide is distinguished from abortion by the fact that the killing of the child happens outside the womb. Its normal definition is "the deliberate extermination of a living human infant either by intentionally ending its life or denying it life-sustaining nourishment." According to the law of those nations that have legislated for abortion, the termination of pregnancy is not considered to be an act of homicide, whereas infanticide is.

After the time has been reached within pregnancy, when the foetus is able to live outside the womb (now considered to be about 24 weeks of gestation[32]), one might well ask, what is the difference between the two? If one of the arguments used against the justification of infanticide is that the infant is so close to being a genuine human being,[33] that killing it should be counted as homicide, what difference to this recognition do the intervening 16 weeks make? Surely the difference is only one of degree. So, an abortionist, logically, would need to come up with a credible set of criteria to convince others that the degree of resemblance, as a human being, between an adult and the infant is sufficient at 40 weeks but not at 24.

This observation is a matter of life and death for a baby that has survived an abortion at 24 weeks (let alone up to the end of pregnancy), is still alive and, therefore, could continue living, if emergency medical care were to be offered. Had the baby been born early during a planned pregnancy, it would have been promptly taken to a pre-natal care unit designed to promote its long-term survival and health. Again, we are confronted with the conclusion that the only real difference between an aborted foetus and a new born infant is the mother's choice to keep the one and dispose of the other. It is hard to be persuaded that this is a very convincing moral choice.

Not everyone who supports the right to an abortion also outlaws infanticide

---

[32] There are a number of cases, where the foetus has survived an even earlier deliverance (of between 21-24 weeks) and eventually developed into a healthy baby.
[33] See, Mary Anne Warren, 'On the Moral and Legal Status of Abortion', in Ethics in Practice, 80.

in every instance. Mary Anne Warren, in her discussion of the morality of abortion, contradicts herself in an inconsistent argument about the fate of the new-born infant. On the one hand, she says,

> "If an infant is unadoptable (e.g., because of some severe physical disability), it is still wrong to kill it. For most of us value the lives of infants, and would greatly prefer to pay taxes to support foster care and state institutions for disabled children, rather than to allow them to be killed or abandoned. So long as most people feel this way, and so long as it is possible to provide care for infants who are unwanted, or who have special needs that their parents cannot meet without assistance, it is wrong to let any infant die who has a chance of living a reasonably good life."

She goes on, however, to contrast her general affirmation that "our legal system is (perhaps) correct in its classification of infanticide as murder, since no other legal category adequately expresses the force of our disapproval of this action," with late-term abortion:

> "There is an important difference between these two cases: once the infant is born, its continued life cannot pose any threat to the woman's life or health, since she is free to put it up for adoption or to place it in foster care...In contrast, a pregnant woman's right to protect her own life and health outweighs other people's desire that the foetus be preserved."

She continues her argument by using an analogy that many people would consider highly distasteful, because of the incompatibility of the comparison made:

> "Just as, when a person's life or health is threatened by an animal, and when the threat cannot be removed without killing the animal, that person's right to self-defence outweighs the desires of those who would prefer that the animal not be

killed."

The conclusion of her discussion demonstrates the kind of muddled thinking that abortionists put forward to defend their thesis:

"Thus, while the moment of birth may mark no sharp discontinuity in the degree to which an infant resembles a person, it does mark the end of a mother's right to determine its fate. Indeed, if a late abortion can be safely performed without harming the fetus, *the mother has in most cases no right to insist upon its death, for the same reason that she has no right to insist that a viable infant be killed or allowed to die.*"

So, she ends up defending the very real possibility that infanticide could be legalised in certain circumstances:

"When a society cannot possibly care for all of the children who are born, without endangering the survival of adults and older children, allowing some infants to die may be the best of a bad set of options."[34]

The words rendered in italics demonstrate the inconsistencies in her arguments for the right of abortion by showing that the distinctions made between abortion and infanticide are contradictory. In reality, a mother, at any time during her pregnancy, is free to consider putting up the infant, once born, for adoption or fostering, if she believes that it would enjoy a more fruitful life than under her care. The confusion arises out of believing falsely that there is an obvious distinction between merely being biologically

---

[34] All the quotes come from 'On the Moral and Legal Status of Abortion' (emphasis added), 80-81

human and being a person.[35]

As for the analogy drawn between an animal threatening to harm or kill a human being and an unborn baby threatening the same is ludicrous. Since when did the baby decide to threaten its mother's life? There is no parallel. Of such is the illogicality of a pro-abortionist argument.

Moreover, attempting to confirm the moment when personhood can be declared is yet another example of muddled thinking. The criteria for affirming the transition do not easily change from one day to the next. No one criterion is sufficiently certain and settled to tip the balance marking a designated change from one alleged category to another.

A future like ours?

The flaw in this argument is said to be overcome by putting forward an ethical theory that builds on the personhood potentiality of the foetus from the moment of conception. This thesis, according to its advocates, seeks to by-pass the moral impasse set up by the confrontation between pro-life and pro-choice advocates. People who hold these two approaches to abortion agree that it is wrong to kill a human person, for killing imposes on the person the irreversible calamity of a premature death. Once dead, a unique life has ceased. Every aborted baby's future is deliberately eradicated. That is the consequence of being pro-choice. This conclusion is manifestly

---

[35] Mary Anne Warren's views summarised here are set forth in greater depth in her book, Moral Status (Oxford: OUP, 2000). Since that time, the defence of infanticide has become more widespread. In a recent article, authored by The Parliamentary Network for Critical Issues, 'The macabre proposal to tolerate infanticide, in the name of abortion rights', August 31, 2020, a case study of infanticide in El Salvador was instanced as an example. In this article, Professor Ligia De Jesus Castaldi commented on false reports by pro-abortionist groups (including Amnesty International) that 17 women were imprisoned for mischaracterised miscarriages, abortions or obstetric emergency: "Decriminalization of infanticide seems to be the new frontier in pro-abortion advocacy, both nationally and internationally...The treatment of abortion and infanticide as equivalents in this litigation is obviously meant to deceive the public: but it also seems to be based on equal disregard for the life of the unborn and newly born child".

unsustainable morally.

The premise of this argument against abortion rests on a logical point of comparison: the difference between a foetus and a fully-fledged human person is only a matter of time. The briefness of a life before birth is no reason for interfering with the normal, natural process of growth, as though an aborted foetus could be compared to a ripening fruit that is plucked before it has become mature. A foetus has a 'Future Like Ours' (FLO). This way of looking at the reality of abortion does not have to specify which properties another individual must possess, in order that the killing of the individual is morally reprehensible. The wrongness of killing an individual, whether in the womb or outside, is self-evident, because its life is always embryologically valuable.[36]

The FLO claim is a heroic attempt to sidestep what is considered by some people to be a sterile pro-choice/pro-life stalemate. Nevertheless, its argumentation is based on a purely human view of the debate, which equates the prolongation of the life of a foetus with the value of its latent future. It could still be argued that, if its conscious life will become intolerable, perhaps through severe, permanent brain-damage, death would not be a calamity.[37] The argument implies that, in such cases, killing (euthanasia) would not be wrong. When life no longer has any meaningful value to the one who suffers (conceivably anyone who is distressingly disabled or traumatised), it is not axiomatic that intentionally ending its life would be a tragedy and, therefore, wrong.

---

[36] This premise is developed by Don Marquis in an article, 'An Argument that Abortion is Wrong' in Ethics in Practice, 86-91; note the use of the term embryological from the reality of the embryo.
[37] Only one example from real life is sufficient to overturn the presumption that massive brain damage renders a human being's life meaningless. Proof of the immense value of such a life is given in the case of Jonathan Bryan, who suffered great loss of blood to the brain during an early birth brought on by a car-accident. Through the unbelievable patience and the incredible skill of his parents and the medics who attended to the consequences of the post-traumatic event, Jonathan survived and learnt to read and write. In spite of suffering from locked-in syndrome, preventing him from being able to communicate in a normal fashion, by the age of 12 he was able to write a book about his experiences; see, Eye Can Write: A memoir of a child's silent soul emerging (London: Lagom, 2018).

So, only the nature of the foetus from God's perspective, as an individual made in God's likeness, having thereby an inherent, sacrosanct value, gives an adequate account of the evil of abortion. Ultimately, FLO as a theory does not outlaw either abortion or infanticide, because it makes worthwhileness depend on human devised criteria, not on the given, inviolable nature of a person from conception onwards.

There are a number of other reasons why deliberate infanticide (including leaving aborted embryos to die, even though they have survived the attempt to kill them, and are capable of living) is always wrong.[38] A child with grave physical and mental disabilities can experience a number of emotions, such as happiness, fright, gratitude and love; therefore, the child shows that its care, even when counting its incapacities, is rewarding. Infanticide is completely contrary to the concept of physicians as healers, charged with an overwhelming duty of care. Their primary responsibility, in so far as they are able to achieve it, is the well-being of their patients, to alleviate their suffering and save lives. The medical profession is not able to make infallible decisions about the future well-being or capabilities of a seriously traumatised young infant. Congenital defects of young children can be corrected by proper surgical procedure, even within the womb.[39] On a pragmatic note, premature infanticide by hastening an infant's death would limit ongoing medical research aimed at discovering more sophisticated treatments in the future.

---

[38] Allowing a living being to die, when all achievable ways of preserving its life have been exhausted, is not to be equated with infanticide. It is vital ethically to distinguish the inevitable physical consequence of a medical trauma, for which there is no current remedy, from pro-actively ending life. One decision is allowing to die the other is intentional killing. This is an easy distinction to make in theory. However, in practice, as several court cases about the legal ambiguity of turning off life-supporting machines has witnessed, there are profound questions still to be answered, such as what counts as a still possible chance of recovery and how is irremediable death to be defined.

[39] Amazing in-utero surgery to correct the defects that lead to spina bifida has been pioneered in Brazil and the USA; see, Usha Lee McFarling, 'She's wiggling her toes: new fetal surgery for spina bifida may be safer for both baby and mom, Stat, May 28, 2019.

Abortion, the law and moral virtue

It is a well-known fact that changes in the law on fundamental social issues often contribute to changes of attitude towards these issues among a given population. Once an action, previously forbidden, was made legal, people's perception of the validity of that action often gradually changes. So it has been with the official overturning of the legal prohibition of abortion in a number of countries. What once was considered by the majority of a nation's citizens to be intolerable has gradually become acceptable. Those opposing abortion now find themselves in a minority.

Laws are modified when most people believe that the old laws are no longer serviceable, because they no longer fit the moral climate of the times. Law changes have often been heavily influenced by determined campaigns, orchestrated by a small group of influential people, who have managed to persuade the nation's legislature that their opinions warrant the desired changes.[40]

Fundamentally, as this discussion has emphasised, abortion was legalised on the basis of an autocratic, ideologically determined decision concerning the distinction between the biologically human and the person in the first two trimesters of the pre-born embryo. No higher law, which would put the matter to rest by declaring that no such distinction pertains, is considered to be relevant and applicable.

Pressure was exerted on those who make laws, and those who administer them, by small groups who often based their arguments for change by reference to extremely few examples of secretly performed (back-street) abortions, where a mother's life was under severe threat from the inadequate methods being used. The result, however, has been that the law itself (legalising abortion) has lowered the value placed on human life. The law

---

[40] A case in point was the UK Parliament's arbitrary imposition of the right of abortion (up to birth on those deemed to be physically impaired) on Northern Ireland in 2020. This was against the wishes of 75% of the population and a majority of the members of the reconstituted Northern Ireland Assembly

could only be passed, once the legislators were persuaded to accept the abortion lobby's argument. The result has been that the intrinsic worth of a pre-born human life in its early stages of development has been discounted. Thus, the instinctive impulse to protect the life of a foetus at any stage of development, was overruled by a false dogma about the baby's status as a human being.

Inevitably, the unconditional sanctity of human life has become eroded. The negative educational impact of abortion on respect for life cannot be ignored. We have shown how, for example, the legitimising of the killing of the unborn has become part of a drive to decriminalise abortion altogether, even up to the day of birth, and even beyond its birth. At its most extreme, abortions are now carried out if parents of the child consider its sex to be unacceptable to them or if, once detected, the physical well-being of the foetus is considered to be compromised. In the latter case, eugenics raises its ugly head.

Unfortunately, a law can be enacted for purely pragmatic reasons, which have not been properly judged by inherently justifiable principles of right and wrong. This is the case with abortion. On grounds of the inherent dignity of the new life in the womb, due to its conception by two persons, there is now no symmetry between the rights of the foetus and that of the mother. The limited rights of a woman to control her own reproductive processes do not entail her right to end another individual's life. The consequence of her inability to fulfil the way she wants to live, as she perceives it, unencumbered by the obligation of caring for another, is not a relevant argument. The life lost is that of the new living individual not that of the woman. It should be self-evident that the loss of life is a much greater wrong than the loss of the ability to be free from motherhood till the optimum time of her convenience.

The original intention of the law on abortion was to allow for certain extreme circumstances, when ending the life of the unborn might be considered the lesser of two evils. Tragically, this has now developed into a situation of practising abortion-on-demand, i.e. abortion in the case of an unwanted pregnancy, for any reason. Current law has overridden the moral assumption that a decision may have to be taken between two evils, for, according to the abortionist demands, only one remains – that pertaining to the mother. Within the last fifty years, the truth about what it means to be human and a person has been changed in its essence. It is hard not to conclude that today, in the context of the inadequate arguments served up to continue the legalisation of abortion against the reasons advocated to end the 'drive towards death',[41] contemporary Western law-makers are actually promoting more than one falsehood.

---

[41] This is a theory expounded by Sigmund Freud in the latter half of his life, which he called Thanatos, the Greek word for death; see, J. Andrew Kirk, Being Human: An Historical Inquiry into Who We Are (Eugene, OR: Wipf and Stock, 2019), 273-274. I will return to his theory in chapter 11. Abortion, save for a tiny minority of cases, manifests a particular drive towards inducing a cruel, painful death.

CHAPTER 2
Human Sexuality (Part I): Truths and Illusions

"Those who can make you believe absurdities can make you commit atrocities" (Voltaire, Questions sur les Miracles)

Why this subject?

Reasons for including this topic in a book, whose principal purpose is to discern, interpret and respond to causes that are widening the gulf between two contrasting worlds, need to be justified. The issues surrounding sexuality, currently being passionately debated within Western nations, have become increasingly strident; in recent political and legal decisions, they have reached fever-pitch.

It is a curious anomaly that, although in recent years Christians have often been accused of placing undue emphasis on the centrality of sex in their engagement with the world. To put it more bluntly, they have been denounced for their tendency to hyper-ventilate on the subject. Now, however, the pendulum has swung in a different direction. Judging by the amount of time dedicated to matters of sexual interest and morals on TV, in the printed and spoken media, in films, on stage, in political forums, in briefing papers, in schools, and by no means least on the internet (as witnessed by the exponential increase of young people watching pornography), the non-Christian world is now much more prolific in its treatment of the subject. Christians now find themselves doing little more than respond to a number of false understandings about sex, sexuality and gender being propagated by groups that wish to free their take on reality from all natural and moral constraints.

The Importance of Sexuality

From a Christian stand-point, sexuality is part of the reality of how humans are constituted. The subject includes the development in children of the awareness of the bipolarity of the human race, similarities and distinctions between boys and girls, the changes in sexual consciousness brought on by the onset of puberty, the need to understand appropriate ways of treating the opposite sex, the right and wrong ways of engaging in sexual intimacy, sexual attraction as a given impulse and the many advantageous reasons for maintaining permanent heterosexual bonds within the covenant of marriage.

The overriding consideration for Christians is that sexuality is a beautiful gift from God which, when properly treated, is a wonderful endowment to be gratefully enjoyed. Due to its supreme significance and importance in human relationships and the depressing and harmful ways in which it has been distorted (about which evidence will be given in this and following chapters), sexuality has to be placed under the jurisdiction of well-founded moral principles that protect its favourable outcomes and curtail its destructive tendencies. This is a major reason for using the subject of sexuality as a pre-eminent example of the harmful confusions that arise when reality, reason and well-proven, beneficial values are rejected by a disordered world. The Christian message of a new world coming, if it were believed and acted on, presents a different reality that has the power to promote healthy living at all levels of human existence.

A sea-change in views of human sexuality

It is easy to trace the ways in which the moral principles that used to guide sexual behaviour and safeguard its delight and wholesomeness have been deconstructed in the last half-century. One of the best examples of how a former consensus about sexual morality has been dismantled is given in *A*

Manifesto of the Gay Liberation Front [42], published in 1971. It is a campaign document whose purpose is "to work for the replacement of the family unit" (considered to be governed by an unchangeable patriarchal framework). The Manifesto presents a strong critique of "compulsive monogamy," an apologetic for "compulsive licentiousness", a strategy for overcoming the "sub-human status" of homosexuals within society, the disbanding of Christianity's teaching on sexuality, deemed to be archaic and irrational. Most significant, perhaps, is its intent to overturn the psychiatric community's former opinion that homosexual and transgender orientations are pathological deviations from healthy sexual relations. Above all, it seeks to promote "a new life-style" in all matters sexual.

The "new life-style" in this Manifesto is predicated on the superiority of homosexual over heterosexual conduct in sexual behaviour, in that gay men do not need to oppress women to fulfil their psycho-sexual needs, nor do gay women need to relate sexually to male oppressors by fulfilling their alleged role of being sex objects. With regard to the reputed character of the ideal family, gay liberation advocates the end of the pursuit of life-long monogamy, which in its opinion is based on man's ownership of the woman. She, apparently, sells her services to a man in return for security for herself and her children. Although never spelt out precisely, the theory states that marriage is "entirely bound up with man's idea of property." Finally the document declares that "the long-term goal of the Gay Liberation Front is to rid society of the gender-role system by abolishing the traditional family as a unit in which children are brought up."

This particular Manifesto pronounces an extreme version of the demolition of the hitherto accepted practice of family life and sexual relations by caricaturing both and insisting that the worst possible interpretation of both accords with daily reality. Not all advocates of a change from society's rejection to its acceptance of the normality of gay attraction, relationships and identity would wish to overturn so radically the inherited pattern of

---

[42] See, www.equalityalliance.org.uk/articles. All quotes in inverted commas come directly from the Manifesto.

family life. More typically, they simply wish to be accorded the same rights, privileges and affirmation as those who are comfortable in their heterosexual existence.

However, as will be pointed out later in the chapter, in recent years legal provisions that grant to committed homosexual couples the same rights and privileges as those given to heterosexual couples, on the basis of an equality of consideration, have had the effect of redefining marriage and the family. This new consideration goes a long way beyond the desire to have two parallel structures of equal value existing side by side. 'Gay marriage' and 'gay family life' actually constitute a fundamental cultural shift for the whole of society. The reasons for redesigning hitherto accepted norms will be set out later.

Approaches to the verification of truths about human sexuality

The methods that I propose to adopt in considering the topic before us are both negative and positive. The issues are so profound and the polemical way in which they are often treated so intense that it is essential that assumptions on which they are based are carefully clarified. Otherwise, what should be a civil debate between people who are deeply opposed in their opinions becomes a mere shouting-match, in which abuse of the 'enemy' becomes the weapon of choice.[43]

So, negatively, I will attempt not to use any kind of ad hominem argument, i.e. any assertion that is based on the alleged character or behaviour of the people whose views I wish to counter. Condemning the personal integrity of people, on account of their beliefs and actions, and thereby dismissing their reasoning, is not acceptable. It avoids rational engagement and, in its place, substitutes unsubstantiated invective.

---

[43] I have set out in detail how language, in a number of cases, has increasingly become distorted by its abusive use; see, The Abuse of Language. In the cultural conflicts of our times, the one who shouts loudest, and most conspicuously turns a deaf ear to the opinions of others, is taken to have won the argument.

I will not appeal to any self-authenticating authority (whatever its source) as a knock-down way of settling a controversy. I will not hide my own moral assumptions and the basis on which they are formed. I will not claim to speak, as though from a wholly neutral vantage-point, because I know that such an allegation is impossible. When discussing concerns that are set out in terms of right and wrong, good and evil, amorality is simply not an option. I will endeavour not to use statistics to demonstrate a point of view, if and when they appear simply to echo prejudices.

Positively, I will rely on the importance of data, when it comes as the result of the most up-to-date and rigorous research, tested by the accepted methods of scientific investigation, such as repeatability, control mechanisms, the extent and longevity of population surveys, and findings based on inferences to the best explanation. In other words, the data will be used, only when founded on the best possible evidence available and have passed the test of not having been distorted by undeclared ideological presuppositions.

I will not assume that the kind of scientific evidence, that is independently reviewed and rationally demonstrated, is the only sort of input that is of consequence in deciding the truth about human sexuality. As we are talking about a matter of such fundamental significance to every member of the human race, other sources of truth, such as those gleaned from history, philosophy, religion, moral discourse and experience are also valid witnesses to what is real and what false.

I will attempt always to be fair to beliefs and reasoning that I do not share. I will endeavour to set them out in such a way that anybody who holds them agrees that justice has been done and that I have been as objective and even-handed as any fallible human being is capable of.

I trust that these approaches to a question of such enormous import as human sexuality will alleviate the suspicion that my deductions reflect nothing more than a set of invincible, prior prejudices and bigotry. Being explicit about one's evaluative framework should at least provide reason to believe that the research is founded on the desire to be honest in an area of such over-heated controversy.

Sexual orientation
The value of scientific findings

This section owes a good deal of its content to a lengthy report, written as a global survey of the latest scientific research on sexuality and gender.[44] Its importance lies particularly in its aim to be as objective as possible in assessing the scientific evidence now in the public domain. The authors are well aware of the fact that "few topics are as complex and controversial as human sexual orientation and gender identity. These matters touch upon our most intimate thoughts and feelings, and help to define us as both individuals and social beings"[45]

The intention of the authors is to search out, as widely as possible, those sources that have delved into the various aspects of the two main topics (sexual orientation and gender alignment) and to analyse their findings. It is unlikely that such a comprehensive undertaking has been attempted before, partly because the amount of literature available is immense. It requires much patience in the reading of the various manuscripts, ordering their subject-matter, providing a careful summary of their discoveries and offering clear and fair explanations of their conclusions.

Throughout the survey, they hold themselves to have focussed exclusively "on the scientific evidence – what its shows and...does not show."[46] Their general conclusion is that "sexual orientation and gender identity resist explanation by simple theories. There is a large gap between the certainty

---

[44] Lawrence S. Mayer and Paul R. McHugh, 'Sexuality and Gender: Findings from the Biological, Psychological and Social Sciences', The New Atlantis, Fall 2016. In case anyone considers a report now seven years old is no longer reliable and cogent, I will also refer to a number of more recent publications. I think, nevertheless, that the analyses and judgements of the document remain well-founded.
[45] 'Sexuality and Gender,' 9.
[46] 'Sexuality and Gender,' 9.

with which beliefs are held (within the general populace) about these matters and what a sober assessment of the sciences reveal."[47] They are well aware that their "report is not an exhaustive analysis nor the last word on the subjects addressed," nor is it "the only avenue of understanding that we can rely on – there are other sources of wisdom and knowledge."[48]

Scientific explorations never stand still. What may be conceived as a consensus on the reliability of research outcomes by one generation may be modified or overturned by the next. In this particular field of inquiry, the very nature of the methods of investigation may be quite problematical, so on occasions the findings have to be pronounced as provisional. Nevertheless, what scientific evidence has so far thrown up on such matters as sexual orientation, the consequences of adopting a particular sexual life-style and the vexed question of gender identity should be taken seriously. If it does not conform to the beliefs of certain sectors of the population, it should not be lightly dismissed, as though individual, subjective feelings and presumptions outweigh a wealth of objective data. In the vehemence of debate, the solid findings of scientifically-accepted methods of analysis are sometimes dismissed disdainfully as though irrelevant to personal perceptions and opinions. Such reactions make pursuit of true reality impossible to achieve. All that is left, regrettably, is abuse, defamation and incoherence.

Is sexual orientation a helpful, explanatory category?

If we may begin by assuming that no personal convictions can be either taken for granted or excluded from the real possibility that they may be mistaken, then the very notion of sexual orientation itself may be misplaced. It may be that the term is just a myth. A number of historians and anthropologists, for example, even those who affirm the division of sexuality into at least three main categories (hetero, homo and bisexual)

---

[47] 'Sexuality and Gender,' 12.
[48] 'Sexuality and Gender,' 12.

believe that such a neat division is a recent social construction, arising in the Western world some 150 years ago. There is little evidence that any society, prior to the mid-19th century, acknowledged the existence of a gay minority, discernibly gay-oriented individuals or even 'straight' people.[49] The word heterosexuality itself arose at the end of the 19th century. Whenever people of the same sex declared their love for each other, or included such relationships in the novels they wrote, there is a tendency to read back into earlier history, say the 18th century, the formulations of a later discourse.

Some believe that both hetero and homosexuality are misnomers, based on the now conclusively demonstrated false premise that one's sexuality is defined genetically, prior to birth, and then fixed for the rest of one's life.[50] The reality is that sexual manifestations do not exist as fixed polarities – either straight or gay. They fall along a continuum between what might be called two extremities. This is particularly true of adolescents, who are most likely to be working through the confusions they experience about their sexual identities. It is quite possible that they have romantic notions and sexual fantasies about people of both sexes. However, when they reach a more stable adulthood, they usually settle on a strong preference for the opposite sex; only a small minority identify themselves as exclusively and permanently attracted to the same sex.

The Royal College of Psychiatrists (RCP) in the UK published a new position paper in 2014, which amounted to a revision of its previous position on sexual orientation. The College used to affirm that it is innate and irreversible. Now, however, it announces that a person's sexual orientation is shaped by post-natal experiences and may change during a person's life.[51] In other words, orientation is a flexible reality that encounters different degrees of attraction for one or the other sex. Changes of

---

[49] See, Jonathan Katz, The Invention of Heterosexuality (Chicago: University of Chicago Press, 2007/2), chapter 3, 'Before Heterosexuality: looking backwards,' 33-56.
[50] I will return to this commonly held notion later in the discussion.
[51] www.rcp.ac.uk/pdf/PS02_2014.pdf : "sexual orientation is determined by a combination of biological and post-natal environmental factors...It is not the case that sexual orientation is immutable or might not vary to some extent in a person's life".

direction are confirmed by observed practice and self-identification.

The widespread assumption that has filtered into current folklore is that both heterosexual and homosexual orientations are fixed from birth and are permanent and unchangeable, has by no means vanished. Some people in the LGBT (lesbian, gay, bi-sexual, trans-gender) community strongly affirm that it is impossible for a same-sex attracted person to move to a more open heterosexual disposition over a period of time, with or without carefully managed and monitored professional therapeutic counselling.[52]

This has led to a vigorous campaign by some professional psychiatric bodies and gay lobbying groups to have such counselling prohibited by law. Thus the RCP, having declared that sexual orientations may change, i.e. that they are not inborn, irrevocable and irreversible, nevertheless declares that, although change may be possible, it should not be permitted by means of the guidance of psycho-therapeutic counsellors. A similar position is held by the UK's Council for Psychotherapy.[53]

Born that way?

Many studies have been carried out on the claims that some people possess an enduring gay identity from birth - "they are born that way." It has been

---

[52] It is interesting to note that the same group acknowledges that the reverse step, from hetero-sexual to homo-sexual orientation, is quite possible and to be endorsed.
[53] "The College would not support a therapy for converting people from homosexuality any more than we would do so from heterosexuality. Psychiatrists should be committed to reducing inequalities, not supporting practices that are explicitly based on pathologising homosexuality. As such, the College remains in favour of legislative efforts to ban such conversion therapies," www.rcpsych.ac.uk/pdf/PS02_2014.pdf.
Later in the chapter I will return to a discussion of this apparent anomaly. Also, see, College for Sexual and Relationship Psychotherapy, 'Code of Ethics and Practice, Ethic principles of the CSRP (5 e):
"Respect for the dignity, autonomy and right to self-determination of the Client;"
"Anti-discriminatory practice, autonomy and right to self-determination of the Client and of others with whom they may be involved must be protected and respected in all interactions, "see, https://www.psychotherapy.org.uk/wp-content/uploads/2018/10/Code-of-Ethics-and-Practice-for-CSRP.pdf.

suggested, for example, that such a trait may be carried in a person's genetic make-up. However, the wide survey already mentioned comes to the conclusion that "the largest attempt to identify genetic variants associated with homosexuality...found no linkages reaching genome-wide significance for same sex sexual identity for males or females."[54] The report continues that there may be genetic contributions towards homosexual inclinations or behaviours, but that a phenotypical expression of genes is usually influenced by environmental factors: different environments may lead to different phenotypes, even for the same genes, including emotional, physical or sexual abuse".[55]

The debate shaped by "nature v. nurture" has been abandoned by scientists who have no particular interests to defend. Genetic influences affecting complex human behaviour depend in part on an individual's life experiences as they mature. So, the present conclusion of the scientific engagement with genetic theory is that the evidence for a direct connection between genes and attributes is extremely modest.[56] "Born that way" is a highly simplistic narrative.

Not satisfied with the paucity of well-established, longitudinal and controlled-group research on the possible origins of homosexual orientation, some advocates of its irreversibility have turned to the possible effects of pre-born hormonal activity in the development of the foetus. It has been suggested, for example, that hormones may, in some cases,

---

[54] 'Sexual Orientation', 33.
[55] A more recent comprehensive, longitudinal and numerically-significant piece of research has been published which comes to the conclusion that "all tested genetic variations accounted for 8 to 25% of variation in same-sex behavior...and do not allow meaningful prediction of an individual's sexual behavior", see, 'Large-scale GWAS reveals insights into the genetic architecture of same-sex sexual behavior', Science, 30 August 2019, Vol. 365. This was interpreted, in an article by Claire Hansen, US News, August 29, 2019, to signify that "the research...found that genetic influence is not determinative (of non-heterosexual orientation) and non-genetic factors are also likely to be involved, making it impossible to use genetics to predict individuals same-sex behavior."
[56] The reasonable conclusion to the debate seems to be that there may be genetic influences on homosexual orientation, when combined with other environmental influences. However, the idea that any one gene causes this orientation has to be dropped, at least as far as present scientific research indicates.

produce permanent changes in the sensitive wiring of the brain, which then become immutable. Another theory that has been advanced is that a mother's stress patterns during pregnancy, through neuro-biological effects stimulated by inter-uterine hormonal dysfunction, may affect sexual orientation at a later stage in the child's development.[57]

Attempts have also been made to show that there are "structural or functional differences between the brains of homosexual and heterosexual individuals (using a variety of criteria to define these categories)." One of the problems with this kind of investigation is that any brain differences could just as easily, perhaps more easily, be the result rather than the cause of distinctive patterns of behaviour and personal identity classification.[58] To identify differences in brain structure or function between those who identify themselves as gay or straight, even if the numbers selected in both cases cohere and are of a sufficient size to make them statistically significant, as being invariably the cause rather than the result of different sexual attractions, is to commit a methodological fallacy. It is well-known that the morphology and activity of the brain is malleable, according to many different life experiences, one of these could be the decision, perhaps after much thought and emotional anguish, to declare oneself homo-sexual or bisexual.

Same-sex attraction and possible abuse in childhood

The origin of same-sex attraction and self-identification is incredibly difficult to locate. A number of theories have been suggested, once the all-inclusive presumption that it is due principally to biological causes has been dismissed as lacking demonstrable evidence. One of the most common theories to explain homosexual orientation, and also one of the most controversial, is the possibility that excessive abuse suffered during the development of a child towards adulthood could be a major cause. In studies on the subject it has been discovered that gays and lesbians had 1.7 times and bisexuals 1.6 times the rate of adverse childhood experiences in comparison to those who declared themselves to be heterosexual in their

---

[57] 'Sexual Orientation,' 23-27.
[58] 'Sexual Orientation', 40-41.

attractions, behaviour and identity.

However, the difficulty of garnering reliable evidence from participants in the survey, because of the limitations of recalling childhood experiences, makes the link somewhat weak. Moreover, the majority of people who suffered childhood trauma of one kind or another do not become attracted to the same sex or think of themselves as bisexual. Nevertheless, in two fairly exhaustive studies of the connection between childhood abuse and non-heterosexual preference a higher proportion of the latter than those who showed no such preference was discovered:

> "In both males and females, significantly higher rates of non-heterosexuality were found in participants who experienced childhood abuse and in those with a risky childhood environment."[59]

The comparative figures were, in the case of homosexual males 41% compared to 24% of heterosexual and in females 42% compared to 30%.

Having demonstrated that there is some kind of co-relation between childhood sexual traumas and homosexual attraction, behaviour or self-declared identity, research has not yet advanced much beyond the stage of conjecture. It could be that early sexual maltreatment may cause boys to believe that they are gay or make girls averse to sexual contact with men. The social stigmatisation felt for the abuse they suffered might push young adults into same-sex relationships. The adverse effect of poor-parenting, shown by the failure of parents or guardians to safe-guard the children in their care, can effect chemical and hormonal receptors in childhood that might influence sexuality through changes in brain regions that regulate social behaviour.

One of the reports cited in the survey of research into sexuality states that "same sex attractions and partnering may result from the drive for intimacy and sex to repair depressed, stressed or angry moods." [60] Any of these factors could be a cause of same-sex attraction in some cases. On the other

---

[59] 'Sexuality', 47.
[60] 'Sexuality', 50.

hand, "without more research, the idea that sexual abuse may be a causal factor in sexual orientation remains speculative."[61]

Another theory that bears the names of the fathers of psychoanalysis, Freud, Jung and Adler, and the initial research findings of Anna Freud, one of Sigmund Freud's daughters, locates homosexual drives in an unconscious, unresolved childhood conflict between the child and one of the parents in a dysfunctional relationship. Jung, for example, summed up the trauma in the following way:

"A homosexual man is incapable of finding maleness deep within his inner being. He, therefore attempts to find it at the biological-sexual level."

Anna Freud identified an important motivational factor for homosexual desire:

"By entering into homosexual activities, a man seeks to 'repair' his identification with the male gender which he failed to achieve as a boy."

Irving Bieber found that

"A failed relationship between father and son in the early years constitutes a typical feature in the biography of a homo-sexually oriented man."[62]

These views were based on the prior assumption that homosexual leanings were symptomatic of a deviance from the norm of a healthy heterosexual attraction and, therefore, constituted a pathology.

The publication of research in this mode was cut short at the beginning of

---

[61] 'Sexuality', 50.
[62] All three quotes are taken from the following study, Christi. R. Vonholdt, 'The Deconstruction of Marriage and Family', German Institute for Youth and Society, March 2003, see, Irving Bieber (et al.), Homosexuality: A Psychoanalytic Study of Male Homosexuals (New York: Basic Books, 1962). The book received a mixed reception, partly because of disagreements about the soundness of the methodological approach and partly because the findings were biased, because the authors were presumed to have presupposed the outcome before the research was undertaken.

the 1970s, when the American Psychiatric Association (APA) declared that homosexual orientation should no longer be considered a mental health disorder. Its summary conclusion was that "homosexual behaviour is simply a perfectly natural, well-adjusted alternative to heterosexual relations".[63] This opinion has gradually worked itself into the collective conscience of many Western societies as a kind of indisputable fact. To deny this verdict is interpreted as manifesting a 'homophobic' attitude against self-confessed homosexuals, equivalent to that of racism and sexism. However, to dismiss any of these possible explanations out of hand, without cogent evidence, lacks honesty and impartiality. The APA's declaration was not the result of sound scientific investigation but rather a political move under the intense pressure of homosexual support groups.

According to the greatest weight of reliable scientific evidence the matter of orientation is not settled. Lawrence S. Mayer and Paul R. McHugh, in the first part of their extensive multi-disciplinary survey of relevant research on sexual orientation come to the following conclusions:

> "The concept of sexual orientation is unusually ambiguous compared to other psychological traits. It typically refers to one of three things: attractions, behaviour or identity. Sexual orientation can refer to several other things as well: belonging to a certain community, fantasies...longings, strivings, felt needs for certain forms of companionship...Even specifying one of the basic senses of orientation...is insufficient for doing justice to the richly varied phenomenon of human sexuality. In this part we have criticised the common assumption that desires, attraction or longings reveal some innate and fixed feature of our biological or psychological constitution... Further more we have some reasons to doubt the common assumption that in

---

[63] Ronald Bayer in his book, Homosexuality and American Psychiatry: The Politics of Diagnosis (Princeton: Princeton University Press, 1987) states that the decision was not based on the appropriation of scientific evidence based on research, but on action demanded by the ideological temper of the times. The main issue was political, namely the question of who decides what is normal sexuality. Seeing that, according to the protagonists of change, this cannot be decided scientifically, then it has to be resolved in the arena of public opinion.

order to live happy and flourishing lives, we must somehow discover this innate fact about ourselves that we call sexuality or sexual orientation and invariably express it through particular patterns of behavior or... life trajectory. Perhaps, we ought instead to explore what sorts of behaviors...tend to be conducive to health and flourishing and what kinds undermine a healthy and flourishing life."[64]

Sexuality, Mental Health Outcomes and Social Stress

The final sentence, just quoted, of the Conclusion to the first part of the ('Sexuality and Gender') study is a guide to how we should judge morally the rightness and goodness of all forms of sexuality. The second part of the study encourages us to be cautious about the desirability of choosing a same-sex identity and life-style. The opening sentence of this section, which sums up the findings of the "robust and growing body of research," confirms that

> "Compared to the general population, non-heterosexual and transgender populations have higher rates of mental health problems such as anxiety, depression and suicide, as well as behavior and social problems such as substance abuse and intimate partner violence."

The study then goes on to survey the literature that presents and validates the evidence for this disparity and explores the possible causes of its occurrence.

By way of a brief interjection at this juncture, if the more pronounced poor mental health and social consequences of homosexual orientation and behaviour, in comparison to heterosexual, is due to the choice of a gay, lesbian or bisexual life-style then it confirms what the message of the Christian faith would expect. The message states that the optimum state of

---

[64] Sexuality, 57-58.

human flourishing is determined by following the moral guidelines laid down by the one who created human beings in a special way. Deviations from the divine model will lead inevitably to the malfunctioning of human relationships and personal well-being. To be able to predict familiar outcomes of a particular set of circumstances should carry some weight in arriving at correct interpretations of the evidence.

One would not expect LGBT supporters to accept this interpretation of the data. It is convinced that homosexual orientation is as normal and valuable a way of expressing one's sexuality as that of a heterosexual disposition. Yet concrete evidence shows that the outcome of homosexual activity clearly produces greater psychological distress. Hence, for LGBT advocates, there must be other explanations for this phenomenon that do not force the conclusion that same-sex orientation runs counter to the fundamental make-up of human nature.

The literature, that confirms statistically that LGBT self-identifying youth experience a higher rate of "depression, as well as suicide attempts and suicidal ideation (inclination)" than heterosexual youth and that "LGB individuals in early or middle adulthood are more prone to mood and anxiety disorders, depression, suicidal ideation and suicide attempts," is summed up in the 2011 report from the US Institute of Medicine (IOM), 'The Health of Lesbian, Gay, Bisexual and Transgender People: Building A Foundation for Better Understanding'.[65] "This report is an extensive review of scientific literature citing hundreds of studies that examine the health status of LGBT populations. The authors are scientists who are well versed in these issues."[66]

In fairness to the data, the report also acknowledges that there are a few studies that do not concur with the vast majority of case-studies that demonstrate the much higher percentage of risk factors, in relation to favourable health outcomes, in non-heterosexual attraction, behaviour and

---

[65] Robert Graham (et al.), (Washington, DC: The National Academies Press, 2011).
[66] 'Sexuality,' 64.

self-identification. Nevertheless, "acknowledging...the studies that do not support the general trend, the vast majority of studies cited in the report point to a generally higher risk of poor mental health status in LGBT populations compared to heterosexual populations.[67]

An explanation for higher adverse health outcomes in the homosexual population compared to the heterosexual.

Given the overwhelming peer-reviewed scientific evidence for the above conclusion, the causes still have to be ascertained. The most convincing theory to explain this phenomenon is the 'Social Stress Model.' It is said that

> "sexual minorities face distinct social challenges such as stigma, overt discrimination and harassment, and, often struggle with reconciling their sexual behaviours and identities with the norms of their families and communities...They tend to be subject to challenges similar to those of some minority populations arising from marginalisation by or conflict with the larger part of society in ways that may adversely impact their health."[68]

This model is sometimes referred to as 'a social or minority stress hypothesis.' Stress may carry a number of different meanings "ranging from a description of a physiological condition to a mental or emotional state of anger or anxiety to a difficult social, economic or interpersonal situation."[69] The model is not intended to put forth a complete explanation for disparities between non-heterosexuals and heterosexuals, nor does it explain the mental health problems of a particular patient, for there may be other factors in play, not directly related to sexual orientation. Its purpose is to advance a theory that describes social factors that might directly, or indirectly, influence health risks for LGBT people. The stresses may be due

---

[67] 'Sexuality', 64.
[68] 'Sexuality', 76.
[69] 'Sexuality', 76.

to external pressures, such as other people's perceptions of homosexuality, or internal, such as the fear of disapproval and a feeling of shame.

The external predicaments can be summed up in the one word, stigma. Stigma is an attitude that, in particular social contexts, reduces a person's worth in the eyes of others. It arises out of negative evaluations that become the basis for excluding or treating differently stigmatised individuals, because their choices are deemed to exhibit a character flaw or moral disorder. The judgements heaped on such persons may find that the cause is considered to be a blemish in their make-up or the utter disgrace of their opinions, decisions and behaviour. Such a reaction may lead them to conceal what they perceive about themselves, leading in turn to experiencing increased mental conflict.

To date, there is little empirical research on the mental effects of stigma on LGBT people. One of the difficulties, in providing objective evidence of cause and effect, is that research depends so much on people's subjective self-assessment – for example, how they evaluate their feelings of being devalued and rejected.

How may the model be tested? Everything else being equal, one might well assume that the opposition of family, friends and colleagues to those who openly declare their homosexual orientation would cause their increased sense of being contemptible. However, it is almost impossible to gauge the effect of stigmatisation on a large population of non-heterosexuals, considering that each individual who takes part in a mass survey remains an individual. Each person, with his or her own unique family and wider social background, may respond differently to the various factors that could be the cause of increased mental distress. One example, already indicated, might be sexual and mental abuse in childhood. Such experiences could well have contributed to both the homosexual inclination and the increased likelihood of mental anxiety and pain in later life. How this abuse was handled by adult carers, at the child's most vulnerable stage of emotional development, will also have either a mitigating effect or one that multiplies the sense of loss and hopelessness.

In order for the stigmatisation model to be fairly tested, means have to be designed that are able to isolate the one factor of homosexual identity that causes the stigma. In their conclusion to a survey of the limited research done in making this connection, Mayer and McHugh say this:

"The social stress model probably accounts for some of the poor mental health outcomes experienced by sexual minorities, though the evidence supporting the model is limited, inconsistent and incomplete... There is evidence linking some forms of mistreatment, stigmatization, and discrimination to some of the poor mental health outcomes experienced by non-heterosexuals, but it is far from clear that these factors account for all of the disparities between the heterosexual and non-heterosexual populations. Those poor mental health outcomes may be mitigated to some extent by reducing social stressors, but this strategy is unlikely to eliminate all of the disparities in mental health status between sexual minorities and the wider population. Other factors, such as the elevated rates of sexual abuse-victimization among the LGBT population...may also account for some of these mental health disparities, as research has consistently shown that survivors of childhood sexual abuse are significantly at risk of a wide range of medical, psychological, behavioural, and sexual disorders."[70]

"Just as it does a disservice to non-heterosexual sub-populations to ignore or downplay the statistically higher risks of negative mental health outcomes they face, so it does them a disservice to misattribute the causes of these elevated risks, or to ignore other potential factors that may be at work. Assuming that a single model can explain all of the mental health risks faced by non-heterosexuals can mislead clinicians and therapists charged with helping this vulnerable sub-population. The social stress model deserves further research, but should not be assumed to offer a complete explanation of the causes of mental health disparities if clinicians and policy-

---

[70] 'Sexuality', 85.

makers want to adequately address the mental health challenges faced by the LGBT community. More research is needed to explore the causes of, and solutions to, these important public health challenges."[71]

Gender identity and transgenderism

So far, we have been considering some of the principal elements involved in a long debate about whether homosexual attraction of a small minority of people living in contemporary societies is natural or abnormal. We have noted that, from an historical perspective, the gradual boost in the public acceptance of homosexual practices has coincided with socio-political tendencies that promote a redefinition of marriage and the family. This has occurred over a period of about 60 years (from 1963-2023). In roughly the last three decades of this time-sequence, the various issues connected to sexuality have been augmented by those related to gender identity.

An increasing number of people, born either male or female, according to all the distinctive biological features of the two sexes, are now declaring that they wish to be identified as belonging to the opposite gender. So, the idea that sexual exclusiveness does not necessarily correspond to a personally-perceived gender has gained traction in some societies. Thus, when a person declares that their self-perceived gender has changed, it is assumed by them that everyone should be glad to recognise this new reality.

Gender change is not the same as gender non-conformity. The latter is the refusal to accept the various stereo-typical social and cultural images of what it means to be a boy or a girl. These should not be aligned with the

---

[71] 'Sexuality', 85.

strictly physical facts of being either male or female.[72] One definition of the sense of belonging to a different gender from that of one's birth is a marked incongruence between one's expressed/experienced and assigned gender. In order for the state of the person to be considered further as a 'gender-identity disorder' or 'gender dysphoria'[73] they must "experience distress or impairment in social, occupational or other important areas of functioning associated with these incongruent feelings."[74]

The notion that gender identity is fluid, and not necessarily binary, has become much more prominent in popular culture in the last three decades. Now, forceful campaigning groups are insisting that how a person feels about themselves is the overwhelming criterion for how they should be treated. This indicates that they should be accepted in the gender they feel comfortable with, for this expresses their authentic self. The theory lying behind this belief is that a specific gender is a socially-constructed artifice imposed upon children from an early age, in order that they may conform to patterns of sexuality dictated for moral and political ends.[75]

The outcome of this new, topical and unusual trend has led to intense campaigning to get laws changed that adhere to the historically consistent

---

[72] "Gender describes a social system that varies over time and location and involves shaping a set of behaviours deemed appropriate for one's sex. It operates on an unconscious level via strong social norms, yet it is also rigidly enforced by coercive controls and sometimes violence", Lucy Griffin, Katie Clyde, Richard Byng and Susan Bewley, 'Sex, gender and gender identity: a re-evaluation of the evidence', BJPsych Bulletin, 2020, doi: 10.1192/bjb.2020. 73, 3.
[73] The use of language, to describe a transgender disposition, has acquired a certain fluidity in the current political debate about the 'correct' use of terminology. For example, "new terminology reflects a conceptual shift from clinical disorder to personal identity. Crucially, gender dysphoria is no longer integral to the condition. The World Health Organisation has renamed 'gender identity disorder' as 'gender incongruence' and reclassified it as a 'condition related to sexual health' rather than retaining it in the chapter pertaining to 'mental and behavioural disorders', a somewhat discrepant replacement, reflecting a political rather than scientific decision-making process", 'Sex, gender and gender identity, 2.
[74] Sexuality', 94-95.
[75] This idea shows the confusion between categories within the transgender movement. What is being described is not a transgender remodelling but gender non-conformity. It fails to distinguish between the fact of immutable biological sex and the transitory patterns of gender compliance expected in some cultures. On this failure hangs much of the transgender movement's misinterpretation of the real world.

view, supported by incontrovertible scientific facts, that the two sexes are not inter-changeable. This advocacy has led to a strong demand that documents, including birth certificates, passports and other identity papers, should be changed on the mere say-so of an individual who wishes to be recognised as belonging to a gender different from their birth sex.[76] This has escalated into the demand that, if non-recognition of the change offends the person concerned, it should be a legal offence to refer to that person by their sex pronoun.

Likewise, a person occupying a public office should be dismissed from their job if they persist in referring to a person, who is a sexual male, but who has transitioned in their gender identity, as he or a sexual female as she. Even further down the line of this trend, is the belief that actually gender is so fluid that to speak of only two is to deny the right of someone to declare themselves multi-gendered. This imagined unreality is believed to be true, despite the fact that sex has an indelible genetic construction, formed during the gestation of a new human being, which simply cannot be changed. Gender, however, is apparently subject only to how individuals feel about themselves at any particular moment.

The consequences of this new inclination, to fashion one's identity by just how one perceives oneself, can be grave. For example, gender transition does not make an adolescent boy with same sex attraction into a heterosexual woman, nor a girl into a heterosexual man. People who believe that it is possible to change gender simply by making a declaration and then undergoing hormone treatment, surgery and/or therapy in the attempt to align one's physical attributes to the chosen gender are unhappily living a delusion:

"The cold biological truth is that sex changes are impossible.

---

[76] At the present moment (December 2022) a new law (Gender Recognition Reform (Scotland) Bill), making the acquisition of a Gender Recognition Certificate easier to be granted than hitherto, is passing through the Scottish Parliament. The age of an application for this certificate is lowered to 16 years and the person concerned has to testify that they have lived in their acquired gender for at least three months.

Every single cell of the human body remains coded with one's gender for life..."[77]

The author of this article goes on to make the salient observation that

"It is certainly ironic how liberals who posture as defenders of science when it comes to global warming flee all reference to biology when it comes to gender."

The result of the attempt to deny one's birth sex and transition to the opposite sex is to mutilate one's sexual reality and damage one's natural fertility. Given the extraordinary lengths legislators seem willing to go, in order to affirm 'non-discrimination' and endorse 'inclusivity', it is now possible to become legally a member of the opposite sex, whilst biologically remaining in one's birth sex. However, legal status does not alter biological status. So, if they were now permitted legally to enter into a civil partnership or marriage with someone of the opposite legal sex, but the same biological sex, this would not constitute a heterosexual relationship.

In a recent study,[78] a cohort of just under 1,000 participants were asked in a survey who they might ever date, given the choice of a cisgender woman or man, a transgender person or a person with a non-binary gender identification. An overwhelming majority (87.5%) only ticked the cisgender boxes. This was interpreted by the article's authors as indicating an unacceptable 'transphobic' attitude on the part of nearly 90% of the participants in the survey.

Unfortunately, for the sake of the integrity of the conclusions drawn, the reasons for their refusal were not required as part of the study. Thus, for example, one commentator on the results concludes that "the results indicate that biology-affirming people fail to be attracted, sexually or

---

[77] Camille Paglia, 'Sex at Birth and Choice of Gender', The Weekly Standard, 15 June 2017.
[78] Blair, K. L., & Hoskin, R. A. (2019), 'Transgender exclusion from the world of dating: Patterns of acceptance and rejection of hypothetical trans-dating partners as a function of sexual and gender identity,' *Journal of Social and Personal Relationships, 36* (7), 2074-2095.

romantically, to people who have chosen to live outside biological norms. This (attitude) is not only ideologically sound but biologically normal and healthy."[79] It would be better, therefore, for transgender people and their ideological supporters to acknowledge that adhering to biological norms increases their psychological health. For this reason it is right, and also the kindest way of responding to the accusation of discrimination, not to recognise their transition status.

It is paradoxical that advocates of the philosophy of transgenderism argue that maintaining one's birth sex throughout life is based on a socially-constructed reality that does not adhere to changes in one's emotional and psychological circumstances, whilst not admitting that the philosophy itself is the only, real, socially-constructed truth of the matter. The reason for coming to this conclusion is that the binary form of biological sex is clearly defined by the part that men and women play in the reproductive system, whilst gender transition entails the loss of either a male or female identity, or perhaps both. 'Transgenderism' is a tragic, heart-rending attempt to deny and alter a permanent fact of human nature:

> "The scientific definition of biological sex is, for almost all human beings, clear, binary, and stable, reflecting an underlying biological reality that is not contradicted by exceptions to sex-typical behavior, and cannot be altered by surgery or social conditioning."[80]

To encourage young children to believe, in the midst of their already stressful development into mature adults, that they may have been born in the 'wrong' body is, surely, a form of child-abuse. As they are discovering the reality of what it means to be either male or female, the kindest and most constructive response of those closest to them is to affirm them in their biological sex. Thus, to emphasise, for example, that being a boy is a wonderful feature of their entire existence and that being a girl is, likewise, a

---

[79] Nicole Russell, 'Psychologists can't figure out why hardly anyone wants to date a trans person' *www.thefederalist.com*, June 24, 2019.
[80] Sexuality, 93.

magnificent reality of which they may be proud is the most humane approach to their, probably momentary, confusion. To confirm them in their newly self-assigned identity simply adds to their disorientation. If it leads to hormonal and surgical interventions to give a semblance of having changed from one sex to the other it means becoming an infertile adult and leads to a life-long dependence on hormones and medical care for the rest of their lives.[81] Such an affirmation is both insensitive and unkind.

Attempts have been made to suggest that there are physiological explanations for cross-gender identification. For example, the theory that such identity transference is due to having a brain structure more in accord with their gender perception than to their biological sex is sometimes quoted. This, presumably, is based on the premise that there are identifiable differences between male and female brains. There is, however, little support in scientific literature, for this theory.[82] As far as current research is considered:

> "The current studies on associations between brain structure and transgender identity are small, methodologically limited, inconclusive, and sometimes contradictory. Even if they were more methodologically reliable, they would be insufficient to demonstrate that brain structure is a cause, rather than an effect, of the gender-identity behavior. They would likewise lack predictive power, the real challenge for any theory in science."[83]

In the rare cases, when babies are born with ambiguous forms of genitalia (inter-sex disorders), at a later stage in their development they are more likely to act in accordance with their chromosomal or hormonal make-up.[84]

---

[81] Marcus Evans, 'Freedom to think: the need for a thorough assessment and treatment of gender dysphoric children', BJPsych Bulletin, doi:10.1192/bjb.2020.72, 3.
[82] The evidence of a sample of research studies into the possible connection between different brain constitutions and transgender identity can be found in Sexuality, 100-102; "there is little or no evidence to support fundamental differences between the brains of females and males"; also, 'Sex, gender and gender identity', 3.
[83] Sexuality, 104.
[84] Sexuality, 100.

A Timely Warning

The final conclusion of the extensive study of scientific research on gender-confusion gives the following warning against the ease with which sectors of present society are prepared to welcome sex-reassignment without counting the potentially unwholesome and unwelcome consequences:

> "The scientific evidence summarized suggests we take a sceptical view toward the claim that sex-reassignment procedures provide the hoped-for benefits or resolve the underlying issues that contribute to elevated mental health risks among the transgender population. While we work to stop maltreatment and misunderstanding, we should also work to study and understand whatever factors may contribute to the high rates of suicide and other psychological and behavioural health problems among the transgender population, and to think more clearly about the treatment options that are available."[85]

Surely, society owes to vulnerable young people a much better insight into the range of issues on sexuality than that being advocated by LGBTQ+ pressure groups.

In summary, it is hard to avoid the conclusion that cross-gender identity is based entirely on subjective assertions. If this is the case, then transgender allegations are in reality idiosyncratic phenomena. Is it not, then, a distressing and painful misapprehension to imagine that attempting to confirm individuals in their chosen gender, through irreversible hormone treatment, surgical procedures or therapy, rather than according to their biological sex, is to increase their suffering, rather than to heal it?

---

[85] 'Sexuality', 112-113.

CHAPTER 3
Human Sexuality (Part II): Real and False Conclusions

"Illusions commend themselves to us because they save us pain and allow us to enjoy pleasure instead. We must therefore accept it without complaint when they sometimes collide with a bit of reality against which they are dashed to pieces" (Sigmund Freud, Reflections on War and Death).
"Illusion is the first pleasure" (Voltaire, La Pucelle d'Orleans).

It is hard to imagine a debate centred on the truths about human sexuality that could be more controversial, or even malicious, than the current conflict between two mutually incompatible views of human nature. These reflect, consciously or unconsciously, the two worlds that exist side by side within present world history. To understand the presuppositions that direct the contradictory opinions and actions that make the debate so indecisive and unsatisfactory may help to clarify people's starting-point. Unfortunately, it will not resolve the intense polemic that characterises much of the debate and the unscrupulous methods being used to try to silence opinions considered distasteful or repugnant.

The opposing world-views

The Western world has been deeply influenced by the Judeo-Christian view of the truth about the origin of the universe, the existence of life, the appearance of human beings on the Earth, the entry of evil into the world, the nature of what is good and what corrupt, and many other aspects of what makes human life meaningful. However, throughout its some four-thousand year history, it has been opposed by other philosophies, ideologies, thought-processes, values and principles. In the last five hundred years at first a gradual and then accelerating sea-change has taken hold of intellectual and moral belief, deeply hostile to this world-view. This began to emerge in its original form during the 18th century (the denominated 'Age of Enlightenment')[86] and gathered momentum during the following two centuries to such an extent that an entirely different world-view now holds sway over those nations that have emerged directly from European history.

For the purposes of this study, we will outline the essential, significant differences of the two worlds that now exist side by side and yet are incompatible in their foundational beliefs and outlooks. The Judaeo-Christian vision of reality starts with the existence of an eternal, self-subsisting Supreme Being, who has brought the whole material universe into existence out of nothing through his own, independently designed, will. He has created it according to his purposes and formed it to function according to certain plans (laws) which are inherent in the structures of the natural world. If these plans are not adhered to, the world humans live in will become dysfunctional, and the result will be manifold patterns of self-inflicted suffering.

This system of belief maintains that the scientific enterprise, which explores material reality in all its myriad manifestations, according to certain well-defined methods, follows as part of God the Creator's gift of the power of human observation and reasoning. It is not surprising, then, that the human mind is able to understand the workings of nature, for God created them both. Science, therefore, is able to open up the truth about much of the real world. However, there are certain areas of human experience that are not transparent to scientific fact-finding, the most obvious being the

---

[86] In fact there are one or two examples, prior to the 18th century, of such anti-Christian beliefs. One classical case would be that of the philosopher, Spinoza (1632-1677). Spinoza declared himself to be "a pupil of the light", by which he meant a follower of the inner power of reason alone to emancipate humans from the tyranny of superstition and the false beliefs of orthodox Christian faith; see, Tom Holland, Dominion: The Making of the Western Mind (London: Little, Brown, 2019) 358-363.

foundations for discerning the moral distinction between good and evil and the purpose of human life.

The non-Christian system of belief has taken the form in the Western world of what is often referred to as Secular Humanism (SH).[87] In many ways SH is based on a rejection of the Judaeo-Christian world-view. It

> "States that there is no reality beyond the natural world. As far as can be determined, human beings know themselves to be alone...Earthly humanity is the highest form of life that we are aware of... No other dimension beyond the physical exists... Such a conviction leads to human beings having to set their own agendas, and carry them out without any external support."[88]

> "If there is no creator...human life has no personal origin. Personality has evolved somehow through the fortuitous but random development of the human brain. Once a theistic account of the universe is rejected, there is no other viable anthropology to lay hold of. Humans are bound, by this assumption, to make sense of their world by dint of using reason and their own experience; there is a vacuum to be filled."[89]

One of the consequences of this framework of belief has been expounded by the French philosopher, Jean-Paul Sartre, in his book, Existentialism is a Humanism.[90] He coined the famous catchphrase, "existence precedes essence." By this he means that human beings first become living beings in a particular context in the world. As they grow into mature adults they encounter themselves and, only later, define themselves. They cannot define themselves, according to some pre-determined essence, because to begin

---

[87] I have explored the basic reality of this divergence from Christian belief in one of the chapters of my book, Being Human: chapter 10.
[88] Being Human, 277-278.
[89] Being Human, 279.
[90] (New Haven, CT: Yale University Press, 2007).

with they are nothing:

> He will not be anything until later, and then he will be what he makes of himself. Thus, there is no human nature since there is no God to conceive of it...Man is nothing than what he makes of himself."[91]

This existentialist philosophy, first aired in the 1950s and 1960s, fits well the development of a radically different view of human sexuality. The chronological concurrence is striking. During the decade of the sixties, a sexual revolution appeared within the consciousness of Western culture. Fifty years ago (1969), for example, the Stonewall riots in Greenwich Village, New York, heralded the beginning of a persistent counter-cultural movement by those in favour of treating homosexual beliefs and activities as equal to those of heterosexuals. Homosexual identity took on the existentialist mantra of being the person one chooses to be.

So, the Western world has become the arena for two divergent worlds, which hold radically opposed understandings of what it means to be human. Strangely enough the differences do not only comprise distinct basic narratives about human reality, but also embrace contrasting views about science, when it enters into the domain of human sexuality. One would imagine that the SH approach to scientific expertise would be extremely favourable, assuming that its established findings point to the reality of what is. However, in practice, when it comes to the defence of alleged LGBT rights, the publicity often ignores the findings of valid scientific research, and in its place promotes disinformation.

The crucial areas, where false information is disseminated, concern the supposed immutable nature of homosexual orientation - that it is innate from birth -, that people born this way cannot change and that it must not be characterised as a disorder. Rather, it should be recognised as a healthy alternative way of living out a person's given sexual essence. It echoes

---

[91] Existentialism, 22.

faithfully Sartre's dictum that, as mature human beings, homosexuals discover who they are in real terms.

All these claims have been refuted by objectively demonstrated scientific evidence. What seems to have happened is that subjective assertions, reputed to be based on people's indisputable experience, have been substituted for actual existence. This allows people the prerogative of asserting individual and collective demands, and using language incorrectly. In the latter case, how else does one account for the use of the epithet, homophobia/homophobic, as a parallel designation to sexism, racism, disabilityism and agcism, all of which are clearly aligned to objective physiological features? There is no need for anyone born a woman, black, to suffer a disability or to have attained middle-age to 'come out,' i.e. to declare their assumed identity.

Ex-gay? Post-gay?

Possibly nothing infuriates LGBT campaigners more than the claim that people, who once declared themselves to be innately same-sex inclined, later overcame that perception about themselves. We have already noted, however, that in real life sexual orientation is variable, mutable and unsettled. Particularly among adolescents it is volatile and unstable. One of the main reasons why LGBT activists are hostile to some people's claim that they are ex-gay is the latter's belief that heterosexuality should be considered sexually normative. It is reckoned inconceivable, then, that anyone, who once declared themselves to be homosexual, should ever wish to reject their previously asserted orientation.

The reality, however, is that a good number of those, who having professed a homosexual orientation, wish subsequently to change the drive of their same-sex attraction. There may be various reasons for this choice. One could be due to a person's religious and/or moral beliefs.

"(Some) maintain the conviction that their homoerotic feelings are not a part of who God created them to be. They instead see their homosexual behavior as falling short of the ideals for sexual conduct reflected in the sacred texts of their faith communities. Other individuals may seek to change same-sex attraction because of their moral beliefs and cultural values, which may or may not be connected to a religious worldview."[92]

Another reason might be that it allows either

"The opportunity for or the maintenance of an existing (heterosexual) marriage and family. So, the desire to have or keep a traditional marriage and family is another powerful impetus for individuals to seek out therapy for unwanted homoerotic feelings."[93]

Finally,

"Many individuals (especially men) who desire to modify homoerotic attraction strongly value monogamy and are motivated by dissatisfaction with their experience of a more sexually open homosexual culture. Even for self-identified, closed-coupled gay men non-monogamy appears to be a frequent occurrence, possibly reflecting a tendency to define commitment in emotional rather than sexual terms."[94]

In this latter case, the observed tendency towards a higher rate of sexual promiscuity in the homosexual community has led to the fear of acquiring one or another contagious sexually transmitted disease.

---

[92] Christopher Rosick, 'Motivational, Ethical and Epistemological Foundations in the Treatment of Unwanted Homoerotic Attraction,' Journal of Mental and Family Therapy, Vol. 29, 1, 13, January 2003, 14.
[93] Rosick, 14.
[94] Rosick, 15.

There can be no doubt that, in some cases, homosexual tendencies may be genuinely unwanted by those who voluntarily seek out therapeutic counselling with a view to increasing their heterosexual attraction. It is perverse, therefore, that a substantial number of professional psychiatric and psycho-therapeutic associations seek to ban re-orientation therapy altogether. They threaten practitioners with being expelled from the association, just because they respond to the desire of their clients for change.

It is true that there have been unfortunate cases, where therapy has been mishandled by not adopting clear-cut, and clinically-standard guidelines for treatment.[95] These latter include informed consent, the absence of external coercion to seek therapeutic help, information about the kind of treatment available, discussion of the probability, or its lack, of it leading to the desired change, respecting client autonomy and diversity, and the

> "Identification of unrealistic expectations, education regarding potential outcomes (e.g., behavioural and/or affectional change), and discussion of how failure to achieve the desired degree of change would be experienced,"[96]

The evidence that some people have left their former homosexual convictions and life-styles is, in the nature of the case, somewhat anecdotal and incomplete. It relies on individuals' own testimony of the change they have undergone in their self-understanding. It marks a similar problem to that which shows up in much research on human sexuality, because the data on which evidence is based is dependent on the honesty of the people interviewed. The only possible objective insight into people's self-declared

---

[95] Many of the abuses listed by the proponents, wishing to ban sexual orientation-changing therapy, have happened a long time ago. Today there is a code of practice in place that strictly adheres to approved psychotherapeutic methods of treatment. All that banning such measures will achieve is to confirm a false ideological set of beliefs, designed to uphold the mistaken view that same-sex attraction is immutable, to perpetuate harm on the well-being of many individuals and to deny a genuine right to seek help for a dysfunctional sense of identity.
[96] Rosick, 18.

inner feelings and desires is their behaviour. At least conduct can be observed. How it is to be interpreted, from the individual's perspective, is again a matter of the person concerned being candid and sincere in what they communicate.

In spite of the methodological difficulties of acquiring reliable evidence, there is sufficient reason to believe that, when people say they have changed their perspective and life-style, as the result of professional therapeutic counselling, from homosexual identity towards a heterosexual self-understanding, they are telling the truth. There are a number of studies that have come to the conclusion that the transition has been made, or is in the process of being made due to competent, qualified guidance and support. In a fairly recent, statistically-sensitive review of several pieces of research into the effects of therapy on aiding a non-coerced desire to transition from homo- to hetero-attraction and relationships, the authors came to the following conclusion:

> "In our study, most of those who participated in group or professional help had heterosexual shifts in sexual attraction, sexual identity and behaviour, with large statistical effect sizes, towards moderate-to-marked decreases in suicidality, depression, substance abuse, and increases in social functioning and self-esteem. Almost all harmful effects were none to slight. Prevalence of help or hindrance, and effect size, were comparable with those for conventional psychotherapy for unrelated mental health issues."[97]

Another conclusion, that contradicts the dogma that sexual orientation change efforts (SOCE) are almost always harmful in their effects, is based on a review by Stanton Jones and Mark Yarhouse, who carried out a longitudinal study of those going through reparative therapy. It states that

---

[97] Paul L. Santero, Neil E. Whitehead, and Dolores Ballesteros, 'Effects of Therapy on Religious Men Who Have Unwanted Same-Sex Attraction', The Linacre Quarterly XX(X), 2018, 1-17.

"Certainly, the best longitudinal study we have so far indicates that there is no evidence that such therapy is psychologically damaging, even where it does not necessarily achieve the results the participant wanted and it can have other benefits such as reducing the person's distress."[98]

The main conclusion that can be deduced from the limited amount of accurate and consistent evidence available on the question of sexual orientation change is that it happens. There are many people who truthfully witness this change in their own lives, almost always from same-sex attraction, behaviour and/or identity to that of the opposite sex. Whether, or not, LGBT activists are willing to accept the truth is irrelevant, for the truth of the case is not settled by what people may wish were the truth, but by a system of verification based on demonstrable evidence. This does not mean that all people who wish to change find it a painless procedure or that it works completely in all circumstances. Evidence suggests that there is a scale of effective change and that it may be a long process.

It is absolutely crucial that the clinical practices involved in change-therapy[99] are in accord with the highest professional standards and not attempted by those with little or no proper training. This being so, professional bodies have no mandate for excluding qualified practitioners who respond compassionately to those who have demonstrated a genuine wish to move from same-sex to opposite-sex attractions and relationships.[100] An outright

---

[98] Peter Ould, 'Can Your Sexuality Change', Living Out, based on the study done by Stanton Jones and Mark Yarhouse, 'A Longitudinal Study of Attempted Religiously Mediated Sexual Orientation Change." Journal of Sex and Marital Therapy, 37 (5), 2011, 404–27.
[99] The epithet sometimes used of 'conversion therapy' is a misnomer, simply because the word conversion has multiple uses and comes with a series of negatively loaded interpretations.
[100] It is worth emphasising again two important instructions, embedded in the code of ethics and practice mandated by The College for Sexual and Relationship Psychotherapy (see chapter 2, note 12): "Respect for the dignity, autonomy and right to self-determination of the Client;" "Anti-discriminatory practice, autonomy and right to self-determination of the Client and of others with whom they may be involved must be protected and respected in all interactions ". It must be clear that a ban on offering re-orientation therapy (a) denies the client's autonomy and the right to self-determination and (b) manifests discriminatory practice. In both cases it disregards two of the College's own codes.

ban on change therapy has been shown conclusively to fail the test of properly accumulated scientific evidence. It is based mainly on a set of misinterpreted personal anecdotes.

Whether or not sexual orientation of any kind is either perfectly normal or, in some cases, represents an emotional and psychological disorder, is not a matter that science, within its own parameters, can solve. It is a human question that ultimately depends on the best, well-founded account of what it means to be human. Science, undoubtedly has much to say in answer to this question, but there are also other factors to consider, beyond the reach of science to decide.

Sexuality and marriage

Perhaps never before in human history has the use of one word been as powerful in changing a time-honoured definition of a fundamental institution of individual and social life as the word 'equal'. Once the word equal became attached to marriage and applied to a particular relationship between people of the same-sex the whole understanding of marriage was subverted from within. Until approximately thirty years ago, marriage was understood by the majority of populations across the world as "the voluntary life-long union of one man and one woman to the exclusion of all others."[101] It has been likened to a four-legged stool: between two people; of the opposite sex; sexually exclusive, and with a life-time commitment."

The definition

Changing the definition of marriage is, in part, the result of a confusion of categories. Marriage has become identified with the actual ceremony that

---

[101] This has been, until recently, the definition of marriage in English common law; see, Jonathan Chaplin, 'A Time to Marry – Twice', Ethics in Brief, Vol. 18, No. 2, 2012; Julian Rivers, 'Redefining Marriage: the case for caution,' Cambridge Papers, Vol. 21, No. 3, September 2012.

solemnises it. The latter may happen in a religious setting or in a totally secular, civic context. The change in laws legitimising same-sex marriage confuses the meaning of marriage with the wording that underlies the rite that administers it. In this way, two distinct definitions of marriage are given equal standing – a religious one and a civic one. So, the alternative definition becomes something like "the legal formalising of an intimate relationship between two people who wish to express openly their commitment to one another." Until recently, the law of almost all societies has only recognised one definition of marriage, not a distinction (religious and secular) between two varieties.

The Christian view of marriage is not about a separate species called 'Christian marriage', but about marriage full-stop. In terms of the Judaeo-Christian heritage, it is about the way humans have been created ("male and female God created them"). In other words, marriage is about forming a union between two people of the opposite sex who will complement one another by their psychological, emotional and biological diversity in an equal partnership. The purpose is to create a mutually fulfilling bond and bring to birth and care for a new generation.

Same-sex marriage is a terminological impossibility for it cannot fulfil these requirements. The union of biological opposites is what unites two people in a new, creative relationship. A same-sex relationship that seeks to imitate such a bond between two people of the opposite sex is unbalanced; it lacks the complementarity between male and female that alone enriches this particular relationship.

The sexual act between the biologically same (especially between men) is, to speak bluntly, a travesty of nature: one man inserts that part of his body that signifies the potential of new life into the orifice of another man that signifies decay and expulsion. How could this act possibly be compared with that of a man and a woman that gives meaning to the word intercourse with its general notion of communion and intercommunication? All these reasons show why aligning the word marriage with same-sex unions, however committed they may be, undermines the institution of marriage.

Marriage is constituted for a number of individual and social purposes. Society is concerned to protect marriage as the formation of a new community designated by the interlocking of two people of the opposite sex who alone can produce a new generation of human beings. It is a significant part of the means of 'safe-guarding' vulnerable members of society. Anything that diminishes the status of heterosexual marriage threatens the well-being of children. Children flourish best in a community, where there is a biological father and mother, who are also husband and wife, living in a harmonious relationship.[102] No amount of intellectual and emotional bluster can eliminate a reality built into the warp and woof of human reality, by pretending that other people's sperm, eggs or wombs are substitutes for the couple who have been joined together in a heterosexual marriage.

Marriage is designed to emphasise the equal 'otherness' of the two sexes. This is absolutely foundational to the meaning of the institution. It is embodied in the binding consummation expressed in physical sexual union. Non-consummation has been a ground for the annulling of a marriage. Sexual union by either the man or the woman, outside of marriage, with another person is adultery. Until recently this was the main ground for divorce. Neither of these legal entailments fit in the case of same-sex marriages: unfaithfulness to a same-sex partner is not considered to be adultery; consummation of the marriage bond makes no sense, when the sex act cannot be reproductive. The illogicality of referring to same-sex legal commitments as marriages is highlighted in the following quote:

> "Pursuit of equality has thus overturned the heterosexual definition of marriage, but has neither abolished nor reconfigured those essentially heterosexual elements. New 'inequalities' will, therefore, arise in marriage law due to maintaining elements of the 'thick' understanding of marriage which stress the importance of physical otherness and sexual union not just mutual love and commitment."[103]

---

[102] See, for example, a document that samples research studies on the question of how biological parents living together, or apart, affect the emotional and psychological health of children and adolescents, Sara MacLanahan, Laura Tach and Daniel Schneider, 'The Causal Effects of Father Absence,' Annual Review of Sociology, 39, (July 2013), 399-427.

[103] Andrew Goddard, 'Reframing the Same-sex Marriage Debate', Ethics in Brief, vol. 18, no. 4, 2013. I have presented four reasons, based on looking at synonyms, why equality does not apply to same-sex marriage in The Abuse of Language, 59-64.

The argument in favour of legislating for same-sex marriage on the basis of 'fairness,' 'rights' and 'non-discrimination' assumes what needs to be proved:

> "Any law, which sets criteria for anything, is bound to discriminate. There are laws, for example, that discriminate on grounds of protected characteristics. Laws of marriage discriminate on grounds of age...(and) kindred-affinity."[104]

Discrimination?

The use of the concept of discrimination has become a weapon of attack in the war of words about equality. It is often entirely misplaced, for the argument does not differentiate between the drawing of any distinction and making inappropriate distinctions. Discrimination may be the result of an unfounded negative view of a particular situation on the basis of misleading or mistaken information, false reasoning or cynical propaganda. However, it may also be necessary as a means of distinguishing between what is true and false, good and bad. It does not seem to occur to those who use the notion always in a negative sense that it also means discernment, acute perception, insight and refined judgement.

> "If no distinction is made between the content of a belief and the person holding it, all criticisms of beliefs are, logically, a censure of the person... This interpretation of discrimination is false. Not all beliefs are equally valid. Beliefs that contradict others cannot all be true. Some beliefs must be judged acceptable and others inadmissible. In the last analysis, a society does not and should not respect all beliefs equally."[105]

In the complete contemporary muddle around the notion of phobias, the wayward use of discrimination scores highly even among otherwise

---

[104] Julian Rivers, 'Redefining Marriage.'
[105] The Abuse of Language, 58-59.

intelligent people.[106]

What should children be taught about sexuality?

The lack of a coherent, 'thick' vision of what it means to be human in today's secularist-oriented societies is resulting in great confusion about how children should be introduced to the subject of sexuality.[107] The following discussion will not attempt to determine whether the subject should be on a school curriculum at all or should be confined to the guidance of parents or carers, since in many nations now the state has intervened by promulgating laws that make sex education a mandatory part of all educational syllabuses at primary and secondary school levels.[108] Since sex-education will be taught in some form or other from an early age, the question boils down to, what should be taught?[109]

It would seem to be logical, and morally compelling, to assert that the basic requirement is that only the truth, and nothing but the truth, should be

---

[106] The latest example is a definition of Islamophobia, adopted by a number of high-profile institutions, which does not seem to know the difference between religious beliefs, always open to critical analysis, and racism - a personal distaste, contempt and disparagement for others based on their skin colour, ethnic origin and ways of expressing their cultural heritage. Critical analysis of Islam cannot be equated with racism, any more than is the case with Christianity or Buddhism. This misuse of the language of 'phobia' in this case is just another example of a confusion of categories.

[107] The curriculum usually speaks about relationships and sexuality. Relationships encompass themes centred on how to behave in a society that wishes to promote civilised norms in interpersonal connections. This is well and good. For the purposes of this study, I will concentrate on the subject of teaching about sexuality, which does not command a similar degree of consent throughout contemporary societies.

[108] The question of whether parents have the right to withdraw their children from sex-education classes still has not been settled. It appears that they have such a right. However, certain powers are granted to head-teachers to refuse the right "in exceptional cases." The cases, however, are not specified.

[109] The question of whether the State has a due claim to be able to require a particular form of sex education for young people remains controversial. Some interpret the mandate as an attempt to take away a responsibility which lies solely with parents. Others go further and accuse democratically elected governments of drifting towards an authoritarian stance that negates what Karl Popper called the 'Open Society'.

conveyed. From a Christian perspective there are two kinds of interlocking truths that need to be considered. There is the truth about the natural world we live in, often referred to as the reality of what exists. We can discover this truth through our life-experiences, observation, the knowledge and understanding of others (primarily through our families and formal and informal education) and through the multi-faceted work of scientific research.

Then there is the truth about ourselves – what does it mean to be human? Who are we? Why are we here? What is the purpose of our lives? How should we live? This form of truth goes beyond the ability of the senses to disclose, or experience to discern. In order to arrive at this dimension of truth, we need to hold to a comprehensive and coherent world-view able to give the best explanation of every aspect of human life.

This world-view needs to be able to interpret and clarify consistently, at least the following realities: the origin and uniqueness of human beings within a diverse natural order; humans' moral sense of right and wrong; the nature and cause of evil; the widespread belief in the existence of a supreme being (within and beyond the material world); human powers of reason; self-consciousness; aesthetic aspirations and accomplishments.[110] Learning and understanding is a life-long enterprise. It begins when young children become aware of things outside themselves and their immediate needs. It ends with our last breath.

So, children in pre-school, primary and secondary education establishments are at the beginning of a life-long exercise of exploration that encompasses both these aspects of truth. The goal can be summed up in terms of discerning "whatever is true, noble, right, pure, lovely, admirable, excellent or praiseworthy."[111] How, then, should these educational establishments interpret the questions: what should children be taught about sexuality, and

---

[110] See, Being Human, chapter 1, 5-20.
[111] The list is taken from the Letter that the Apostle Paul wrote to the Church in Philippi (chapter 4, verse 8) in the first century. It continues to represent a benchmark of high moral virtue.

at what stage in their development? The answer, as cosmopolitan, diverse and divergent societies are now realising, is complex and problematical. The reality being experienced in Western societies is that the two dimensions of inferred truth – life experiences gained by observation and internal reflection, together with the fullest and most persuasive explanation of them available, – may well conflict. Diversity and tolerance may be virtues that are often trumpeted in so-called liberal, multicultural societies. However, they often relate more to theoretical wish-fulfilments than to practical realities, never more so than in the question of the truths about sexuality.

The landscape around questions of sex, sexuality and gender have shifted monumentally in the last fifty years in secular, Western societies. What used to be taught as a consensus belief about the bi-polarity of human beings as either male or female, the meaning of marriage, the normativity of heterosexual relationships and the abnormality and deviant nature of homosexual relationships, is no longer accepted by a large number of the inhabitants of Western nations.[112] The traditional beliefs that were assumed to be true, on the grounds of the prevailing world-view, have all been challenged and, to a certain extent, overturned by new laws, under-girded by a radically different perspective on human nature.

Diversity may be proclaimed as a self-evident virtue; in practice, however, it is not actually tolerated, unless it promotes a view that diverges from the preceding norm. To give one recent example: a teen-age boy, in Scotland, was expelled from his school for daring to suggest, and refusing to deny, that there are only two genders, one is either a boy or a girl, a man or a woman; there are no other categories available in the real world. As soon as he received the order to leave the school, diversity, in a narrow sense, may have been upheld – call yourself whatever you wish -, but proper diversity, including the boys true belief, tolerance and non-prejudice flew out of the

---

[112] However, majorities outside the Western nations, and even some within Europe, do not agree with the secular humanist consensus. In a typically paternalistic way, many in the West declare that, precisely because of this divergence, other societies have much 'catching-up' still to do.

window. In other words, a new 'truth' is being proclaimed: the validity and authenticity of trans- and multi-sexuality. This is the belief that must be adhered to, on pain of severe discrimination.

This is the overall reality that exists in a society, where the government of the day wishes to introduce children to a particular set of beliefs about relationships and sexuality that accords with the world-view of a specific, minority faction (LGBTQ+ pressure-groups) in society.[113] So, what should we deduce from this background to the great controversy that governments' requirements have precipitated? I will suggest a few points.

Firstly, children should be exposed, simply as a matter of fact, to the now divergent examples of family life: with two biological parents of the opposite sex in a marriage-partnership; or with one parent, previously either married, in a civil partnership or cohabiting (the other having left); or with one parent mainly responsible for the care of children, but where the other parent is involved (at a distance) in their well-being; or with two 'parents' or carers, where one may be biologically related to the child/children, but the other is not (either because the relationship is between two people of the same sex, or one biological parent has a different partner); or with two biological parents, neither married nor in a civil partnership, but co-habiting.

It is possible that children are already aware of any or all of these arrangements. At a young age they may not question the diversity; only at a later stage of development might they wonder why such a variety of family life patterns exist. So, what should they be taught? Simply, this is the way things are, but in no way are children responsible for the choices of their parents. Whatever kind of family their friends and play-mates are part of, all children are to be valued equally. Their worth as human beings does not depend on the circumstances of their lives, but transcends whatever their background may include.

---

[113] A summary of this position is presented on the web-site of the campaigning group, Stonewall; see, Fay Bartram, 'An Introduction to Supporting LGBT young people: A Guide for Schools.'

Secondly, in this regard, what should they not be taught? They should not be taught that all these family arrangements are of equal value; that it does not really matter how a couple with children, or who wish to have children, contrive their relationship. Accumulating evidence shows that any bond other than a settled, long-term, monogamous, heterosexual marriage is likely to be damaging to children. Many who have grown up in other forms of family have testified to this fact later in life. There is an ideal and there are a number of deviations from the ideal. To pretend that all is well, whatever the situation of two or one adult(s) who have the care of their children, when so much evidence exits that a dysfunctional relationship causes children to suffer, is not to be considerate or kind.

However, at the same time, educators who are aware of the malfunctioning of the family to which one, or more, of their pupils belong need to be highly sensitive and sympathetic to the child in question.[114] Above all else, it is vital to assure the child that they personally are not to blame for any major disruption in the relationship between those expected to care for them. Clearly, the age at which this discussion is introduced, and the delicate way in which it is handled, is of the utmost importance for the child's well-being.

Thirdly, they should not be subjected to information on sexuality, in any of its forms, that is not confirmed by rigorous scientific findings. If the information claims to be based on strict scientific methodology, it should be open to being tested for the criteria that have been used.[115] In the case of same-sex orientation this means that young people should not be told that homosexual orientation is an inherited characteristic that does not and cannot change, either as a matter of normal sexual development or through external counselling. The assertion, for example, *"that some young people will realise that they are lesbian, gay, bisexual or trans"*, meaning that their sexual orientation or gender

---

[114] This is crucial in the light of the fact that numbers of children being referred to clinics dealing with mental distress is increasing exponentially.

[115] The criteria in question will include longitudinal research studies, based on statistically significant numbers of participants, chosen carefully (including a control group), so as not to presuppose the outcomes, before the research is undertaken, or distort its findings.

identity may be different from many of their peers,"[116] is a misinterpretation of a much more complex situation for young people, already seeking a settled resolution to their uncertainties. These claims deny what extensive research has revealed conclusively that sexual orientation at a young age is fluid and changeable, not static and fixed.

Fourthly, they should not be taught that a person can change their gender by simply asserting that they do not belong to their birth sex. Their sex is an irreversible biological fact: they were born either male or female for life. It is not a matter of how they may feel in their innermost being at any moment in time. How, for example, can a young male-bodied individual "feel like a girl," when they have no experience of being an actual girl, or vice-versa? It is an irrational idea. It may seem plausible to the person concerned, but in reality belongs to the world of fantasy.

Gender reality is not the result of a social-construct, suggested by the phrase "sex as assigned at birth," as some people imagine. Such an idea simply panders to contemporary post-modern relativism. Thus, so- called gender re-assignment through processes such as environmental conditioning, puberty-blockers, hormone treatment, surgery and/or therapy is a tragic misrepresentation of what is possible. To pretend otherwise in the hearing of young people whose intellectual, moral and emotional maturity is, as yet, unformed is an abuse from which they should be safeguarded.

For adults to confirm youngsters' feelings about being transgender is not a compassionate action to take, since it assumes that subjective emotions, that may well be fleeting, and even change from day to day, are more important than the objective scientific certainty that one's birth sex is unchangeable. Moreover, extensive research concludes that the majority of young people who declare themselves to be lesbian, gay, bisexual or transgender revert in a short while to their original heterosexual identity and birth sex. The support they most need is to realise that their feelings, although they may express

---

[116] 'An Introduction to Supporting LGBT young people' (italics added). This statement compartmentalises and stereotypes young people in identities they may well wish to relinquish within a short space of time.

real personal convictions, may also be momentary signs of a process through which they grow into mature adults.[117]

Fifthly, they should not be taught that their assumed sexuality is the main factor that defines their identity. Their proper and lasting identity is established, from the moment of conception until they die, by their humanity. One of the main problems with the whole discussion of homosexual orientation and transgender notions is that those who promote the theories that back them up have a 'thin' view of what it means to be human. Only the belief that every human being, without exception, irrespective of their sex, racial category, ethnicity, cultural background, physical health, mental abilities, chosen lifestyles, preferred sexual orientation, moral, philosophical or religious beliefs, is created in the image of an eternal, all-wise, totally virtuous and trustworthy God, can provide a lasting answer to the question of human identity. God loves them for who they are in his sight, not how they may be categorised or judged by flawed human standards. This represents a thoroughly 'thick' view of human nature and, incidentally, is the only sound basis for talking about human rights.[118]

Sixthly, it is for this latter reason that all young people should be taught to grant to those of their peers who have adopted a homosexual or transgender identity all the respect their humanity in God's image demands. This is not on the basis that their particular sexual identity is to be accepted as perfectly normal, in their best interests and of the same value as that of heterosexually inclined people, but on the basis of their much more profound identity as equal human beings.

---

[117] I look at the controversy about transgender matters, fairly recently raised in some societies, in greater depth in the following chapter.
[118] See, The Abuse of Language, chapter 5, 'Rights and Obligations, 102-122.

Department of Education Briefing Paper (Relationships and Sex Education in Schools (England))

It is for these reasons that the Department of Education in England is quite misguided to insist that all pupils, whether educated within public or private educational institutions, are expected "to have been taught LGBT content at a timely point."[119] The content of its Briefing Paper is false at strategic points, promotes beliefs that many parents rightly reject and does not give a balanced view of what is right to conclude about human sexuality. It has been correctly defined as unwanted indoctrination and propaganda. As such, where its views are plainly mistaken, they should not be part of any future school curriculum.

The Paper on the government's new regulations on relationships and sex education in schools may be helpful in clarifying what the government's intentions are. However, it is also defective in a number of assumptions that it makes. The statement, for example, that the education should ensure that it "encompasses an understanding of the ways in which humans love each other" with reference to same-sex relationships, is to beg the question hugely about what love means.

In contemporary society it tends to be a slogan emotionally thrown about like confetti, landing anywhere, and picked up according to people's individual tastes. The fact that people fall in and out of love on a number of occasions, when relationships, claimed to be under-girded by love, end in break-up, testifies to the superficial view of love that pervades modern culture. The slogan of 'Pride' marches that "love is all" is about as banal as it is possible to imagine. The word, love, used as a slogan, is meaningless and destructive, unless it is given a solidly founded content that takes into account its proper application, far beyond the conventional stereotypes of Hollywood. Love encompasses far more than attraction, enchantment or

---

[119] See, Robert Long, Relationships and Sex Education in Schools (England), Department of Education Briefing Paper No. 06103, 28th February 2019. Since this Briefing paper was published, the Department of Education has toned down some of its more extravagant requirements, not least the implied promotion of the extreme LGBT agenda.

captivation. It is a strong notion that entails tenderness, cherishing, delight, self-sacrifice, generosity, forgiveness and deep friendship all of which combine to ensure that a relationship is able to survive the rocky moments that usually occur in even the most enduring of relationships.

The Regulations speak a number of times about the importance of marriage and stable relationships for family life and bringing up children, "as key building blocks of community and society."[120] However, the present and recent governments have continually destabilised marriage, by re-inventing and re-defining it to include same-sex unions, by introducing civil partnerships as an alternative, and most recently by changing laws on divorce, influenced by the spurious notion that marriage breakdowns can be free of anybody's fault.

In the latter case, the one who has been wronged has no recourse in law to the likelihood of having been the victim of another's infidelity, control, abusive attitude or even physical violence. Nor has this person any possibility of attempting to save the marriage, if the husband or wife is determined to file for divorce. How anybody can think that any of these actions enhances the institution of marriage and the family is beyond comprehension. They all follow a pattern that was disclosed in the previous chapter, of wishing to overturn the understanding of marriage as a life-long, freely chosen, monogamous union between two people of the opposite sex.

The Regulations do not mention, alongside cyber-bullying, 'sexting' and staying safe online, the risks to young people of affirming that same-sex orientation is perfectly normal or that transgender realignment is an acceptable option for young children or adolescents. Without a doubt, what they are taught about the whole issue of sexuality is where the rubber hits

---

[120] This is, perhaps, a throw-back to Article 16 (3) of the Universal Declaration of Human Rights which asserts that "The family is the natural and fundamental group unit of society and is entitled to protection by society and the State." At the time of its pronouncement in 1948, the family would have been understood as a unit, comprising a married man and woman, one or more children, and close relatives. It would not have countenanced the common contemporary assertion that the family comes in many different guises, all to be valued equally.

the road. If they are not taught the truth, and nothing but the truth, they are likely to grow up with ideas and practices that, in the shorter or longer term, are damaging to their individual well-being and, collectively, to society as a whole. No school should be willing to teach a syllabus that may encourage young people to believe messages that could encourage them to engage in practices that lead to self-harm.

A Timely Warning

The final conclusion of the extensive study of scientific research on gender-confusion gives the following warning against the ease with which sectors of present society are prepared to welcome sex-reassignment without counting the potentially unwholesome and unwelcome consequences:

> "The scientific evidence summarized suggests we take a sceptical view toward the claim that sex-reassignment procedures provide the hoped-for benefits or resolve the underlying issues that contribute to elevated mental health risks among the transgender population. While we work to stop maltreatment and misunderstanding, we should also work to study and understand whatever factors may contribute to the high rates of suicide and other psychological and behavioural health problems among the transgender population, and to think more clearly about the treatment options that are available."[121]

Surely, society owes to vulnerable young people a much better insight into the range of issues on sexuality than that being advocated by LGBTQ+ pressure groups.

---

[121] Sexuality', 112-113.

Postscript

An intriguing article, whose significance for the discussion about transgenderism is such that it is worth-while to summarise what the author affirmed.[122] His autobiographical synopsis tells the reader that in the earliest years of his academic research he bought into the belief, popularised by the French philosopher, Foucault that the way most people read the past is the result of their present ideological commitments. What is being asserted is that the possession of knowledge, gleaned from historical research, is loaded and distorted to promote the interests of those who are its beneficiaries.

So, knowledge, apparently, is not something to be discovered as a universally valid proposition, which is not open to doubt by anyone adequately exercising their reasoning-faculties.[123] Rather, it is the outcome of a set of rules that an influential group of people have managed to impose on society as a whole. Truth and falsehood are, it is asserted, matters of negotiation among those who draw up the rules.

According to this theory, in order to understand what may be affirmed or denied, it is necessary to engage in the kind of research by which the political, social and cultural factors that determine the knowledge professed can be uncovered. Often, what is claimed to be right, for example that the basic family unit has always been considered the fundamental bed-rock of a healthy society, is no more than a social construction instituted and defended by those who gain by its patriarchal structure. In a case like this, the historian is duty bound to uncover and deconstruct the underlying ideology in question, in order to replace it with another that is of benefit to those hitherto oppressed by the false ideology.

In terms of the history of gender, round about the beginning of the 1990s, the theory that the reality of gender was a human construct that did not conform to any certain, universal judgement became dominant in many

---

[122] Christopher Dummitt, 'I Basically Just Made It Up: Confessions of a Social Constructionist', Quillette, September 17, 2019.
[123] A widely given definition in philosophy is that knowledge amounts to "justified, true belief".

scholarly circles. Academics, mainly from the social, cultural and gender-studies departments of Universities, asserted that the way gender-identity has been constructed is all about the power that certain social elites exercised at particular moments in history. They opposed the strict binary definition of sex to forward their own interests.

What is often forgotten, in the debate about socially constructed beliefs, is that the basis for the criticism, by the same argument, is equally socially constructed. All that is left is a complete lack of criteria for judging the truth of a statement; one so-called social-construction theory makes the other void, and vice-versa.

Christopher Dummitt explains, as he sees it, the situation and its consequences:

> "Almost nobody, who hadn't been exposed to such theories at a university, could bring themselves to believe that sex was wholly a social construct, because such beliefs went against common sense."

> "(The theory) shows up especially in the talking points about trans-rights, and policy regarding trans-athletes in sports. It is being written into laws that essentially threaten repercussions for anyone who suggests that sex might be a biological reality. Such a statement, for many activists, is tantamount to hate speech. If you take the position that many of my '90s-era debating opponents took—that gender is at least partly based on sex, and that there really are two sexes (male and female), as biologists have known since the dawn of their science—, uber-progressives will claim you are denying a trans person's identity, which is to say, wishing ontological harm upon another human being."

> "Ideology is what it was, and is: a set of pre-formed beliefs that are built into the gender-studies disciplinary penumbra."

Dummitt finishes his admission that he had been a part of this deception with these words:

"This confession should not be interpreted as arguing that gender is not, in many cases, socially constructed. But critics of the social constructionists are right to raise their eyebrows at the so-called proof presented by alleged experts. My own flawed reasoning was never called out—and, in fact, only became more ideologically inflected through the process of peer review... Until peer review can be something more than a form of ideological in-group screening—then we ought to be very sceptical indeed about much of what counts as "expertise" on the social construction of sex and gender."

Dummitt, who has tenure in his University post, is, therefore, unlikely to be dismissed for his changed view-point He has had the courage to condemn what is, tragically for the well-being of many children and young adults, the noxious misuse of epithets, such as trans-phobia and hate-speech.

In the course of the present 'cultural war' around transgenderism, gender non-conformity has been conflated with gender-dysphoria. It is perfectly legitimate to reject some of the stereotypes often applied to femininity and masculinity, i.e. what society in general accepts as social conventions about the innate characteristics embedded in the nature of womanhood or manhood. However, it is quite another matter to pretend that a girl or a boy can seriously believe they were "born in the wrong body." In point of fact, the latter belief is tantamount to accepting the stereotypes!

Transgenderism is a tragic and harmful means of compounding the disorientation a person may experience in being able to identify with their real sex. When transgender campaigners dispute the reality of their birth sex to young, vulnerable, identity-seeking children, even before the physiological changes that happen at puberty, and promote gender-transition as a life-changing alternative, it becomes a toxic and pernicious doctrine.

As Christopher Dummitt has realised, the whole ideology is just made up. According to his own self-confession, it is just the kind of social-construct condemned by post-modern thinking.[124] In this case, it is exemplified by the absurd statement that one's sex is *assigned* at birth. In the real world it is recognised as being what one is, either female or male. Those who, having had their gender 're -allocated' and wish to have the designation on their birth-certificates changed, live in a fantasy world. The law cannot alter a true fact.

---

[124] I consider in more critical depth in Appendix B the origin and depth of this current, pervasive ideology.

Chapter 4
'In Praise of Folly?'

"There are some people who live in a dream world, and there are some who face reality; and then there are those who turn one into the other." (Desiderius Erasmus).

Preface

In 1509 Desiderius Erasmus, the well-known Dutch Renaissance Scholar, whilst staying in Sir Thomas More's house in London, wrote a satirical essay in Latin, condemning the superstitious practices and absurd beliefs of the Western Church and European society of the time.[125] Much to his surprise, it became his most well-read book. This was due, perhaps, to ordinary people's natural appreciation and relish for an expose of the idiotic beliefs and practices of contemporary persons who occupied influential positions in the church, governments, academia and other institutions.

My reason for borrowing this title as a heading for this chapter is simple: there are, it seems to me, many instances of absurd beliefs and senseless practices in contemporary Western societies that rightly attract the epithet of folly. Some of these have already been portrayed in the previous three chapters; they will be further discussed in this chapter. There are others, such as recreational drug-taking, gambling, climate change denial and vaccine denial which could also be mentioned, but space is too limited. I do

---

[125] Moriae Encomium. There are many English translations, for example, Erasmus, Desiderius, Praise of Folly (Harmondsworth, UK: Penguin, 1993/2); The Praise of Folly (Princeton, NJ: Princeton University Press, 2015/3).

not pretend to possess the same quality of wit or inventiveness as displayed by Erasmus in exposing the follies of his day, nor will I attempt to copy the satirical prose which he used. However, a good deal of contemporary Western cultural, social, political and moral life appears to have reached a level of scatterbrained idiocy that, if pursued without correction, will impel its societies into a terminal decline. I do not claim myself to be free of personal follies. So, I offer the subsequent comments in a spirit of self-criticism.

Erasmus's essay

Erasmus conceived his essay, not only as a satire against foolish beliefs and practices, but also as an extended piece of mockery. Folly, herself, is the narrator and praises all things that humans, in their right minds and according to well-considered experiences, know to be nonsensical. She pits folly against wisdom, the emotions against reason:

> "In the first place consider how providently nature has taken care of us that in all her works there should be some piquant smack and relish of Folly: for since the Stoics define wisdom to be conducted by reason, and folly nothing else but the being hurried by passion, lest our life should otherwise have been too dull and inactive, that creator, who...made us up, put into the composition of our humanity more than a pound of passions to an ounce of reason; and reason he confined within the narrow cells of the brain, whereas he left passions the whole body to range in."[126]

The gist of Folly's fulsome praise of herself is that everything that seems reasonable and full of common sense leads to disenchantment, frustration and distress; better, therefore, to pursue a course of action that abhors the

---

[126] See, Erasmus, In Praise of Folly (translated by W. Kennet) (London: Reeves and Turner, 1876), 26.

disillusionment that philosophical meanderings will undoubtedly bring:

> "Folly – Erasmus' mouthpiece – praises herself endlessly, arguing that life would be dull, colourless, and plain boring without her. In her work she is aided by assistants: Self Love, Flattery, Oblivion and Pleasure, whom she believes promote friendship and tolerance within society... Folly praises foolishness, levity, humour, nonsense, and even madness...her entire speech is an endless invective which sets foolishness against authority and pseudo wisdom."[127]

My take on Erasmus's derisive caricature of much that happens in the way of the old world is to focus on contemporary examples of folly. The purpose is not to be attracted to Folly, as in this pyrogenic from the 16th century, but shunned because of the depressing consequences that it inevitably brings.

So, how should we best understand the meaning of folly and foolishness? There is probably not a synonym that exactly matches the precise significance of its finer meanings. Perhaps, the word stupidity comes closest to the sense of what is conveyed, as when we admit to ourselves what a folly we have committed in making a choice whose detrimental consequences we never anticipated. A good contemporary example might be falling inadvertently for a scam, which has deprived us of a considerable sum of unrecoverable money. We shunned the rational and experiential warnings against the false claims and promises of unsolicited invitations, by investing savings in bogus deals. What drove us was not intelligent forethought but the clever appeal to the emotion of excitement at the possibility of gaining a windfall.

Foolishness has a number of synonyms that bring out the range of its repertoire, such as senselessness, ineptness, absurdity, short-sightedness. We tend to use the word to refer to other people, rather than ourselves, when

---

[127] Desiderius Erasmus, Praise of Folly in Contemporary American English (Mary Marc Translations): 'About the Praise of Folly' (Leipzig: Amazon Distribution, 2013), v.

something they have said or done appears to us to be contrary to well-informed, sensible reasoning. It is along these lines, that I would use the term in relation to the way in which abortion is defended and sexuality has been cut adrift from its secure moorings in properly controlled, scientific research findings and coherent belief systems.

The Case of Abortion
Confusing the language

One of the moral justifications used by pro-abortionists for carrying out what amounts to a death sentence on a living, biological human being alive in its mother's womb is that it is not yet a human person. For those desirous of aiding mothers to end their unwanted pregnancy, the living being is referred to euphemistically as a foetus or embryo, or sometimes as just a bundle of tissues. The latest euphemism to be used is a product of conception, i.e. a commodity or piece of merchandise. When it is not wanted, there are businesses available who will dispose of it for a profit.[128]

In complete contrast, however, to this way of speaking about the living being in utero, a woman who becomes pregnant, because she and her male partner are longing for a child they have produced together, will speak about her baby. How, though, is it possible to contrast the definition of two identical physical forms within the wombs of two different women, say at 10 weeks of gestation, simply because the mother (often advised by abortion services or coerced by the prospective father) wishes, in the first case, to rid herself of the living being or, in the second case, to carry it to birth? The mother's decision is logically irrelevant to the personal status of the being recently conceived. Whether aborted or cherished, the being is equally human in both cases.

---

[128] During a recent debate on a Bill in the New Mexico State Assembly, legalising abortion up to birth, State Senator Jacob Candelaria called a model given to him of a 12-week pre-born baby "offensive" and told the Assembly how he "threw it in the trash", The Daily Citizen, February 14, 2021. What used to be considered a person is now deemed to be rubbish, fit for the scrap heap or, in the case of home abortions, excrement to be flushed down the toilet.

The human status of an aborted foetus

Relevant to this discussion is the way society deals with the remains of an aborted body. Following the discovery of the remains of 2,246 aborted body parts in the home of former abortionist Ulrich Klopfer, a new Bill has been introduced in the US Senate, sponsored by Senator Mike Braun called 'The Dignity for Aborted Children Act':

> "The bill mandates that abortion providers obtain informed consent from any woman who undergoes an abortion procedure, giving her the choice either to take possession of the fetal remains or to release them to the clinic. *In the latter case, the clinic must then "provide for the final disposition of the human fetal tissue... consistent with State law regarding the disposal of human remains...in the same way that State laws require burial or cremation of the remains of adult humans*"[129]

Although this law, if passed, would be a progressive step in the controversy about the moral warrant for abortion or its inadmissible moral basis, it shows the great confusion surrounding the reason for and practice of abortion in the first place. On the one hand, it confirms the legality of abortion in certain circumstances. On the other hand, it confers human status on the living being just aborted, implying that the act of terminating the life of the pre-born is actually an act of homicide. A similar conclusion is drawn when a baby is killed in the womb by an external act of extreme violence on the mother. In the US, at least, the perpetrator can be prosecuted for murder, according to 'The Unborn Victims of Violence Act' of 2004:

> "This law recognizes an embryo or fetus in utero as a legal victim, if they are injured or killed during the commission of any of over 60 listed federal crimes of violence. *The law defines*

---

[129] Report by Alexandra DeSanctis in The National Review, October 1, 2019 (emphasis added).

"child in utero" as *"a member of the species Homo sapiens, at any stage of development, who is carried in the womb.""*[130]

This leads us to consider the argument, designed to vindicate abortion, that the presumed distinction between something that, from conception, has the emerging characteristics of being human, particularly its genetic make-up and the formation of its brain, and a person is valid. Apparently, on the basis of this contention, abortion is legitimised, as long as the fetus has not yet crossed the threshold, deemed necessary by abortionists, to become a person. However, the absurdity of this line of reasoning is contained in the reality that the before and after of personhood is quite impossible to define.[131] From the moment of conception to the moment of death there is an uninterrupted, continuous line of development from one stage to another of a personal, unique being. The moment of birth marks the beginning of a new stage; it does not signify that personhood has suddenly commenced. Such a pronouncement cannot be defended on any rational basis. The distinction is incoherent. It is foolish to pretend otherwise.

---

[130] Text taken from the Wikipedia article, 'The Unborn Victims of Violence Act' (emphasis added). At the time of the passing of the Act, even though abortion was excluded from the provisions of the Act, pro-abortionists rightly concluded that the wording conferred personhood on the unborn child "at any stage of development," thus contradicting the famous ruling of the Supreme Court, Roe v. Wade (1973), "in which the Court ruled that the Constitution of the United States protects a pregnant woman's liberty to choose to have an abortion without excessive government restriction." The Court's ruling was based on two considerations, the right of a mother to privacy (i.e. the non-interference of the state in the mother's decision to choose to undergo an abortion or continue with the pregnancy) and the judgement that a pre-born infant did not yet possess the status of a person.

[131] This reality was acknowledged in the famous case of Roe v. Wade. The Court based its decision against the personhood of the unborn child, at least until the moment of viability, on a negative argument: "The Court found that there was no indication that the Constitution's uses of the word "person" were meant to include fetuses." It concluded that "We need not resolve the difficult question of when life begins. When those trained in the respective disciplines of medicine, philosophy, and theology are unable to arrive at any consensus, the judiciary, in this point in the development of man's knowledge, is not in a position to speculate as to the answer." It was admitted in the Court's submission that any point chosen was arbitrary. This bears out the logical conclusion that the distinction between personhood and non-personhood cannot be sustained. That being the case, the Court should have ruled against abortion, on the grounds that it cannot be upheld by appealing to a highly questionable distinguishing characteristic.

A third line of reasoning appeals to the alleged integrity of the mother's body. What she is carrying is deemed to be a part of her body over which she should have complete control. Such a notion runs counter to the fact that the conception of another living being is easily distinguishable from every other organ in her body. The being has been implanted by the external intervention of another human being. The fertilised egg is part of her body. However, the sperm that fertilises the egg to produce another human is not part of her body.

Before the sexual act which brings the two together she possessed all the parts of a body that make up a woman's physiology. Those constitute a complete physical inventory, unless one or another has been removed (e.g. teeth, appendix, a kidney). The introduction of something new in her womb, which will remain for approximately nine months and then leave her body, is of a different category. To pretend that this belongs to her body is a conclusion based on rhetoric for the sake of defending what cannot be defended. The notion is nonsensical, because it implies that the birth of the child signifies the loss of a body part. Logically, the consummation of the pregnancy would then signify a physical deprivation for the mother.

The argument is designed to suggest that the state has no legitimate authority to intervene in the decision she makes about her body,[132] as though it were of a similar nature to the colour she dyes her hair, whether she has tattoos or not, or how she feeds herself. If that is the argument, then the pro-abortionist lobby is sorely mistaken.

It is evident in the polemic aroused by this lobby that there is virtually no protection conferred on the new, independent, living being. Any rights possessed by such a being are ignored or dismissed; the only rights admitted are those of the mother. The state, however, does have a moral responsibility to protect the life of the pre-born human, because it is of a different class to everything else in her body and because the mother,

---

[132] At the present moment usually up to 24 weeks of the pregnancy (in the UK, but several weeks less in most European countries). However, there is an increasing clamour by organisations that gain financially by offering abortions, to extend the period up to birth.

seeking an abortion, has refused her responsibility to protect it. To categorise it as of a similar kind, just another part of her body, is to commit a category-error. The idea that the liver or heart, for example, might have independent rights would be ludicrous.[133]

Moreover, abortions, except in the extremely rare special circumstance of a threat to the life of the mother, are the very opposite of essential health care. Health care means protecting, curing, extending and improving lives, not killing them. Medical professionals, therefore, who are engaged in the occupation of ending baby's lives, are committing a dereliction of duty. To attempt to cover up the destructive act they perform by using the entirely misplaced phrase, "a woman's health and reproductive rights", is to follow a specious line of reasoning. Pregnancy is not a health problem, unless there are unforeseen complications, in which case the health service has a responsibility to use all reasonable means to save the baby. Nor is there a reproductive right to end the child's life. Abortion is not a human right; it is a human wrong.

The right to choose to be a mother, or not, is claimed as a dogma. The ground of the right is given as the pursuit of equality between women and men. A little thought, however, will show that the rhetorical use of the term equality is invalid when it come to the consideration of motherhood, for obvious biological reasons. The right to choose is indeed present before, but not after, the act of intercourse has happened. It is a right to choose sometime in the future to have a baby or not to have a baby. It is not the right to kill or not to kill the new human being. Abortion cannot, therefore, be conceived as a justified response to the failure of a contraceptive device, or neglecting to use one.

So, the variety of reasoning that is used to justify abortion, now being

---

[133] On the question of protection, any parent who allows a defenceless young child to suffer the kind of violence and trauma that an aborted pre-born living being suffers would be charged with either gross-negligence, or in the case of a resulting death, manslaughter or murder.

extended by some legislations[134] beyond the time of viability (normally considered to be 24 weeks of gestation) up to birth, for reasons of convenience, is unsuccessful on all counts. The original ground for decriminalising abortion was when the pregnancy became a profound threat to the mother's health. The intellect that considers any other reasoning well-informed in the real world can only be characterised as foolish. It is ill-considered and inept.

The Case of Sexuality

This is the second profound example of how human moral sensibility differs between those living in the old world and those already inhabiting the new world, now partially hidden, but one day to be fully revealed. The first constitutes a realm, where the rule of a compassionate and just God is not recognised. The second is also a realm, whose inhabitants consciously seek to live by a pattern of existence that delights God. It is also the only place where humans can truly flourish.

How important is sexuality?

One of the main issues that separate the two groups, as has already been discussed in the preceding two chapters, is the serious question about whether the subjects of sexuality and gender should enjoy the kind of prominence they have recently acquired in Western societies. Of late, the centrality of the sexual, in the quest to find a meaningful, personal identity, has come to the fore in secular culture. In the past, the Christian Church used to be accused of over-stating the importance of sexual morality. This is no longer the case. Now the Church tends to mention the subject mainly in response both to the way it is exaggerated in many forms of communication and to the confusing and deceptive manner in which it is

---

[134] Most recently by the New Zealand Parliament (Bill passed on the 19 March, 2020). Organisations that gain financially by offering abortions, are increasingly clamouring for other states to legalise abortion at any time before birth, and for any reason.

often portrayed.

I suspect that the reason for this reversal is that the secular, humanist ideal brings much mystification to the matter of human identity and uses sexuality as a pre-eminent means of trying to come to terms with the resulting predicament of its own creation. Meanwhile, Christians, who believe that God has revealed clearly and fully to humanity what it means to be human, and have found the answer to be true in their experience, have no such quandary. The truth about the sexual dimension of human life is for them a settled matter; it is not open for revision.

Sex is binary

The human race is composed of (only) two sexes. This objective fact is irrefutable. Women and men share many of the same characteristics, such as powers of reason, the ability to solve problems, linguistic dexterity, artistic gifts and memory. In other ways they tend to behave differently, for example in the way they display emotions, relate to children, react to challenging situations, and take responsibility for the care of the elderly. Although there are different characteristics, both within and between women and men, when fully understood they contribute complementary gifts in their relationships. This is the way that God has made them, in order that they may be mutually dependent on one another, using their diverse qualities for the benefit of both and, within the marriage covenant, for offspring they may produce.

The complementary nature of the two sexes, physiologically and psychologically, is why marriage is defined as the union between one man and one woman for life. Sadly, such an understanding is no longer acceptable to the old world, for it is said to deny experimentation. For a number of disputable reasons, this world has blessed other, alternative ways of understanding sexual intimacy. Ever since small minorities of very determined people began to be promote the sexual revolution, same sex attraction, behaviour and self-identity has been proclaimed as a legitimate moral equivalent to that of heterosexuality. Over a period of roughly twenty years, within secular-humanist dominated societies, the standing of same-sex partnerships has been accorded the same legal rights and privileges as those of opposite sex couples. Now a vociferous minority wishes to extend the same legal rights and privileges to polygamy and to other polyamorous arrangements.

Sexuality converted into a political project

On the basis of a dubious interpretation of the meaning of equality, it might be thought that the legally recognised equivalent status of same-sex relationships to those of the opposite sex had been settled to the satisfaction of its protagonists. This is, however, far from the truth. As Douglas Murray has chronicled in his book, The Madness of Crowds,[135] a new militant ideology has been spun out of the imagination of a group of people led captive by the implausible theories of post-modernity.

In a chapter, he calls 'An Interlude, on The Impact of Tech,' he bewails the way that tech companies that dominate social media are prepared to allow distorted information to be disseminated on their platforms. At the end of the chapter, he concludes,

> "The one overwhelming problem with this attitude is that it sacrifices truth in the pursuit of a political goal. Indeed, it decides that truth is part of the problem – a hurdle that must be got over. So where diversity and representation are found to have been inadequate in the past, this can be solved most easily by changing the past. Some users of the world's most popular search engine will have noticed some of this...For most people on a day-to-day level...there may simply be a sense that something strange is happening: that they are being given things they didn't ask for, in line with a project they didn't sign

---

[135] The Madness of Crowds: Gender, Race and Identity (London: Bloomsbury Continuum, 2019).

up for, in pursuit of a goal they may not want."[136]

The two keys words in this paragraph are 'truth' and 'political goal.' The normal, objectively reliable definition of truth, that it encompasses everything that conforms to 'what is the case', is now dismissed in favour of a subjective view, that truth is whatever conforms to how I feel about matters. What is being promoted is a conception of truth as a situation or belief I personally feel comfortable with, even though it may be an untruth rather than what is real. Governments have already or are in the process of legislating for the acceptance of untruths about abortion, same-sex relationships and trans-gender ideas. In certain cases, courts are insisting that the public abide by these false assertions. Later on in his book Murray, in the context of IQ differentials, observes that

> "the fall-back position for refusing to engage with the evidence on IQ differentials is to say that even if the facts are there, and even if they are very clear, it is morally suspicious to want to look into them...The retreat from 'the facts are wrong' to 'the facts are unhelpful' has become the signature retreat of opinion in the face of the growing literature on the subject."[137]

The alternative to the 'facts of the matter' is to perpetuate a contemporary, post-modern myth that past opinions about matters of abortion, sexuality and transgender are simply 'social constructs' hoisted on oppressed minority groups by powerful traditionalists (usually categorised as white, middle-class, middle-aged males) who wish their views to remain dominant in the public sphere.

What is happening, then, is the subtle politicisation of certain novel dogmas, often referred to as 'politically correct' (notice the expression), in the hope that they can become the controlling ideology in a future transformed society. Unfortunately, not only do these dogmas contradict centuries of

---

[136] The Madness of Crowds, 120.
[137] The Madness of Crowds, 171.

established moral values but they also negate solid, well-founded scientific findings that deal with the issues in question: for example, that human life begins at conception, that there is no scientific justification for separating personhood from humanness or for maintaining that sexual orientation and gender are fixed in the womb.

It is truly an amazing happening that in the 21st century, after roughly four hundred years during which a scientific mind-set has dominated rational thought, such a cavalier attitude to scientific methods of verification so easily discards evidence-based proof, simply on the basis that they do not conform to what some people wish to believe. However, the new ideologies are hoisted by their own petard, for their post-modern critique, that 'non-progressive' ideas are merely social constructs, falls into the same trap they have set for others. The whole contemporary 'sexual revolution' is itself a prime example of a social construct that a small minority of basically white, middle-class, middle-aged males (and some females) wish to impose on a rightly sceptical society.

Sexuality and human rights?

One of the biggest deceptions being perpetrated in the field of sexuality is the notion that sexual orientation is analogous to race and sex (gender in its correct sense), when it comes to the rights and privileges that society should accord to those who claim to be gay. So, 'homophobia'[138] is now always conjoined with racism and sexism (and to a lesser extent with ethnicity, nationality, disability and ageism) that must be condemned by laws as an equivalent designation. Conversely, homosexuality meanwhile has been accorded the same kind of protected status in law as race, sex, ethnicity, etc., even though it clearly does not belong to the same category.

However, for obvious reasons, there is no equivalence to be drawn. Firstly, there can be no question about a person's sex or race (ethnicity, nationality,

---

[138] On the way in which the term homophobia/homophobic is being constantly abused, but could be used accurately, see The Abuse of Language, chapter 8.

disability and age). In each case people are certainly 'born that way'; in the case of disability, it may be an inherited medical trauma or due to an unwelcome accident. A gay person is certainly not 'born that way.' Gay orientation is mainly a matter of preference. It is a sense of identity felt by some people at a particular moment of their psychological and mental development. Whereas a person's sex or race is, from the moment of an ultra-sound scan or birth, highly visible and incontrovertible, a person's sexual inclination only becomes visible when self-declared and/or manifested in certain conducts.

Secondly, neither sex nor race is reversible, what one is given in birth remains for the whole of life. In theological terms they are gifts of God to be honoured and enjoyed as part of the diversity and complementarity of human existence. In the case of sexual orientation the case is different. In a person's earliest years, there is no conclusive way of determining how they may decide their sexual orientation in the future. Despite the powerful disinformation put out by the gay lobby, people erotically attracted to people of the same sex can often form normal sexual relationships with people of the opposite sex. There is also sufficient evidence now available, mainly in the personal testimony of individuals who have changed their orientation from homo- to hetero-sexual, and feel better for doing so, to deny the mantra that homo-sexuality is irreversible. As Murray says appropriately,

> "For many gay men and women the idea that sexuality is fluid and that what goes one way may go another...is an attack on their person. And this isn't a fear without basis. Plenty of gay people will hear in the suggestion some echo of those dread words 'it's only a phase.' People who are gay find this suggestion enormously offensive, as well as destabilising in their relationships with parents, family and others. So since the phrase...is offensive for some people, the idea that it might actually be true for some people is unsayable...In some way the perception has developed to once be gay is to have fallen into your true state of nature, whereas to be for ever afterwards

straight is not."[139]

Murray concludes his discussion of the question of sexual identity with an important existential observation:

"The fact that this (fixed points of sexual identity) can change from one fixed identity to another, and from there to fluidity, points to more than a leap around from one dogma to another. It suggests a deep uncertainty about one underlying and rarely mentioned fact, which is that we still don't have much idea as to why some people are gay. After decades of research this is a huge – and potentially destabilizing – question to remain unresolved on an identity question which has arrived at the very forefront of our purported values."[140]

No gay gene

Following on from this observation, it is perhaps pertinent to mention that the very low percentage of those who claim to be gay or bisexual (probably no higher than 2.5% of a given population) would be extremely strange, if same-sex orientation was entirely or mainly caused genetically. Although apparently no convincing evidence exists that shows conclusively any particular cause of same-sex attraction, it is now demonstrated, beyond reasonable doubt, that an earlier belief that it followed innate impulses is no longer sustainable. A genetic analysis of almost half a million people has concluded there is no single "gay gene".

A report posted on the BBC web-site on 29 August, 2019, entitled, ' No Single Gene associated with being Gay,' analysed a study, published in the journal Science, using data from the UK Biobank and the organisation, 23andMe, that found some genetic variants associated with same-sex relationships. But these genetic factors accounted for, at most, 25% of

---

[139] The Madness of Crowds, 23-24.
[140] The Madness of Crowds, 25.

same-sex behaviour. The Harvard University and MIT researchers concluded, when the whole genome is considered, that genetics could account for between 8-25% of same-sex behaviour across a population.

Five specific genetic variants were found to be particularly associated with same-sex behaviour, including one linked to the biological pathway for smell, and others to those for sex hormones. But together they only accounted for under 1% of same-sex behaviour. David Curtis, honorary professor at the Genetics Institute, University College London, said:

> "This study clearly shows that there is no such thing as a 'gay gene'. There is no genetic variant in the population which has any substantial effect on sexual orientation. Rather, what we see is that there are very large numbers of variants which have extremely modest associations."[141]

This being the reality about the role of genetics in sexual orientation, some rather surprising conclusions were drawn by some expert commentators on the findings. Dr. Davis, for example, surmised that "even if homosexuality is not genetically determined, as this study shows, that does not mean that it is not in some way an innate and indispensable part of an individual's personality."[142] It would be interesting to know how a non-genetically determined sexual orientation is "an innate and indispensable part of an individual's personality." One would presume that, if the scientific evidence runs counter to this conclusion, the latter must be an unsupported conjecture.

Ben Neale, an associate professor in the Analytic and Translational Genetics Unit at Massachusetts General Hospital, who worked on the study, said:

> "Genetics is less than half of this story for sexual behaviour,

---

[141] 'No Single Gene', BBC web-site, 29 August, 2019.
[142] 'No Single Gene', BBC web-site, 29 August 2019.

but it's still a very important contributing factor. There is no single gay gene, and a genetic test (to decide whether) you're going to have a same-sex relationship is not going to work. It's effectively impossible to predict an individual's sexual behaviour from their genome."

According to this survey, genetic variations may play some role in homosexual orientation, amounting to a percentage factor of possibly between 8%-25%. This is hardly "a very important contributing factor." There is no conclusive evidence that links genetics to orientation in such a way that no other explanation could possibly be entertained.

Finally, Fah Sathirapongsasuti, senior scientist at 23andMe, concluded that

"This (homosexual orientation) is a natural and normal part of the variation in our species and that should also support precisely the position that we shouldn't try and develop gay 'curism'. That's not in anyone's interest."

Apart from the fact that 'curism' is not an accurate term to use for the generally accepted nomenclature, "sexual orientation change efforts" (SOCE), the assertion "that's not in anyone's interest" is false, seeing that a number of people with unwanted same-sex attraction have been greatly helped by "change therapy." Clearly it is, at least, in *their* interest.

The conclusion that can unequivocally be drawn from the many studies that have been undertaken on the reality of homosexual orientation is that it is not immutable.[143] That being the case, it should not be accorded the special legal designation of being a protected category, as if it shares the same

---

[143] In an extensive article, with the title, 'Evidence Shows Sexual Orientation Can Change: Debunking the Myth of "Immutability," ' Peter Sprigg lays out the extensive evidence, contained in a number of recent studies, that shows conclusively that a particular sexuality is not an innate part of a person's physical and mental make-up from conception onwards; see, Family Research Council, March 2019. Issue Analysis IS19C01.

characteristics as does race, sex, age and disability.[144]

The Case of Gender

I have already begun to discuss some of the issues that surround the notion of transgenderism. So important is the topic and so potentially damaging to young, vulnerable children and adolescents that further reflection is appropriate.

The understanding of what is implied by transgenderism is not controversial. At the least, all sides of the current dispute are agreed that being 'transgender' is a situation in which some people sense in their inner selves that their birth sex does not conform to how they view themselves. As they do not experience the characteristics usually associated with their sex at birth, they believe they were 'born in the wrong body'. This may result in a sense of acute discomfort in attempting to live according to what their biological sex is commonly understood by custom to indicate. This can be clinically diagnosed as 'gender dysphoria' (GD), i.e. a deep feeling of personal unease that demands some form of psycho-therapeutic counselling to alleviate or resolve their identity confusion.

The physical, mental, emotional and moral development of children

The rapid growth amongst young people, who present themselves as suffering the trauma of having to live in a physical body that they disown, is

---

[144] In an article, Lisa M. Diamond and Clifford J. Rosky, 'Scrutinizing Immutability: Research on Sexual Orientation and U.S. Legal Advocacy for Sexual Minorities,' The Journal of Sex Research 53 (2016): 363-391, have written the most comprehensive recent critique of "immutability." Given the nature of the controversy and the consequences often deduced from particular interpretations of the origin of sexuality, it is important in this context to note that Diamond is a self-declared lesbian. She has also written a book that explores the real existence of 'gender fluidity' as a counter to the outdated notion of immutability, Sexual Fluidity: Understanding Women's Love and Desire (Cambridge, Mass.: Harvard University Press, 2008).

a relatively new phenomenon. I will explore later some of the reasons why this proliferation of cases may be happening. First, it would be helpful to consider what developmental studies tend to show, concerning children's appreciation of sexual matters.[145] Young children possess only a superficial understanding of sex and gender. For instance, up until the age of seven, many children often believe that if a boy puts on a dress, he becomes a girl. This suggests a naive appreciation of sex identity.

In order to make sense of subsequent gender dysphoria in a very small minority of children, it is vital to recognise that gender stereotypes can massively influence how some children understand their sex. Thus, society expects male children to display more aggressive behaviour than female. Female children are supposed to show a more compassionate and caring attitude, less prone to dominate in inter-sex activities, more withdrawn into an inner world of imagination. This may be due to the way in which hormonal activity from the time of conception onwards influences the development of both physical bodies and brains. Distinct development pathways are triggered based on the XX (female) and XY (male) chromosomal make-up of neurons. Integration of these sex-related factors with environmental pressures gives rise to an individual's unique personality and preferences.

Importantly in terms of personality traits, an overlap of roughly 30% between the sexes has been revealed. This means that a considerable divergence of sex-related attributes exists within both sexes. One would, therefore, expect in the case of some children that at least some characteristics in a female are more 'male-like' than those exhibited within some males, and vice-versa. This could lead, in a few cases, to a young, female adolescent, whose behaviour, personality and preferences are more 'masculine,' compared to others of her biological sex, believing that she is

---

[145] I will follow a recent article that deals with the uncontroversial findings of socio-scientific research in the area of children's physical, mental and emotional growth, see William J. Malone, Colin M. Wright and Julia Robertson, 'No One is Born in the Wrong Body,' Quillette (24 September, 2019).

trapped in the wrong body; whereas, in reality, she simply exists towards one end of a behavioural spectrum. This amounts to no more than the fact that 'sex-atypical' behaviour is part of a natural variation exhibited both within and between the two sexes.

There is, therefore, no reason to think that either personality, preferences or behaviour defines one's sex. Sex is defined biologically by the reproductive organs, the chromosome difference, and the hormonal activity with which one is born. If a biological male displays characteristics more usually identified by a particular culture as belonging to a biological female that indicates a certain gender fluidity. It does not make him a female. It simply confirms a wide spectrum of interests and concerns between the two sexes. That is all there is to it.

It has been calculated that about 10% of a given population of young people possess 'sex-atypical' personality profiles. They are, however, all contained within the natural distribution of personalities within each sex. Gender identity, therefore, is likely to follow the way in which an individual perceives his or her own sex-related and environmentally influenced personality in comparison with that of the opposite sex they mix with. In other words, it is built on an individual's self-assessment of his or her stereotypical degree of masculinity or of femininity. It is unfortunate, and psychologically damaging, that this can be wrongly conflated with their biological sex.

This analysis, when used sensitively in counselling by psychotherapists properly trained in children's psychological development, can alleviate the distress caused by a perceived incongruence between one's biological sex and perceived gender. A child or young adult can be encouraged to reflect on the ways in which social and cultural pressures have brought about an unfortunate and inappropriate conventionalising of gender differences. These pressures, not based on well-informed objective evidence, have produced an added confusion into a young person's mind at just the time when they are experiencing immense, unforeseen physiological changes in their make-up.

Fortunately, most young people who are inclined to believe the myth that they inhabit the wrong body, with proper counselling are able to resolve any trauma or thought-processes that have caused them to desire an opposite sex body. As they progress with treatment they are gradually able to feel increasingly more comfortable with their real gender. Gender dysphoria then becomes an occurrence of the past.[146]

'Gender affirmation'

Unfortunately, in the present climate, in which a small minority of radical ideologues are seeking to impose their contrived version of a sexual revolution, the reality of child sexual development, as summarised above, is being transformed into a fiction. In place of good, standard psychotherapy practice, a different model, called 'gender affirmation' is being practised, much to the further confusion and detriment of young people. In this model, often a minimum of clinical assessment is undertaken concerning the real causes of gender dysphoria, before irreversible medical intervention is recommended. It is based on the fictional assumption that a young person's disorientated sense of identity must be believed and acted on just because, in one moment of time, that is what they say they wish.[147]

---

[146] A fascinating and eye-opening account of two such anonymous cases (one male and one female) has been recounted by two therapists working with the renowned Tavistock Clinic in London; see, Anna Churcher-Clarke and Anastassis Spiliadis, 'The Value of Extended Clinical Assessment for Adolescents presenting with Gender Identity Difficulties' (Research Article) in Clinical Child Psychology and Psychiatry (February 6, 2019).

[147] "The affirmative approach to gender dysphoria has been adopted by the majority of children's services in the UK. This approach endorses the child's belief that they were born in the wrong body and practitioners are required to support the child's self-identification...This is despite research findings which strongly suggest that most of the cases would eventually desist if left untreated", see 'Freedom to think', 1. However there are signs that this approach is slowly changing, partly owing to the pending closure of the Tavistock Clinic after an extensive, interim report by Dr Hilary Cass, a consultant in Paediatric Disability at Evelina London Children's Hospital, produced negative findings of its caseloads. One major finding was that health staff felt under pressure to adopt an "unquestioning affirmative approach," see https://www.bbc.co.uk/news/uk-62335665.

Naturally, any skilled, professional counsellor will take seriously the individual's self-appraisal of his or her condition. They will certainly not dismiss it out of hand. They will listen carefully to the person's story. However, they will not jump to the conclusion that a person, who affirms their different gender, needs their belief at once to be validated as true for them.[148] Rather, they seek to understand more deeply what has brought the young person to seek a gender change which denies the normal presumption that one's sex corresponds to that of one's birth.

'Gender affirmation' as a therapeutic practice

In recent years this procedure, attempting to deal with gender confusion, can lead to serious life-changing, irreversible procedures that a young person cannot begin to appreciate fully. The normal path to a complete transition from a person's birth-sex to a gender-change, that can only imitate that of the opposite sex, seems to follow a particular pattern. The first stage involves a social change when the young person is encouraged, sometimes by parents, other times by teachers or social media platforms, to adopt the outer trappings of the opposite sex, such as the use of clothes and the demand to be addressed with the pronoun of the preferred gender. This gives an indication of the desire for change. A second stage then follows at the onset of puberty, as the adult male and female characteristics of the child begin to show in the adolescent's body: menstruation and the enlargement of breasts in the female and voice-breaking, facial hair growth and genital emissions in the male. It is often at this stage that a few young people, who are serious about allowing their bodies to be conformed to their chosen gender, press their parents or guardians to arrange an appointment with a gender identity development service (GIDS) like the Tavistock Clinic.

---

[148] "We must deal with our patients with compassion but also make safe medical decisions, when demonstrable material reality is at odds with a patient's subjectivity", 'Sex, gender and gender identity', 3.

Depending on the advice given, a third stage may be recommended, namely a course of treatment by puberty blockers. The reasoning behind this proposal is that it allows time for the young person to explore more carefully whether they wish to proceed with further medical interventions. The logic behind this thinking is that it delays the powerful changes that confirm girls and boys in the physiological reality of their biological sex. At the same time, the treatment may be stopped and the normal changes of puberty can continue without any harm having been incurred. Further on, I will look at whether this thinking about potential harm has any actual scientific evidence to confirm its expected outcome.

A fourth stage sets in motion treatments that profoundly change the young person's further physical development. A male young person would start taking the female hormone, oestrogen, and anti-androgens (to inhibit the effect of testosterone). Likewise, the female would do the reverse. The effect in both cases would be to invert their normal sexual development. A final stage would be to undergo surgical procedures that would massively re-arrange their distinguishing physical parts: a female would undergo a mastectomy (the removal of the breasts) and a hysterectomy (the removal of the womb); a male would be castrated, i.e. have his penis and testicles removed.

The folly of 'gender affirmation'

If all the stages (even if the final one was omitted) were carried through, it is obvious that a full-blooded transition from birth sex to preferred gender is a massive and largely irreversible procedure. Common sense would suggest that, willingly undertaking such a radical transformation, would be the epitome of folly. In the first place, the practice is not medically warranted. The young person concerned is not suffering from some physical disease or bodily malfunction. They present themselves as physically healthy with a body that, if left to itself, would develop normally into a robust adulthood. There is, therefore, no medical justification for such interventions.

Secondly, the outcome of the interference with normal, healthy growth is largely unknown. One of the reasons given for making the changes is the young person's threat to commit suicide, if some or all are refused. However, there is plenty of evidence to show that the rate of suicide actually increases after the treatment.[149] An Australian paediatrician, Prof. John Whitehall, in a series of articles in the Journal Quadrant (2018), pointed out that 'The Australian Standards of Care and Treatment Guidelines for Trans and Gender Diverse Children and Adolescents' are

"Not based on the usual standards that justify Western medical therapy, including biological plausibility, proof of effect and absence of complications in bench studies, animal experiments and human trials. Rather, they are based on a 'clinical consensus...and a limited number of non-randomised clinical guidelines and observational studies'"[150]

In other words, they are founded on the 'expert' opinion of doctors running

---

[149] "One 20-year Swedish longitudinal cohort study, Dhejne, et al, 'Long-term follow-up of transsexual persons undergoing sex reassignment surgery: cohort study in Sweden'. Scott J (editor), PloS ONE, 2011: 6(2), showed 'persisting high levels of psychiatric morbidity, suicidal acts and complete suicide many years after medical transitions had taken place. These results are not reassuring and might suggest that more complex intra-psychic conflicts remain unresolved by living as the opposite sex', see, 'Sex, gender and gender identity,' 5. (Italics added).
The American Journal of Psychiatry published in its October 2019 journal a large study of transgender patients in Sweden who had undergone sex-reassignment surgery. The results of the study found that surgery improved patients' mental health. However, the Journal retracted the findings, when the original authors of the study admitted that a second look at the subject found there was no improvement; see, Richard Branstrom, John E. Pachankis, 'Reduction in Mental health Treatment Utilization Among Transgender Individuals after Gender-Affirming Surgeries: A Total Population Study' and Sven C. Mueller, 'Mental health Treatment Utilization in Transgender Persons: What we Know and What We Don't Know (editorial), both articles in American Journal of Psychiatry, Vol. 177, Issue 8, published online, 1 August, 2020. The conclusion of the revised interpretation of the data is cited by Mueller: *"treatment for anxiety disorders was higher in persons diagnosed with gender incongruence and who had received gender-affirming surgery* relative to persons diagnosed with gender incongruence and who had not received gender-affirming surgery" (Italics added).
[150] See, Michael Cook, 'There's nothing fake about the dangers of transgender medication,' Mercantornet, 1 October, 2019.

the clinics. The prescribing of untested medical procedures to otherwise healthy young people could be considered a dereliction of proper medical health-care. The idea that the administration of puberty blockers (gonadrophin-releasing hormones (GnRH)) gives a young person a neutral space to consider any further course of medical intervention does not take into account the known effect of this particular hormone on the development of the brain. It is now believed that GnRH appears in cerebrospinal fluids, cardiovascular and intestinal systems and gonads. In other words, it is widely involved in a range of functions from sexuality to cognition, memory to emotion and executive function. Prof. Whitehall comments,

> "There are no relevant studies of the effect...of cross-sex hormones on a growing brain. However, the imaging of brains of adult-trans (people) revealed shrinkage of male brains exposed to oestrogens at a rate 10x faster than would occur in ageing and revealed hypertrophy of female brains exposed to testosterone."[151]

He questions, therefore, how a young person is able to think straight about gender and fundamental changes to their physical make-up when their cognitive faculty is being disturbed by an unnecessary external force.

Thirdly, following on from these objections is the reality that the young person's belief that transitioning is the answer to his or her anguish about identity is not a strictly medical care issue, but a psychological one. Sensitive, prolonged counselling, without medical intervention, has shown time and again that young people who say they wish to transition come to realise that their distress is due to other factors in their environment than an unhappiness with their birth sex. Even without counselling, a very large percentage of trans-inclined young people realise after a fairly short time that they will be much more content if they can become convinced that there real sex (gender) is something positive to be admired and fostered.

---

[151] 'There's nothing fake'.

Fourthly, the combination of puberty-blocking drugs, followed by cross-sex hormones, will result in permanent infertility. This means that a trans-person, having undergone prescribed medical interruption, can never be a natural father or mother. Why would any caring clinician ever prescribe a course of action whose outcome was so dramatically life-frustrating and counter-productive?

Fifthly, how is it possible that a person of one sex can ever experience what it is like to belong to the opposite sex? The mantra that, "though I am a boy, I feel like a girl", or vice-versa, has no toe-hold in reality. The fact that a child may prefer the company of the opposite sex and manifest aspects of their characteristics does not mean that they belong to that sex. To affirm that they no longer belong to their biological sex, simply by an act of the will, is to live in a fantasy world; one in which the existence of unicorns and fairies would be just as real.[152] Imagination is a great gift and, to a certain extent, should be encouraged in children and made to flourish. At the same time, children need to be able to distinguish between what is actual and what is make-believe fiction. This is part of the process of growing up.

Sixthly, the experience of trans-people who, having taken steps to change physically their real sex for a preferred gender and then regret the results, should be carefully observed. It would be another matter of folly not to follow the reasons that have driven them to reconsider seriously the harm they have inflicted on themselves by taking the wrong advice.[153]

---

[152] A number of clinicians have pointed to anorexia nervosa as a plausible comparison, based on the disjunction between reality and a young person's fantasy. In this case it is the belief that, although unusually slim, they are overweight and therefore need to follow a stringent diet. No professional psychiatrist would deem it right clinical practice to confirm them in their belief.

[153] It is perhaps significant that the word transition, in the context of trans-genderism, belongs to the same linguistic family as transitional, whose synonyms are provisional, temporary, passing, changing, fluid and unsettled; see, Chambers Thesaurus (Edinburgh: Chambers Harrap Publishers, 2003).

Possible causes of the desire to live as someone of a different gender

If one starts with the way a child is brought up by the adults whose responsibility it is to look after the child, then the first possible cause of a gender identity disorder may be the way in which the child is socially conditioned. The carer(s) may have come under the influence of trans-activists who propose that signs of gender non-conformity are in reality indications of being uncomfortable in one's 'assigned' sex.[154]

As already discussed, gender identity disorder is confused with gender non-conformity. A child could, and sometimes does, express some stereotypical gender behaviours of the opposite sex (for example, the case of a, so-called, female 'tom-boy'), but without identifying herself with the opposite sex. Behaving as boys are characteristically thought to behave is not symptomatic of a girl defining herself as a boy. When the child's carers misinterpret what is happening and try to encourage the child to think of themselves as belonging to the opposite sex, they are on the way to causing irreparable damage to the child.

A theory has been floated that transgender-inclined children could be subject to conditions that stimulate the brain to develop in a way more characteristic of the opposite sex. However, research supporting this theory is, at the best, minimal and quite unproven.[155] It is again a misapprehension of transgender activists to suggest that at some stage in a child's development the body has to be made to conform to the brain, in order to harmonise the entirety of a person's make-up. The theory may provide a potentially attractive explanation for cross-gender identification, especially for individuals not affected by any known genetic, hormonal or psychosocial abnormalities. The issue, however, is not whether people imagine they are

---

[154] It is worth pointing out that the use of the word 'assigned' to describe what happens, when a birth certificate is filled in, is completely misplaced. The sex of the baby just born is not assigned, as if there was some doubt about it. The correct word to use is 'recognised.' The sex is what the respective genitals indicate, being in entire conformity with every other aspect of their maleness or femaleness. The word 'assigned' simply follows the misconceived social constructionist theory, clearly shown to be disproved in the case of birth.

[155] "There is little or no convincing evidence to support fundamental differences between the brains of females and males", 'Sex, gender and gender identity', 3.

of a different gender, but whether they are in fact.[156]

Detailed and prolonged counselling sessions by clinically-trained experts have thrown up a number of other possible causes of gender identity disorder, as the article by two clinicians working with the Tavistock Clinic has identified.[157] They explain that gender-identity confusion has to be set in the context of a broader disoriented identity, histories of social exclusion and persistent bullying when younger, accompanied by social anxiety and depression, most often with self-harm and the threat of suicide. The young people they meet are often socially and academically marginalised. They come often with high expectations that medical interventions for GD would solve their difficulties. Young referrals are predominantly female-bodied with high levels of social communication difficulties, mental health complexity and neuro-diversity. A considerable number come with an autism spectrum condition (ASC).

Extended counselling has been able to identify a whole series of social, adaptive, self-awareness and communications factors that could be the main reasons why young people believe that gender transition could well be the answer to their problems. The consultants recommended an extended diagnostic period, in which clinical decisions should proceed slowly. As together they explored the possibility that their referrals could live comfortably in the gender role of their birth sex, rather than foreclosing prematurely their struggle with gender identity, they have created a space in between the internal and external worlds of these young people. They have, in other words, allowed for an exploration of the inescapable 'in-betweeness' of adolescence. Although these authors might not adopt the language, it is the mind that needs repairing, not the body. A healthy mind will accept the body's unchangeable reality and thus avoid the suffering caused by wayward thinking.

---

[156] A full survey of the current scientific consensus on associations between brain structure and transgender identity is contained in 'Sexuality and Gender', 102-105. The authors conclude, "Scientific evidence overwhelmingly supports the proposition that a physically and developmentally normal boy or girl is indeed what he or she appears at birth. Evidence from brain imaging and genetics does not demonstrate that the development of gender identity as different from sex is innate."
[157] See, note 139.

The ideological origin of transgender belief [158]

The whole preceding discussion is based on the assumption that sexual identity is binary, i.e. there are, in the real world, only two sexes.[159] This fact is paradoxically born out by the desire to transition from one sex to the other. However, a number of people do not undergo any of the medical and surgical procedures they believe will transform their gender. They simply assert that they no longer belong to the sex identified either before or at birth. As Douglas Murray has phrased it,

> "At one end of the spectrum there are people who are born intersex...the rest of the trans issue is clearly on a spectrum...from people who have visible, biological justification for being described as between the sexes to those with no proof of difference other than testimony."[160]

He uses the analogy, taken from the computer, between hard and software. Hardware is the basic driving mechanism necessary for computers to operate; software represents the enormous variety of programmes that can be invented that enable a diversification of the computer's myriad uses. The decision to declare oneself to be the opposite sex is an invention – a software matter. However, the analogy breaks down at this point, because the software does not fit the original hardware of one's biological sex. In other words, the software (gender-transition) simply messes-up the human hardware system, making the computer inoperable. The invention of a sex-change is, then, better described as a malfunctioning programme; even one corrupted from outside (by malware):

---

[158] I delve deeper into this subject in Appendix B.
[159] The fact that an infinitely small number of people are born bearing the physical attributes of both sexes (inter-sex) does not alter the debate about transgenderism. At some stage in their physical development a decision will be taken as to which sex they should belong and surgical procedures will be undertaken to harmonise their physicality with this choice. These cases are anomalies that have no bearing on the debate about transgender beliefs, because the latter lack all reference to tangible, physical actuality.
[160] The Madness of Crowds, 195

"The question becomes about whether what one person or even a lot of people believe to be true about themselves has to be accepted as true by other people or not. This lack of evidence is one reason why some people believe that the whole Trans issue is a delusion."[161]

How a person feels on the inside is not applicable to the question of the biological self. Every chromosome, every cell in a trans-person remains as they were at birth.

The fundamental element in the trans-discourse is deconstruction philosophy. Nothing is ever as it appears on the surface. Social and cultural history tells us that we need to dig much deeper, looking for the authentic reasons for concluding 'wrongly' (since the dawn of the appearance of homo sapiens on the earth) that humans are divided into two, and only two, sexes. This account has to be demolished in favour of the social constructionist theory: namely that the cause of the abiding belief in the binary nature of sex is the desire of the physically stronger sex to dominate the weaker one. So, according to the theory, the whole history of the assumed two sexes is reduced to a narrative of subordination and submission. To quote Dummit again:

> "Whenever one comes across someone saying that something was masculine or something was feminine, it was never just about gender. It was always, simultaneously, about power...So if someone denied that gender and sex were variable, if they suggested that there really was something timeless or biological about sex and gender, they were really making excuses for power. They were apologists for oppression... *the same defective thinking, now is being taken up by activists and governments to legislate a new moral code of conduct...*[162]

---

[161] The Madness of Crowds, 199.
[162] 'I Basically Just Made It Up: Confessions of a Social Constructionist' (emphasis added).

Dummit finishes his confession of having been misled in his thinking by acknowledging that the discourse about sex and gender has become hopelessly distorted by a false ideology.

Conclusion

I maintain that the above reasoning that disputes the current dismissal of truth about abortion, sexuality and transgenderism also shows why our Western societies are being impelled towards the kind of abject folly that Erasmus, over five hundred years ago, depicted with razor-sharp wit and derision. It is in the interests of regaining a healthy state of affairs in human communities that it is shown up for what it is, a pack of false fabrications.

Finally, do not let anyone consider that any of the arguments put forward amount to hate speech. Those whose first concern is to speak the truth, and do so to protect and advance the well-being of vulnerable people, certainly hate the false philosophy that underlies and promotes the current misinformation around abortion, sexual and gender identity. However, in the strongest terms, they do not hate the people who have inadvisedly taken on board the ideological distortions being canvassed by a small group of zealots. Nor do they hate the zealots! For Christians the message is unmistakeable: "putting away falsehood, let all of us speak the truth to our neighbours...Be imitators of God, as beloved children, and live in love".[163]

To be involved in campaigns to liberate people from their psychological distress, moral confusion, legal muddle and spiritual misguidance instigated by those promoting the destructive ideologies around human identity is the very opposite of hate. The intention is to free people, caught up in the current social and cultural propagation of perverse thinking, to enjoy in full their real, authentic humanity. Transphobic, as an epithet applied to those who speak the truth about transgenderism in love, is a piece of dishonest abuse of language. In point of fact, those who truly demonstrate

---

[163] Ephesians 4:25; 5:1-2.

intolerance, bigotry, and the loathing of others are the ones seeking to overthrow the truth about what it means to be fully human. They are the ones who show what depths of hatred are possible among those determined to deconstruct reality. Three quotes from two eminent figures from the past throws light on the supreme issue that confronts those who have let their intellect be taken over by a false philosophy:

> "The truth is incontrovertible. Malice may attack it, ignorance may deride it, but in the end, there it is" (Winston Churchill);

> "The further a society drifts from the truth, the more it will hate those who speak it" (George Orwell);

> "In a time of universal deceit, telling the truth is a revolutionary act" (George Orwell).

PART II

THE WISDOM OF A BRAND-NEW WORLD

CHAPTER 5
Why Listen to God's Word?

"In the beginning was the Word, and the Word was with God, and the Word was God...The Word became flesh and lived among us...full of grace and truth".[164]

> "Let the word of Christ dwell in you richly; teach and admonish one another in all wisdom"[165]

Imagine an ocean-going schooner under full sale or a sailing boat attempting to win an Olympic gold medal in one of the various classes of racing vessels. Assuming that there is sufficient wind to propel them forward at a good speed, there we have a picture of how the Bible came to be written. There is a verse in the New Testament which applies the sailing boat imagery to the formation of the written word:

> "No prophecy ever came by human will, but men and women moved by the Holy Spirit spoke from God."[166]

The word translated in this version as "moved" really means "blown along." When one considers that the same word in Greek (pneuma) can signify both spirit and wind, there is a perfect analogy to the impression of a boat with its sails fully extended catching the full force of the wind and being driven forward. In the case of the Bible's prophetic word, it is the Spirit of God

---
[164] John 1:1, 14.
[165] Colossians 3:16.
[166] 2 Peter 1:21.

who propels human beings to speak the Word of God.

The mechanics of how this happens is not important. In another passage, Jesus uses the imagery of wind to depict the Spirit's action:

> "The wind blows where it chooses, and you hear the sound of it, but you do not know where it comes from or where it goes. So it is with...the Spirit."[167]

Finally, in yet another passage, it is said that

> "All Scripture is inspired by God (theopneustos);"[168]

The meaning of divinely-inspired

So, the first, excellent reason for listening to the message of the Bible is that it has its origin in the combination that occurs when human authors are indwelt by God's Spirit as they write down the words that appear in the Hebrew and Greek Testaments of the Bible. The Christian understanding of divine inspiration can be compared to the two natures of Jesus: fully God and fully human. The words have the full approval and authority of God, but they are also cast in the language that the authors chose out of their own imagination. Inspiration is not to be equated with dictation. The authors are not the passive recipients of words from an external source that they simply write down word for word as they are transmitted. The freely chosen words are theirs, but they convey the message exactly as God wishes it to be communicated.

---

[167] John 3: 8
[168] 2 Timothy 3:16

The phenomenon of the Bible[169]

A second convincing reason for listening to God's word is that its core message is unique among the various narratives that give an account of the significance of human life on planet earth.

The Nature of Scripture

This is summed up in the prophecy of Amos:

"Surely the Lord does nothing, without revealing his secret to his servants the prophets.[170]"

According to this text, the Bible claims to be a record of particular events that God accomplishes in the natural world and human history and a detailed explanation of those actions. A similar thought is spelt out by the apostle Paul in the New Testament:

"The mystery was made known to me by revelation...In former generations this mystery was not made known to humankind, as it has now been revealed to his holy apostles and prophets by the Spirit..."[171]

The word "mystery" in this context has a different meaning from the one normally understood in the English language: it is not the equivalent of a secret or an enigma; quite the reverse, it stands for a message made known publicly and clearly. Once, in its full meaning, it was hidden; now in the

---

[169] This section is a revised, updated and shortened version of the chapter I wrote for a symposium on the varied understandings of mission in the Bible; see, Rollin G. Grams, I. Howard Marshall, Peter Penner and Robin Routledge (eds.), Bible and Mission: A Conversation between Biblical Studies and Missiology (Schwarzenfeld, Germany: Neufeld Verlag, 2008), chapter 9, 'How a Missiologist Utilizes the Bible', 246-269.
[170] Amos 3:7; See also, Jeremiah 23: 18, 22.
[171] Ephesians 3:3-5.

fullness of time it is revealed thoroughly.

In brief, the Bible bears witness to special events that bear God's imprint, in that he initiates them and uses them to fulfil his purposes. These acts have precise interpretations related to the reasons for their occurrence. Thus, to give a clear example: (a) (fact) Jesus, an itinerant preacher and healer from Nazareth in Galilee, was crucified at a site called Golgotha just outside Jerusalem (nicknamed 'the place of the skull'). This happened before sundown initiated the Passover celebrations, on the order of the Roman Governor of Palestine; [172](b) (interpretation)"Jesus... suffered outside the city gate in order to sanctify the people by his own blood."[173] Here we see how one particular episode received a precise and distinct explanation.

Clearly the Bible is not interested in every event that happened in the Ancient Near East. What it records is a selected microcosm of the general history of the period. At the risk of over-simplification, it speaks about five fundamental aspects of existence in terms of a story (or drama):

a) The being and nature of God (the ultimate reality of all that is), the universe, planet earth (not a chance occurrence, but designed by its creator for a purpose) and humans (a special creation within the world). God created an ordered existence and made humans in his image. This is the beginning of the story.

b) The manner in which the three distinct entities – God, the natural world and human beings – relate together. This is the purpose of the story.

c) The reason why the relationship has broken down. This represents the story's tragedy.

d) An account of how it has been restored again. This announces the story's good news.

e) A portrayal of what the restoration will finally look like. This is the end of the story.

---

[172] John 19:14, 17-18.
[173] Hebrews 13:12.

The purpose of Scripture

This is summed up in Paul's second letter to his colleague, Timothy:

> "The sacred writings...are able to instruct you for salvation through faith in Christ Jesus. All Scripture is inspired by God and is useful for teaching, for reproof, for correction, and for training in righteousness, so that everyone who belongs to God may be proficient, equipped for every good work."[174]

This passage makes a two-fold claim: the Bible (a) shows the way of salvation, first by making people wise about their need of salvation and, secondly, by explaining how it may become a concrete reality in individual lives, (b) enables us to live according to God's pattern of righteousness and justice. In other words it indicates how we should and can live in his new world, as God's adopted children, in the universal family he, as the Father, is creating.

Interpretation

So, we have explored briefly the nature of the Bible and its two principal purposes. In some ways that is the easiest task. However, over the course of two thousand years, the Christian community has often disagreed about how different passages and teachings should be understood in distinct contexts. How, then, should the universal church deal with divergent interpretations? Are there dependable ways of being able to judge between legitimate and illegitimate readings of the text? Are there methods which can ensure that any particular rendering of the text is more faithful than any other? Is it possible to be sure that we are holding fast truthfully to Jesus teaching, as in the saying:

---

[174] 2 Timothy 3:15-17.

"If you continue in my word, you are truly my disciples; and you will know the truth, and the truth will make you free.[175]

Unlike Pilate, the Roman governor, Jesus' disciples are not sceptical about truth. Nevertheless, how is it possible to have a sure knowledge (justified, true belief) of the content, original meaning and present entailment of Jesus' words? Can we ever be certain that we are not simply dishing up our own prejudices in the solemn guise of 'Thus, says the Lord'? At the risk of making a misleading generalisation, it is possible to discern three complementary, but distinct approaches to understanding the text made by the Christian community in the course of its history.

Scripture alone (sola Scriptura)

The ideal of the sixteenth century reformers was to take the Biblical text, and give it to ordinary members of the church, translated into their local languages. They made significant translations from the original texts into the languages of the common people and distributed them widely.

The catchphrase, 'Scripture alone', implied that every belief and practice of the church had to be tested for its conformity to Scripture: did it agree with or was it contradicted by the plain meaning of its message? The reformers made assumptions about the implications of the principle they announced. First, the church has no authority to impose any teaching that was not explicitly or implicitly found in Scripture. Secondly, the Scriptures are clear in their intention. Thirdly, anyone,[176] coming to the text in a spirit of humility, the desire to learn, and the guidance of the Holy Spirit can understand the text. The sense of Scripture is free from obscurity and ambiguity, self-evident to anyone willing to abide by its teaching. Thus the professional clergy did not have the sole right to clarify its meaning. Fourthly, individuals are required to obey their consciences in matters of belief and practice, enlightened by the Holy Spirit through God's Word.

---

[175] John 8: 31-32.
[176] As a reformer, William Tyndale, famously remarked, "Even the plough-boy".

Tradition

At one time, branches of the Church subscribed to the notion of two sources of revelation – the Word of God in Scripture and the Word in and through the Church. This is no longer the case. The Bible alone is now recognised by the universal Church as the complete source of God's revelation. However, in order to maintain the unity of the faith against individualistic, idiosyncratic and arbitrary interpretations, the Church calls upon its accumulated wisdom as a way of measuring legitimate and illegitimate understandings of the text.

Thus, churches claim to teach only what is always already implicit in Scripture. Due to the divine teaching authority given to duly appointed guardians of the faith by Jesus Christ, it can be made explicit in the fullness of time by revelation of the Holy Spirit. So, some churches have developed, in recent years, a distinction between the original or formal sense of the text and the fuller or subsequent sense. Understanding the task of Biblical interpretation in this way allows the Christian community, by listening to the voice of the Holy Spirit (channelled through the church's teaching authority), to perceive the mind of Christ in every new generation. One text that seems to confirm this approach is that given by Christ to his disciples on the eve of his crucifixion:

> "I still have many things to say to you, but you cannot bear them now. When the Spirit of truth comes, he will guide you into all the truth...He will declare to you the things that are to come."[177]

Tradition is a useful tool in uncovering the meaning of the text and, in particular, how its teaching relates to changed historical situations. However, it never can usurp the overriding authority of the text itself. This means that

---

[177] John 16: 12-14. It has to be acknowledged that this verse tends to be interpreted by Protestant churches as referring only to the writings of the New Testament, subsequent to Jesus resurrection and ascension, not to the Church's teaching after the closing of the Canon of Scripture.

the Church's grasp of what the text is communicating is always to be held accountable to further insights that spring from the text itself. The text is inviolable; tradition may be corrected in the course of time. Listening to the text is, therefore, a never-ending activity of fine-tuning.

Reason

Since the middle of the 18th century, belief in the grand narrative of the Bible, as a true account of human existence in all its manifold variety, began to wane. In its place, the powers of independent human reasoning, based on the ability of 'scientific' methods of investigation to discover the real, natural world, began to take centre stage as the only reliable way of assessing the validity of all claims to truth. Gradually the Biblical message, mainly because it arose in a pre-scientific world, dominated (so it was believed) by all manner of speculation, based on untested legends and myths, became demoted as the ultimate authority on what was correct and safe to believe.

As a new awakening to the reliability of rational thought to discern the difference between genuine knowledge and mere speculation, new social research techniques, claiming scientific objectivity, began to arise: sociology; economics; historical studies; psychology; anthropology; cultural studies and more. Each of these developed sub-sections, out of which new schools of thought and university academic departments were created. Knowledge became hugely diversified and its discovery a matter of ever-increasing specialisation. Biblical and theological studies inevitably became influenced by this new trend that challenged them to submit their methods of intellectual exploration and scrutiny to the findings of the new 'sciences.'

There is a long history of the claims of these sciences to deliver objective, neutral and unbiased conclusions about all the objects of their inquiry. Thus they were deemed assured in being able to offer well-tried and tested methods of ascertaining their findings, when applied to a study of the humanities, such as philosophy, theology, moral theory, political studies, education, law and the like. These disciplines were reckoned to be based on more subjective interpretations of their areas of study than the strict sciences.

There is nothing intrinsically wrong in using contemporary knowledge or widely accepted insights as resources for interpreting accurately the original meaning and current application of the Biblical message:

> "On the contrary, if the purpose of the Bible is to teach us how to live as redeemed people in God's world in God's way, then the wise use of accumulated human experience is indispensable as part of understanding the reality of that world.
>
> However, the use of reason is not one-way traffic. It has been assumed too easily that the Scriptures, because of their ancient provenance, are the main object of critical scrutiny. It has also been assumed too readily that the rational tools that are to hand in a post-Enlightenment society are non-partisan and unprejudiced. In particular, there exists a strong trend...to expand the bounds of scientific method beyond what it is capable of delivering qua science. Thus metaphysical claims are sometimes made, in the name of science, that science...is incapable of verifying or falsifying."[178]

The conclusion to be drawn from this section on the use of reason in interpreting and applying Scripture is that it can be an important instrument, but with some discretion. It can be accorded cautious approval, always bearing in mind that it is not exempt from ambiguity and ideological manipulation.

---

[178] Bible and Mission, 255.

Explanation

A third reason why the Bible should be listened to is, perhaps, its most significant contribution to knowledge about the authentic reality of human life in community. It concerns its proven ability to explain fundamental aspects of human relationships, how they work, should work and why they often fail, and also predict likely future incidents based on present trends. The Bible possesses a mine of wisdom and discernment about what makes human flourishing actually possible and why the human search for the best outcome that matches their given nature is so often thwarted by false reasoning, bad decisions and adverse circumstances.

Not only does the Bible possess this knowledge it can also be compared favourably with alternative explanations. Some scientists propose a theory that knowledge gained through observation of the natural world (including the physical mechanisms of the human brain), by means of controlled experimentation, will be sufficient to explain the sum total of human experience. This belief derives from what has been called 'scientific expansionism,' the conviction that science will, one day, be able to encompass all the knowledge required to give a full account of human life on earth.[179]

However, in the real world, it can be shown incontrovertibly that knowledge derived entirely 'from below,' i.e. from data acquired from material sources alone, is intrinsically incapable of discovering the whole truth about what it means to be human. It can deliver sound knowledge about a wide range of matters, based on its ability to explore the truth about the natural world. At the same time, it needs to be complemented by knowledge 'from outside,' which tells us what we would not otherwise know.

Within the Christian tradition of thought, this is called revelation or divine disclosure. This is precisely what the Biblical message offers. In no way does

---

[179] An outcome which the renowned theoretical physicist and cosmologist, Stephen Hawking, believed would one day become a reality: a so-called 'theory of everything'.

it contradict the proper use of scientific means of gaining understanding. Indeed, the origins of modern science in the West owe their impulses to people, versed in scientific explorations of their era, who were also committed Christian believers. The idea that science and religious belief were ever on an inevitable collision course owes its precept to widely projected misunderstandings, sometimes on both sides.

Conclusions

Philosophical fashions and tendencies of the last sixty or so years have gradually permeated centres of intellectual output, such as universities and research centres, to such an extent that the ability to discover the truth about what it means to practice the good and abhor evil has become increasingly problematical. The rash of publications and the creation of new courses spawned by Lyotard's epic-making book, The Postmodern Condition: A Report on Knowledge,[180] has led to a world where access to truth is no longer determined by objective criteria:

> "unless there is an independent point of reference, truth equates with subjective reckonings and issues are settled by either superior force or persuasive power...(However) the common view of truth is that it pertains to an order of existence which lies outside of subjective desire and ideological manipulation, able to challenge all thought and ideas. In other words, truth-claims are provisional, because they can always be challenged by a fuller appreciation of what is the case. To the contrary, truth claims would always be 'true,' for there would be no proper grounds for considering them false."[181]

---

[180] (Minneapolis, The University of Minnesota Press, 1984) a translation of the original, La condition postmoderne: rapport sur le savoir (Paris: Minuit, 1979).
[181] J. Andrew Kirk, The Future of Reason, Science and Faith, 169.

More than forty years on from Lyotard's influential tour de force much of what he advocated has come to pass. In the two areas of conflicting ideas that form the first part of this study, it is evident that some, strongly-held beliefs are now determined not by concrete, verifiable evidence, but precisely by "subjective desire" and "ideological manipulation." What is 'true' is what anyone finds acceptable to believe and practise. Often the process of arriving at personal convictions about life is influenced by dominant intellectual forces. Decision-making bodies like governments and legal institutions are also often persuaded by persistent lobbying to confirm them. Whether what is believed and practised accords with facts of the matter is irrelevant, as long as they conform to how people feel and what they desire.

Concerning discussion by people who approve of abortion (now basically on demand), same-sex orientation, and transgender transition, all that matters is how a person responds emotionally to the opinions they 'like'.[182] It is a sign of the times that laws can be changed or created on the whim of a group of people who feel that this is how things ought to be, not how they are. We are living in a room full of mirrors, like those found in entertainment locations, that, in order to amuse, distort the reality of what is:

> "The view that truth can no longer be defined in terms of conformity to what is the case, independently of what humans may think is the case or would prefer was the case, is itself a statement about the facts of the matter. Otherwise, it could be legitimately interpreted as the attempt by certain thinkers to gain supremacy over the meaning of truth."[183]

So, how might it be possible to attempt to bring back our Western cultures from the destructive, dead-end of solipsism, i.e. "an order of existence,

---

[182] The first four chapters of this book have demonstrated in manifold ways this radical change towards what constitutes acceptable belief and conduct.
[183] The Future of Reason, 170.

where confidence in representation and correspondence has broken down, (so that) there is no way of telling whether a person's beliefs, held within their head, reflect any reality external to the neuropsychological functioning of the brain cells?"[184] How can the fiction, that holds that people's interpretation of their experience is always legitimate within their own inner world, as long as they can justify it to themselves, be reversed? How can a fantasy world, where no objective standard of measurement of what is the case is presumed to exist, where there is no way of determining for sure whether a statement of belief actually denotes anything, be exchanged for the real one?

In the philosophy of science, a method is used to arrive at the truth of a situation known as inference to the best explanation (technically called abduction). This method works by comparing alternative explanations of the data of experience. It incorporates into its method of working any evidence that seems to be germane to the case. The 'best' explanation is the one most warranted by all relevant evidence and, if true, provides the best understanding.

It works well in a court of law. In order to arrive at a decision about the reliability of a conviction the best explanation of all the relevant evidence has to be determined. Accomplishing this objective takes place through the gathering of data deemed to be relevant to the case under consideration. At the time of the trial, the prosecuting and defence counsels employ a method of cross-examination in which the consistency of a witness's testimony is weighed against its own internal harmony. This is part of the evidence that must be included in the final summing up.

The judge in the case lays out the evidence as clearly as possible, alludes to possible doubts about its reliability in some instances, and then sets out the various alternative interpretations that may be able to explain the phenomena under discussion. He then either gives his own judgement or he directs a jury to come to a balanced decision, beyond all reasonable doubt,

---

[184] The Future of Reason, 166.

concerning a verdict of guilty or not guilty. At no point in the procedure are subjective feelings allowed to intrude into the decision-making process. What counts is a rational, objective estimation of whether the evidence produced is true, false or impossible to determine.

So, in conclusion, the fundamental issue is whether, in the debate about the word of God, as an explanation of lived human experience in all its manifestations, does a better job, i.e. provides the most convincing answers, in comparison with any other known alternatives. The Christian answer is, yes it does, not as a matter of dogmatic certainty, but as something that can be tested in the public arena. The rest of this study will undertake to demonstrate how this is possible by continuing to compare the two worlds. We will now consider what the Biblical message says about these two worlds, existing side by side.

CHAPTER 6

The Announcement of a New World in the Midst of the Old

"This is the judgement, that the light has come into the world, and people loved darkness rather than light because their deeds were evil".[185]

"Jesus spoke to them, saying, 'I am the light of the world. Whoever follows me will never walk in darkness but will have the light of life".[186]

A new regime is declared

Around the year 29 AD, Jesus of Nazareth, a man in his early thirties, appeared on the banks of the river Jordan and was baptised, along with many Jews of the time, by his cousin John. John, called by God to prepare his people for the coming of the Messiah, was preaching a message of God's judgement on all kinds of corruption and deceit, but also the offer of forgiveness to all who turned back to him in repentance from the error of their ways, and committed themselves afresh to follow his purposes.[187] The latter's commitment was signed and sealed by full immersion in the river, signifying the passing from one way of life to another. He also proclaimed that he would be followed by another, "more powerful than I...(who) will baptise you with the Holy Spirit."[188]

---

[185] John 3:19.
[186] John 8:12.
[187] Luke 3:7-18.
[188] Luke 3: 16.

As Jesus came up out of the water, he was greeted by a voice from heaven which pronounced the identity of this exceptionally special person:

"You are my Son, the Beloved; with you I am well pleased."[189]

These words echoed two passages from the Old Testament, which both pointed forward to the Messiah to come.[190]

This decisive event was followed by a sojourn in a desert place, where Jesus' was tempted, by a string of deceptive questions put to him by Satan, the prince of evil, to deny his messianic destiny. After Jesus had refuted Satan's strategy, he began his public preaching, teaching and healing ministry:

"Now after John was arrested, Jesus came to Galilee, proclaiming the good news of God."[191]

The substance of the good news

"The time is fulfilled, and the kingdom of God has come near; repent, and believe in the good news."[192]

The good news spoken by Jesus, and manifested in his public life, centred on the actual arrival of God's reign, announced by the Jewish prophets and fulfilled in Jesus mission. The significance of Jesus interpretation of his part in this fulfilment is clarified in many episodes during his three year ministry. Three of them are particularly worth noting.

---

[189] Mark 1:11.
[190] Psalm 2:7, Isaiah 42:1.
[191] Mark 1:14.
[192] Mark 1:15.

The engagement with Satan[193]

The temptation narrative, recorded in the Gospels of Matthew and Luke, recounts how Jesus on his own in a remote location, was confronted by Satan. The essence of the contest between them concerned Jesus messianic calling. Satan did not deny that he was the Messiah sent by God to his people. Nor did he attempt to induce Jesus into denying his messianic role. Rather, the falsehoods that Satan invented were attempts to provoke Jesus into creating a Messianic function for himself that blatantly contradicted God's will for his future ministry. Satan's enticement is repeated twice, "if you are the Son of God, then..." His purpose was to persuade Jesus, with apparently plausible quotes from the Jewish Scriptures, to deviate from the chosen path. The final effort was to lure Jesus into the trap of taking a quick route to the inauguration of the kingdom:

> "The devil took him to a very high mountain and showed him all the kingdoms of the world and their splendour; and he said to him, 'All these I will give you, if you will fall down and worship me.'"[194]

Satan was not offering Jesus God's kingdom, but his own. He was attempting to entice Jesus into substituting a counterfeit world of his own invention for the genuine article. Jesus was tempted to compromise completely with Satan's blatant falsehood. Luke's account of the exchange of words adds another dimension to what Matthew records:

> "To you I will give their glory and all this authority; for it has been given over to me, and I give it to anyone I please. If you then will worship me, it will all be yours."[195]

Satan's claim is utterly bogus. The only one who could do as he alleges would be God. However, the statement would be a contradiction in terms.

---

[193] Matthew 4:3-10; Luke 4:1-13.
[194] Matthew 4:8-10.
[195] Luke 4:6-7. The emphasis is added.

It would be totally impossible for God to surrender complete control of the kingdoms of this world to his arch-enemy. Satan's lies were not even particularly subtle. The other side to this discussion is that Satan was offering Jesus the kind of kingdom that he had precisely come to replace. The splendour and glory of the earthly nations, in themselves manifestations of corrupted human desires, pride and arrogance, were already under God's judgement. Jesus notion of the kingdom was of a realm of human existence delivered from the illusions propagated by diabolic perversions of the truth.

The conversation with Nicodemus[196]

For reasons we can only guess at, we may presume that Nicodemus, a prominent Jewish leader, visited Jesus because he wished to speak with him about a supreme matter to do with the Jewish faith. The story does not tell us what exactly was the subject he wished to bring up. We can only deduce it from Jesus first words in reply:

> "Very truly I tell you, no one can see the kingdom of God without being born from above" (or "born again"- the word has this double meaning).

I think it is fair to surmise that the topic was the kingdom of God. The kingdom of God was a hugely important issue for the whole Jewish population. Its coming represented the main hope that Israel could permanently regain its independence from the oppressive occupation of a foreign power.

So, one can imagine that Nicodemus wanted to find out whether the Jewish expectation of the coming kingdom was going to be fulfilled by Jesus. Jesus response was, to say the least, surprising. He introduced a notion of kingdom that Nicodemus obviously did not understand: he referred to

---

[196] Recorded in John 3:1-18.

"seeing the kingdom" and "entering the kingdom" through the gift of a second birth from above. There is the natural birth through which every human being enters into this life and, then, there is a further birth through which we may understand the true meaning of God's kingdom ("seeing") and become part of it ("entering"). It is a new world, a distinct way of living, emerging within the old. It is centred on the God whom Jesus has revealed. Jesus, then, is introducing Nicodemus to two different dimensions of human life: a human birth and a birth by God's Spirit; earthly things and heavenly things (verses 6 and 12).

People are fully aware of the physical world around them, and are thoroughly immersed in it. The spiritual world, for the majority of people, is a more indistinct reality. They may recognise hints of it, for themselves, in their dissatisfaction with a common feeling that material goods and services, however useful or sublime, do not ultimately satisfy. That is why they have to be repeated and ever new cravings pursued. It manifests itself as a kind of yearning for something more, a deeper reality beyond the concrete, tangible world. There exists in the constitution of all human beings a wistful hunger for something beyond the material world with all its splendour and glory.

So, Jesus' discussion with Nicodemus is about the reality of God's kingdom, the second birth by the Spirit into this reality and the new life of the spiritual realm. After the work of the Spirit in human lives, the knowledge and experience of God moves from the margin into the centre of those lives. This is what Jesus means when he talks about "having eternal life".

The rest of the passage speaks about how humankind is split into two groups: those who believe that through Jesus we may leave one impoverished realm of existence (the old world) and enter another, and have acted on it, and those who do not believe in Him and remain outside. Jesus marks a great divide among people: either they enter into the great blessing of new life in God's kingdom or they remain under the curse of imagining that the life they have invented for themselves is the whole of existence, its only possibility. When they talked about God's kingdom late at night, Jesus held out to Nicodemus an alternative version of the kingdom to the standard Jewish understanding.

Jesus before Pilate: a mini-discourse on political power[197]

The third episode happened when Jesus stood, at the end of his earthly life, before Pilate, the Roman governor of Judea at the time. Pilate's first question to Jesus, according to John's Gospel, was about whether he claimed to be the king of the Jews. This was the crime brought against him by the Jewish leaders in Jerusalem.[198] His reply helps to clarify the meaning of the kingdom, an interpretation that appeared to Nicodemus at first as a complete conundrum,

> (Yes, I am a king.) "(However), my kingdom is not from this world."[199]

His kingdom represented a quite different reality. The kingdoms of this world (nations, states, civilisations) arise, prosper for a time and then fade away. They are built, like the Tower of Babel, on human ambitions. They do not act according to the ways God has planned, so that people may delight in the world he has created. God's kingdom, then, does not correspond to what this world might imagine.

In Jesus life, the prophetic message he proclaimed excluded recourse to violence. In fact the announcement of God's rule (the kingdom) denied the possibility that it could be accomplished by the use of coercive force. This is the gist of the rest of what Jesus said at his trial:

> "If my kingdom were from this world, my followers would be fighting to keep me from being handed over to the Jews. But, as it is, my kingdom is not from here."[200]

Both the context and the use of the preposition 'from' show that Jesus is affirming that his reign does not have its origin in the way this world habitually thinks about the exercise of power. So, the first statement is

---

[197] John 18:33-38, 19:9-11.
[198] John 19:12.
[199] John 18:36
[200] John. 18:36. The word "from" is a better preposition to use than "of" to translate the Greek ek. The latter suggests that Jesus kingdom does not belong in this world. Whilst the former denotes the nature of the kingdom that it does not spring from out of this world; it is from another place. Nevertheless, it is active within this world.

explained by the second. Were the kingdom of Jesus to be from this world that is governed by the normal procedures of human thought and action, he would have organised his followers into a military force to defy the authorities and defend his cause. In an equivalent saying, recorded in Matthew's Gospel, Jesus rebukes his followers for using violence:

> "All who take the sword will perish by the sword. Do you think that I cannot appeal to my Father, and he will at once send me more than twelve legions of angels?"[201]

Many, both within and outside the Christian church have misinterpreted the saying about the kingdom, understanding it to be claiming that Jesus' kingdom does not belong here, but exists in some mystical, spiritual sphere, removed from normal earthly existence. No Jew of the first century could possibly have misunderstood the meaning of the kingdom (malkuth YHWH) in this way. At issue is the question of origins:

> "Both expressions mean that Jesus' reign does not have its source or origin in this world ... The kingships of this world preserve themselves by force and violence."[202]

In other words, the kingdom of God is a powerful presence within the world, but in a different way from that normally associated with human rule. Many people have advanced the idea that Christianity preaches a message of private, individual, inward, spiritual and future-oriented salvation. Such a view, however, has little to do with a careful reading of the New Testament.

Conclusion

So, in these three episodes we find a number of clues about the reality of the kingdom as taught by Jesus and made concrete in his life. Jesus view of God's new regime coming into being through the sacrifice of his life, which

---

[201] Mt. 26.52-53. In the first century a legion, at full strength, consisted of 5,280 fighting men. 12 legions, therefore, would have made up an army of 63,360 men.
[202] D.A.Carson, The Gospel according to John (Leicester: IVP, 1991), p. 594.

he suffered as the result of his witness, is in radical contrast to the normal way of life in the kingdoms of this world as portrayed by Satan and understood in principle by the Jewish leaders, and by Pilate.

Nicodemus, on the other hand, judging by his subsequent action on behalf of Jesus, at the least began to understand that Jesus represented a persuasive fresh interpretation of God's kingdom. He protested against the way in which the religious leaders of the time condemned Jesus without allowing him a fair hearing in a properly constituted court of law.[203] Then, at the end of Jesus' earthly life, he joined with Joseph of Arimathea in burying Jesus. The incident suggests that Nicodemus, like Joseph, had become a disciple of Jesus, "though a secret one because of his fear of the Jews".[204] History does not tell us anything more about him.

In the next chapter I will explore the reality of the radical distinguishing features that exist between the two worlds or kingdoms, as presented in the Gospels' four accounts of Jesus teaching. The outlook of both the old and the new will begin to become more transparent in the telling of the two stories.

---

[203] John 7:50-52.
[204] John 19: 38-42.

CHAPTER 7

A New Order is in Place

"If anyone is in Christ, there is a new creation: everything old has passed away; see, everything has become new"[205].

The beginnings of a new community

Some six weeks after some of Jesus' followers discovered that the tomb, in which he was placed after his death on a Roman cross, was empty, he appeared to his closest disciples for the last time on earth.[206] Prior to his death, he had been preparing his disciples for the moment he would no longer be with them physically. His teaching encompassed two massive pieces of information: God's new creation under his rule would continue in a new form, and the impetus behind it would be the gift of his Spirit to be a constant presence with the community that Jesus had begun to initiate. And, so it happened.

His last words on earth encompassed teaching both about the kingdom of God and the coming of the Holy Spirit. In answer to the apostles' misconceived question,

> "Lord, is this the time when you will restore the kingdom to Israel?"[207]

---

[205] 2 Corinthians 5:17.
[206] Acts 1:2-11.
[207] Acts 1:6.

Jesus did not directly rebuke them for their continued misunderstanding of the nature and future shape of the kingdom. Instead he left them with a substantial hint of how it would come about. In comparison with the hope engendered among their compatriots, the apostles were still bemused by what for them was Jesus' perplexing reinterpretation of the kingdom. They continued to think along traditional lines of the restoration of an independent political regime comparable to that of David and Solomon. Jesus disabused them of this false hope and, in its place, gave them a different one:

> "You will receive power when the Holy Spirit has come upon you; and you will be my witnesses...to the ends of the earth."[208]

And, so it happened.

On the Day of Pentecost (fifty days after the Passover), when the people of Israel celebrated both the completion of the barley harvest and, possibly, the anniversary of the giving of the law at Mount Sinai,[209] Luke records that the Holy Spirit came upon each of Jesus' followers. Immediately after this manifestation, Peter spoke to a gathered crowd about the significance of Jesus life, death and resurrection. As a result, "about three thousand persons were added" to the company of disciples and a new community came into being.[210] In response to Jesus' promise about what would happen, once he had left them, God's new creation (the kingdom) was activated.

Early in its life, the community was referred to as 'the Way '.[211] The High Priest's lawyer also called it, 'the sect of the Nazarenes.'[212] "In Antioch...the disciples were first called Christians."[213] Luke alludes to the new community

---

[208] Acts 1:8.
[209] There is no absolute certainty that this latter anniversary was acclaimed at this time. At some stage, however, it became recognised among Jews as part of the Feast of Pentecost.
[210] Acts 2: 22-36, 41, 43-47.
[211] Acts 9:2; 19:9, 23; 22:4; 24:22.
[212] Acts 24:5, 14.
[213] Acts 11:26.

as the church for the first time, in relation to the persecution that broke out against Jesus followers after the martyrdom of Stephen. He used the term again after the conversion of Saul of Tarsus, when persecution had ended for the time being.[214] He also mentions Paul's use of the word, when he addressed the Ephesian elders a few years later.[215] Paul also employs the word in his earliest letters (Thessalonians and Galatians), addressing the readers as "the church of the Thessalonians" and "the churches in Galatia."[216] In later letters, (1 Corinthians, Romans, Ephesians and Colossians) he elaborates a more developed doctrine of the church.

The new order in the teaching of Jesus
The Sermon on the Mount

The most far-reaching exposition of the kind of life expected in God's new world is given by Jesus in what is commonly called the 'Sermon on the Mount.'[217] It amounts to a kind of manifesto that sets out in some detail the characteristics of people who submit themselves to God's reign.

The Beatitudes

The teaching begins with a series of pronouncements on what counts as a genuine blessing for human life. The teaching throughout is given in contrast to the way that the old world imagines what a well-ordered life is like.

The first of the blessings belongs to those who are *"poor in spirit."* It is an affirmation about the spiritual nature of those who wish to participate in the new world. The saying echoes two declarations given towards the end of

---

[214] Acts 8:1; 9:31.
[215] Acts 20:28.
[216] 1 Thessalonians 1:1; 2 Thessalonians 1:1; Galatians 1:2.
[217] The full version is found in Matthew 5-7. Luke's Gospel also contains similar teaching, but with some variations; see, Luke 6:20-49.

Isaiah's prophecy:

"For thus says...the one..., whose name is Holy: I dwell in the high and holy place, and also with those who are contrite and humble in spirit".[218]

"Thus says the Lord:...this is the one to whom I will look, to the humble and contrite in spirit, who trembles at my word".[219]

The opposite of "poor in spirit" is "arrogant," "contemptuous", "condescending," self-important," "presumptuous" and "conceited." The "poor in spirit" are contrite people, aware of their failings, deficiencies and weaknesses. They are chastened and repentant.

The rest of the blessings create a pattern of life that fills in, in more detail, the meaning of being poor in spirit within the confines of the old world: *mourning* is to feel pain because of one's own or another's misfortune or folly; *meekness* is to be modest, humble and gentle; *having a hunger and thirst for righteousness* means living by God's standards, i.e. seeking in every situation what is good, honest and virtuous; *being merciful* is the capacity to show compassion, forgiveness and kindness even to those who act dishonestly, callously and inhumanely; *being pure in heart* is about ordering the centre of our being towards moral cleanliness, authenticity and sincerity; *being a peacemaker* means seeking the welfare of others, especially young people, the disabled, the destitute and the elderly, bringing an end to conflicts and enabling reconciliation.

Those who are *persecuted for righteousness sake and reviled* because they are followers of Jesus are those who belong to God's new order. Being persecuted and reviled are signs of the clash of two worlds: the sphere where God reigns and his righteousness is the standard to be followed, to

---

[218] Isaiah 57:15.
[219] Isaiah 66:2.

achieve the highest pinnacle of moral endeavour, and the sphere where Satan reigns, inculcating lies, fabrications, deceptions and illusions. The latter indicates an existence lived on the basis of unreality; the former points to the truth of what genuinely fulfils human well-being.

The disciple of Jesus can expect defamation of all kinds, based on falsehood and misrepresentation. To be associated with Jesus is to be hated and despised. He is the one person in the whole of human history to whom it is absolutely right to give one's entire allegiance. This will imply that, in certain circumstances, unwavering adherence to human authority has to be denied.

Members of the old world largely do not tolerate people, prepared to please God rather than conform their lives to the standards of a world under God's judgement. They scheme against anyone who confesses that Jesus alone is the final arbiter of good and evil, truth and falsehood. Distortion of the truth, based on corrupt evidence, is exactly what a follower of Jesus would expect to experience. People who belong to the old world are inclined not to tolerate those, living among them, who are seeking to practise Jesus' standards of truth, goodness and unconditional love.

The rest of Jesus' teaching in the Sermon covers other elements of a Jesus-centred lifestyle. It is introduced by the claim that in the midst of a crumbling world, disciples will, in the nature of the case, act like salt that keeps food from decomposing and like lights that show a way out of encircling gloom. The teaching comes with a warning, alluded to in different instances throughout the Sermon:

> "Unless your righteousness exceeds that of the scribes and the Pharisees, you will never enter the kingdom of heaven."[220]

The standard of behaviour is nothing less than perfection. Perfection is spelt out in a number of different aspects of everyday living: reconciliation;

---

[220] Matthew 5:20.

sexual desire; marriage fidelity; faithfulness to one's word; retaliation; generosity; one's attitude to one's adversaries; giving to the needy; prayer; ambition; anxiety about the future; hypocrisy; equality of treatment among all people; fulfilling God's will.

In the story at the end of the teaching, Jesus pictures two builders: the first was a wise person who built his house upon a solid, immovable foundation (rock); the second was foolish, for he built his house upon shifting ground (sand). When severe rain storms and high winds (hurricanes/typhoons?) struck, the latter's footing was unable to support the structure. The two house-builders illustrate the bearing of those "who hear these words of mine" and acts on them, or the one who hears them, but "does not act on them."[221] The first group may be travelling on a hard road, but it leads to life; the other group has chosen an easy road, but it leads to destruction.[222] They are distinguished by the outcome of their lives, whether they produce good, nourishing fruit or rotten, unhealthy fruit.[223]

What comes out from a person defiles

Two other pieces of teaching exemplify the distinction that Jesus draws between those dedicated to following him and experiencing the joys of the new world and those who choose to follow their own desires and feel the burden of their follies. On one occasion, a group of Pharisees and scribes engaged in a dispute with Jesus about the failure of his disciples to observe the same traditional practices of those who interpreted the law inflexibly.[224] The particular issue between them was centred on observing the Jewish rituals of cleanliness before eating.

Jesus responded to the guardians of the traditions by pointing to the difference between the intention of God's law as written and the massive

---

[221] Matthew 7:24-27.
[222] Matthew 7: 13-14.
[223] Matthew 7:15-20.
[224] Mark 7:1-23.

accumulation of regulations, not found in the Scriptures. These latter were added apparently to safeguard the correct fulfilment of the original laws. Jesus gave one illustration, to show how the tradition actually negated one of the Ten Commandments, in this case to "honour your father and your mother". He ruthlessly exposed their hypocrisy in "making void the word of God through your tradition."[225]

He then went on to draw a distinction between the outward ritual of cleansing before eating and the true location of what profanes and corrupts human existence:

> "Nothing outside a man can make him 'unclean' by going into him. Rather, it is what comes out... that make him 'unclean'... Nothing that enters a man from the outside can make him 'unclean'. For it doesn't go into his heart but into his stomach, and then out of his body. For from within come evil thoughts".[226]

Jesus finishes his dispute with the Pharisees and the Scribes by listing what might be called a sample selection of evil thoughts that lead remorselessly to corrupt desires and actions:

> "Sexual immorality, theft, murder, adultery, greed, malice, deceit, lewdness, envy, slander, pride, folly".[227]

The implication of his teaching is simple: attempts to avoid what are conventionally considered impure objects from the external world are insignificant in comparison with the need to be rid of the evil imaginations that contaminate the human psyche from within. Only the one true God, through Jesus, is able to cleanse us from the inside out.

---

[225] Mark 7:13.
[226] Mark 7:18 (NIV)
[227] Mark 7:21-23 (NIV)

What will it profit to gain the whole world and forfeit one's life?

The second piece of teaching comes a little later in Jesus ministry. It follows consistently from the argument about cleansing, but also takes it to a further dimension of reality:

> "What will it profit them (those who wish to preserve their lives from making a choice for Jesus and God's new order) to gain the whole world and forfeit their life"?[228]

There is an echo in these words of Satan's temptation of Jesus:

> "All these (the kingdoms of the world and their splendour) I will give you, if you will fall down and worship me".[229]

The temptation to go after the alluring spectacles of the world (i.e. the materialistic project of accumulating goods and experiences) is Satan's bargain.[230] Tzvetan Todorov, a humanist philosopher, suggests the possibility that secularism could be viewed as one of the greatest contributions to evil, echoing the view that the origin of evil is to be found in the misuse of freedom. Humans, he says, may have unwittingly accepted a kind of devil's pact, in which Satan offers them unlimited free-will, meaning the power to choose exactly how they wish to live. However, Satan hides the cost of total autonomy, that it will destroy all relationships:

> "If you want to keep your liberty...you will have to pay a triple price, first by separating yourself from God, then from your neighbour and finally from yourself."

---

[228] Mark 8:36.
[229] Matthew 4:9
[230] A contract offered by the devil to exchange one's soul for the transitory pleasures of this world has been observed since the 16th century in literature, drama, art, opera, symphonic and other types of music, following a legend about a certain Dr. Johann Faust (1480-1540). It is often referred to as 'the Faustian pact'.

"No more God – you will be a 'materialist'. No more neighbour...you will be an 'individualist'...(No more self)...you will be an alienated, inauthentic being."[231]

Eventually humans, having once unwittingly accepted the devils' bargain, accumulate for themselves an enormous debt, which they spend the rest of their life trying to pay back. This debt, Todorov suggests, signifies the moral, spiritual and psychological burdens which are now destroying Western civilisation and which secular humanism cannot lift.

Jesus puts a stark choice before the whole of humanity:

> "Those who want to save their life will lose it, and those who lose their life for my sake, and for the sake of the gospel, will save it".[232]

In other words, the choice is between the old world and its deceptive attractions and the new world, where true human freedom is found only in submission to Jesus. He alone can save us from ourselves.

"The seed that dies"

The apostle John, in his record of Jesus' life and ministry, reports a saying that echoes the one in Mark's Gospel that we have just surveyed:

> "Unless a grain of wheat falls into the earth and dies, it remains just a single grain; but if it dies, it bears much fruit. Those who love their life lose it, and those who hate their life in this world will keep it for eternal life. Whoever serves me must follow me... Whoever serves me, the Father will

---

[231] The Imperfect Garden: The Legacy of Humanism (Princeton, NJ: Princeton University Press, 2002), 2-4.
[232] Mark 8:35.

honour."[233]

The metaphor, taken from common agricultural and horticultural practice, is related to how a person views their existence in relation to Jesus the bringer of God's new order. The choice that is offered to every human being is absolute: either they wish to cling on to the imagined freedom they will enjoy by being in control of their own destiny ("loving their life", just as they wish to organise it), or they will exchange this illusory freedom for the real freedom that Jesus alone offers.

"The truth will make you free"

In Jesus teaching, according to John's account, freedom is directly and intimately related to "knowing the truth." In fact, Jesus reverses the order of the relationship between the two that this world believes to be correct. This world imagines that the gaining of truth requires first and foremost the freedom to follow any paths of enquiry and experimentation, wherever they may lead. Freedom, on this account, means deliverance from the imposition of any belief or behaviour that we have not seen fit to choose for ourselves.

Jesus, on the other hand, asserts that we have first to discover the truth, by listening to his explanation of how it is achieved, and then we will be truly free:

> "If you continue in my word, you are truly my disciples; and you will know the truth, and the truth will make you free...So, if the Son makes you free, you will be free indeed...I declare what I have seen in the Father's presence...If I tell the truth, why do you not believe me. Whoever is from God hears the words of God."[234]

In other words, if we wish to know the truth and follow the truth and thus

---

[233] John 12:23-26.
[234] John 8:31-32, 36, 38, 46-47.

be free from the illusion that we are born into the world free to discover the truth by our own powers of reflection, we must take Jesus at his word. To listen to the teaching of Jesus and take it on board is the beginning of true wisdom.

"For this reason I was born"

We return to the dialogue between Jesus and Pilate, this time considering a different aspect of what is involved. The message about the relationship between freedom and truth is hammered home in the exchange of words between them.[235] The outcome of the discussion is demonstrated clearly in the actions that followed.

The dialogue[236] begins with a controversial question that Pilate put to Jesus, as he sat on his seat of judgement:

> "Are you the King of the Jews?"

Jesus first reply was to ascertain whether the question was sincere, i.e. whether Pilate really wanted to know for himself personally what was Jesus status, or whether the question was posed as a result of the belief of those who brought him to Pilate, that Jesus was making a false claim about himself. So, he replied with his own question:

> "Do you ask this on your own, or did others tell you about me?"

Jesus second reply would have sounded to Pilate quite enigmatic:

---

[235] This passage has already been explored in relation to the nature of the kingdom of God. It also provides a telling reflection on what is truth in the context of political power.
[236] John 18:33-38.

> "My kingdom is not from this world...My kingdom is not from here."

Pilate assumed that, because he had used the phrase "my kingdom," he must be claiming to be a king of some sort:

> "Pilate asked him, 'So you are a king'?"

(Unfortunately, as we do not know how Pilate inflected his voice, we cannot know whether this was a genuine question or actually a cynical statement; either would have been possible in terms of the dialogue).

Jesus final response to this discussion implies that it was a statement, whether contemptuous or not:

> "You say that I am a king."

However, he immediately changes the drift of the dialogue. He moves to the crux of the controversy. It is about power as understood by both the Jewish leaders and the Roman Empire; who knows the nature of what is true?

> "For this I was born, and for this I came into the world, to testify to the truth. Everyone who belongs to the truth listens to my voice."

Pilate finishes the exchange of words with a question that one must suppose he did not feel able to answer:

> "What is truth?"

Now many commentators on this passage remark that Jesus did not reply to the question. The story moves quickly on to Pilate's attempt to release Jesus from custody by asking the crowd gathered in the forecourt of his residence whether they would wish him to fulfil the custom of discharging a prisoner at the time of the Jewish Passover. However, as a matter of fact, Jesus had already answered Pilate's question, although not in the governor's presence. Before his arrest, in his final prayer to his heavenly Father on behalf of his disciples, he affirmed that,

> "I have given them your word and the world has hated them because they do not belong to the world, just I do not belong to the world. I am not asking you to take them out of the world, but I ask you to protect them from the evil one...*Sanctify them in the truth; your word is truth.*"[237]

Now following on the dialogue between Pilate and Jesus we can ask, which of the two was truly free: Pilate, who did not know the meaning of truth, or Jesus who did know? The old world would probably answer, why Pilate, of course. He claimed, in a further interrogation of Jesus, that he had the power to release him and the power to sentence him to death. The authority to exercise his power, delegated by the Senate in Rome, showed that he was free to decide the outcome of the trial. Meanwhile, Jesus had no power over the judicial process, so presumably he was not free. The world's answer, however, would be entirely mistaken. Jesus was the really free person, for he had already chosen freely to allow himself to be put to death in order to atone for the sins of the whole world (including those of Pilate):

> "For this reason the Father loves me, because I lay down my life in order to take it up again. No one takes it from me, but I lay it down of my own accord. I have power to lay it down and I have power to take it up again. I have received this command from my Father."[238]

Pilate eventually is relieved of his mandate and dies ignominiously in Rome. Jesus also dies, wholly innocent of all the charges laid against him, but on

---

[237] John 17:14-17 (emphasis added).
[238] John 10:17-18 (emphasis added).

the third day after his death, he appears alive again and continues for forty days to teach the disciples. He then leaves this life to be with his Father, and will one day return to this world as its judge. The one who knew the truth was also the one who was truly free.

Contrast with the old order[239]

Throughout the story of Jesus, as recorded by John, there is a running commentary by both Jesus and his adversaries about the reality of the old order, summed up in the expression, "this world."

A literal sense

As elsewhere in the Scriptures of both Testaments, the world refers to the whole inhabited planet: "the true light...was coming into the world (*kosmos*)...he was in the world..."[240] It is also used of the human world, the world of social interaction: "as you have sent me into the world, so I have sent them into the world"[241] ...; "that the world may know that you have sent me"[242] ; "he is the atoning sacrifice for our sins, and not for ours only but also for the sins of the whole world"[243] .

Occasionally, John also uses the word earth (*gē*) as a synonym: "I glorified you on earth..."[244] ; "when I am lifted up from the earth..."[245] However, the occurrence of 'the world' in this general sense is limited. The vast majority

---

[239] This section will comprise a summary of how the world is portrayed in the writings of the Apostle John. It will follow a previous study in my book, The Church and the World: Understanding the Meaning of Mission (Milton Keynes, UK: Paternoster Press, 2014), 22-29. This formed part of a longer study on 'The Biblical View of the Cosmos,' 3-29.
[240] John 1:9, 10
[241] John 17:18
[242] John 17:23
[243] 1 John 2:2
[244] John 17:4
[245] John 12:32

of instances of its use in John's writings is of a different order.

A metaphorical sense

When John refers to the world, almost universally he is depicting humanity in its opposition to the plans and purposes of God. It is a sphere of unbelief. It is a worldly system opposed to God.

The world opposes God and resists the redeeming work of God's Son. It not only does not believe in him, but actually hates him:

> "The world...hates me because I testify against it that its works are evil";[246]

> "If the world hates you, be aware that it hated me before it hated you."[247]

The human world, in its resistance to the Father and hostility to the Son is actually ruled by the ruler of this *kosmos*:

> "Now the ruler of this world will be driven out;"[248] "the ruler of this world has been condemned;"[249] "we know...that the whole world is under the power of the evil one."[250]

In the Prologue to the Gospel[251], there is a dramatic shift of emphasis between two parts of verse 10. In the beginning of all things, there was God and there was the Word. They belonged inseparably together. All matter throughout the universe owes its existence exclusively to the initiative and

---
[246] John 7:7
[247] John 15:8
[248] John 12:31
[249] John 16:11
[250] 1 John 5:19
[251] John 1:1-18

creative power of God through his Word. There is no other pre-existent being. He brought life into existence through his own life-giving power, and this life was the one and only means of interpreting the significance of the created order.[252]

A prophetic word was made available through "a man sent from God, whose name was John."[253] The lesser word testified to the greater Word that this was indeed "the true light, which enlightens everyone (and he) was coming into the world."[254] In other words his nature, identity and mission was in the process of being revealed.

Nevertheless, even though he was the life and light of all people, "the world did not know him."[255]. Even more surprising, he was born as one of the people that God had chosen in a special way to represent him to the nations, and yet this people ('his own') did not accept him.[256] In this respect, they behaved no differently from the non-Jewish world. His coming into the world, then, set up a new kind of division: not based on any ethnic or cultural distinctions, but on reception or rejection of Jesus.[257] This contrast remains constant throughout the Johannine writings.

The world in defiance of God and the ones he has sent

The world is a dark place, alienated from God, in bondage to sin. It is blind[258] and unregenerate,[259] a world that resists God's life-giving purposes. This is because it has accepted another ruler to whom it gives allegiance. Its peace, then, is contrary to the peace or wholeness that God provides. It is a travesty of God's shalom:

---

[252] John 1:5
[253] John 1:5
[254] John 1:9
[255] John 1:10
[256] John 1:11
[257] John 1:11-13
[258] John 9:39-42
[259] John 3:3,5

"My peace I give to you. I do not give to you as the world gives."[260]

Here there may be an implied criticism of the *pax romana*, seen as an unjust imperial order:

"The world, then, comprises the hierarchical, unjust society that the ruling authorities have established for their own benefit and defend with violence (John 18:36)".[261]

In John's first letter, there are twenty two references to the world; all but three of them are negative:

"Do not love the world...The love of the Father is not in those who love the world; for all that is in the world — the desire of the flesh, the desire of the eyes, the pride in riches — comes not from the Father but from the world. And the world and its desires are passing away..."[262]

Here there is a clear reference to a sphere of activity that absorbs the energies, motivates the activities and controls the desires of human life in ways which are inimical to the wholesome and worthy purposes of God. The world's problems stem from the fact that those who belong to it do not know God.[263] This world has to be conquered or overcome; otherwise it will draw the children of God away from God's life-enhancing gifts. The instrument with which the world may be rendered ineffective is faith in the reality of Jesus, the Son of God, sent to be the Saviour of the world and to destroy the works of the devil.[264]

---

[260] John 14:27
[261] Warren Carter, John: Storyteller, Interpreter, Evangelist (Peabody: Hendrickson Publishers, 2006), p. 91.
[262] 1 John 2:15-17
[263] 1 John 3:1
[264] I John 5:4-5; 4:14; 3.8

So, the world is a place where God, present in human affairs, is engaged in a contest with spiritual powers that enslave human beings:

> "You are from your father the devil, and you choose to do your father's desires. He was a murderer from the beginning and does not stand in the truth, because there is no truth in him. When he lies, he speaks according to his own nature, for he is a liar and the father of lies."[265]

In this passage John refers to two families: the family of God, through faithful Abraham, and the family of the devil. They are divided from one another on the basis of whether they accept that Jesus is from God, and his words are true, or do not:

> "Whoever is from God hears the words of God. The reason that you do not hear them is that you are not from God."[266]

So, the world is divided between those born of the Word and Spirit of God and those born of the devil.[267] There is a clear demonology throughout the New Testament. It is explicit in John's writings.

When faced with the truth of Jesus Christ, the world as it were 'turns a blind eye'; it cannot see what is in front of it. The tragedy is that it believes that it understands well what is true and false, what is good and bad. Yet the world is blind, precisely because it claims to be able to see and yet fails to recognise God's Messiah in its midst.[268] As long as the world holds to its own version of reality, it is in control. Sadly, however, it completely misses the true nature of things. Only by submitting to the truth transmitted from the Father through the Son, who is 'Lord and Teacher,' will its eyes be open

---

[265] John 8:44-45
[266] John 8:47
[267] 1 John 4;4-6
[268] John 9:39-41

again. This is the world for which Jesus does not pray,[269] and to which he cannot reveal himself, because of its resistance to him and his Spirit.[270]

It is not surprising that, as the world hates the Son, so it also will hate those whom the Son sends in his name.[271] The world's antagonism is grounded in the disciples' non-alliance with the world. This is exacerbated by the fact that Jesus chooses them "out of the world." Since the world persecuted Jesus, it will also persecute his followers.[272]

The world as the object of God's love

In spite of the world's opposition to God's good purposes for its life and well-being, his constant, gratuitous love for what he has created has found a way of offering it a new beginning. In the most often quoted verse of the Gospel, the meaning and extent of this love is spelt out: God sends his Son into the world to offer to all humanity eternal life rather than death.[273] He takes the initiative to save it from its self-inflicted destruction and to transform it.[274] Jesus is the agent of this salvation, who has laid down his life, in order to take away the world's sin.[275] He is the bread and water of life who alone can quench the hunger and thirst of those dissatisfied with mere religious observance.[276]

So, God has done all that could possibly be expected, and all that is necessary, to rescue the world from its blindness and its inability to save itself. Although the world deserves judgement, for it has refused to listen to the truth and see the signs of God's active involvement in the world, Jesus

---

[269] John 17:9
[270] John 1:5-8; 8:23; 17:16
[271] John 15:18; 17:14; 1 John 3:13
[272] John 15:20
[273] John 3:16
[274] John 3:17
[275] John 4:42; 1 John 4:14, John 10:17-18; 1 John 3:16; John 1:29
[276] John 6.35, 7.37-38; 4: 23-24, 39-42

Christ has not come to condemn the world.[277] His purpose has been to give the world every opportunity to believe and be saved.

However, the world is faced with a choice between life and death. If they choose to turn their back on God's offer of life,[278] they condemn themselves. This is the way that God's judgement works on a world that continues to go its own way:

"And this is the judgement, that the light has come into the world, and people loved darkness rather than light because their deeds were evil. For all who do evil hate the light and do not come to the light, so that their deeds may not be exposed."[279]

The self-inflicted judgement is that the world remains in its sin, ignorant of the transforming new life that it could enjoy. Although it believes itself to be free, and not subservient to anyone,[280] it remains a slave to sin and in the grip of lies that it is destined to believe:

"The tragedy of so many in John's day (and in ours) is that they have been so wise in their own estimation that they have rejected the ways of God and have set up their own way as the way to life. Jesus pointed out that some of his hearers did not really "seek the glory that is from the only God" (5:44); they did not "have the love of God in themselves" (5:42).'[281]

The nature of Jesus' kingship

The Jewish leaders faced a serious quandary when confronted with the

---

[277] John 3:17
[278] John 6:66-67
[279] John 3:19-20
[280] John 8:33
[281] Leon Morris, Jesus is the Christ: Studies in the Theology of John (Grand Rapids: Eerdmans, 1989), p. 128.

challenge Jesus posed to their authority, and with the political sensitivity they required, in order to comply with the demands of the occupying power. They reckoned that if they did not intervene very soon, everyone would believe in him.[282] They were faced with an enormous dilemma: how to do away with a person who posed a threat to their rule, and yet had committed no crime worthy of the death-penalty.[283] The answer had to be the trumped-up charge of presenting a danger to the Roman forces of occupation.[284] In any case, they needed the sanction of the Roman procurator, in order to have Jesus put to death.[285]

The so-called trial before Pontius Pilate[286] (in reality a dialogue between Pilate and Jesus, interspersed with the clamour of the Jerusalem leaders and the 'rent-a-mob' they had assembled for the purpose of calling for his crucifixion) proved to be a remarkable piece of drama. Pilate began proceedings by asking whether Jesus claimed to be the king of the Jews. Presumably this title was used by the Sanhedrin to impress Pilate with the reality that Jesus was a dangerous, subversive liability. In point of fact, their real grievance was that Jesus claimed to be the Son of God, thereby committing blasphemy and deserving to die. Now, the title Son of God might also have been interpreted as a threat to Roman hegemony, seeing that the Emperor was regarded as *divi filius* (son of the divine). Either way, whether king of the Jews or Son of God, they hoped to portray Jesus as an unacceptable risk to the authority of Rome.

There are two kinds of logic at work, which illustrate the gulf that exists between the two worlds: the logic of Barabbas, the Jewish leaders and the Roman Empire that violence is a legitimate means of advancing one's cause in the world, and the logic of Jesus that human-devised violence is inimical to God's sovereign presence in the world. In the former case, the ends are calculated to justify whatever means are considered appropriate. In the latter case, the means are in total harmony with the ends. When comparing both

---

[282] John 11:47-48
[283] John 8:46
[284] John 11:48
[285] John 18:31
[286] John 18:33-19:16

the ends and means they are found to diverge radically from one another. In other words, the conflict between his peaceable kingdom and the aggressive kingdoms of this world is not carried out on the world's terms. Jesus followers cannot establish his kingdom by intimidation or compulsion of any kind. Their weapon is to bear witness to the truth. Jesus in his person and in his witness is the truth.[287]

Nowhere in John's Gospel does Jesus deny being a king; only that, given the misconceptions surrounding the notion,[288] he is very careful to distance himself from the normal understanding. His kingdom is not established by any worldly power, but by the power of God. The authority and power of Caesar and his representatives are derivative, limited to the earthly sphere and intended to be used in the service of truth and justice. Even then, they are accountable to God:

> "You would have no power over me unless it had been given you from above."[289]

It appears, therefore, that the contrast between the two kingdoms is intended as a critique of the way in which the profane kingdom operates. The teaching of Jesus, as recorded in John's Gospel, is absolutely explicit that two opposing worlds operate within the reality of just one existence on this planet. The two worlds function according to conflicting principles. A new order is breaking into the old. However, the old still retains a residual power, which it disseminates in order to try to eliminate the new. The task, however, is ultimately doomed to failure, for it belongs to the past, not to the future.[290]

---

[287] John 14:6; 8:31-32
[288] John 6:15
[289] John 19:11; Romans 13: 1-7; 1 Peter 2:13-14; Titus 3:1.
[290] In the final section of the book's last chapter, I dwell on the church's mission calling with respect to the transient world. In the light of Jesus' consistent pronouncement of judgement on the modus vivendi of this world, it would be easy to conclude that Jesus' disciples ought then to withdraw from contact with and involvement in this world's affairs. This, however, would be a wrong deduction, taking into account the whole sweep of the apostolic teaching; see, as one example, Paul's statement in 2 Corinthians 10:5.

CHAPTER 8
The Contours of the New World

"The grace of God has appeared, bringing salvation to all, training us to renounce impiety and worldly passions, and in the present age to live lives that are self-controlled, upright and godly...Jesus Christ...gave himself for us that he might redeem us from all iniquity and purify for himself a people of his own who are zealous for good deeds".[291]

"To set the mind on the flesh is death, but to set the mind on the Spirit is life and peace...Those who are in the flesh cannot please God".[292]

The new community grows and expands

Building on the promises contained in the Old Testament, reinterpreted by Jesus in terms of his own calling and ministry, a new community bearing unconditional allegiance to his own self-designation as "Teacher and Lord,"[293] begins to arise within the old community of Israel. This is exactly as Jesus had planned. Immediately prior to his death and resurrection, his teaching became increasingly directed to the future, when he would no longer be with his disciples in a limited, physical form:

"Little children, I am with you only a little longer...Where I am going you cannot come".[294]

---

[291] Titus 2:11, 14.
[292] Romans 8:6, 8.
[293] John 13: 13.
[294] John 13:33.

"Now I am no longer in the world, but they are in the world, and I am coming to you".[295]

Jesus promises his followers another presence to be with them, that of God's Spirit, the Spirit of truth:

"When the Advocate (*Parakletos*) comes, whom I will send to you from the Father, the Spirit of truth...he will testify on my behalf".[296]

"When the Spirit of truth comes, he will guide you into all truth, for he will not speak on his own, but will speak whatever he hears...".[297]

Jesus, after he was raised from the dead, sent his disciples out on a universal mission "to make disciples of all nations, baptising them in the name of the Father and the Son and the Holy Spirit, and teaching them to obey everything that I have commanded you".[298] Such a mandate implies the formation of a multi-ethnic and multi-cultural community, beyond the confines of the geographically-located nation of Israel or of Jewish groups scattered around the Mediterranean basin. And so the new community was born, to incorporate new Jesus-centred converts into its midst and to continue to teach them whatever the Spirit of truth was revealing.

The ordering of the new community

After a period of time had passed, some of the leaders of this new community began to set down in writing how its members should order their lives, individually and as a fellowship. There is much material found in the letters they wrote to churches located in Asia Minor, Greece and Rome.

---

[295] John 17:11.
[296] John 15:26.
[297] John 16:13.
[298] Matthew 28:19-20.

The most comprehensive teaching was given by Saul of Tarsus (the apostle Paul) to the Christian believers in Rome. He begins by what might be described as an orderly exposition of the good news (the gospel) of and about Jesus Christ, the Son of God.[299] It represents, he says,

> "The power of God for salvation to everyone who has faith, to the Jew first and also to the Greek. For in it the righteousness of God is revealed through faith for faith".[300]

First, however, he contrasts this message of God's righteousness to the ungodliness and wickedness of those who belong to the old order.[301] The latter are characterised by their suppression of the truth about the reality of God and the world. In addition, Paul identifies some of the practical consequences of their false belief. The origin of their fundamental inclination to believe what is not true lies, firstly, in their wrong moral choices.

These erroneous choices are due to their rejection of the wise and good Creator who put in place the workings of his creation:

> "Though they knew God, they did not honour him as God".

So,

> "They became futile in their thinking and their senseless minds were darkened. Claiming to be wise, they became fools".

The outcome was that

> "God gave them up in the lusts of their hearts to impurity, to

---

[299] Romans 1:9
[300] Romans 1:16-17.
[301] All the following quotes are taken from the passage, Romans 1:18-32.

the degrading of their bodies among themselves...to degrading passions...to a debased mind and to things that should not be done".

In this passage, Paul is relating, from a Jewish-Christian perspective, the underlying philosophy of the old order and the destructive consequences of its folly. All that he says, from this point onwards, is grounded on this interpretation of the way the old world functions. It can be summarised in the one word '*exchange*', repeated three times:

"They exchanged the glory of the immortal God for images..."

"They exchanged the truth about God for a lie";

"Their women exchanged natural intercourse for unnatural, and in the same way also the men".

In a sense, the wrong moral choices and the destructive consequences that inevitably flow from them are a wake-up call to humanity to turn from the futility of creating a world built ultimately on a fundamental lie. They are called to turn to the truth about a real world in which humans can find again their authentic humanity, created in God's image. The fundamental problem is that people have "not seen fit to acknowledge God".

Breaking free from the old world

Paul's letter to the Christians in Rome is rich in its presentation of many different motifs. It is not possible in the space of one chapter to attempt to do justice to all of them. From the perspective of the main thesis of this whole study, he follows his summary of the disarray which characterises the present world with the ways by which God has provided a 'departure gate' to escape from its false certainties and destructive habits, and to enter into the new world.

The first pathway to a new life is signalled by the symbols of death and resurrection. Through trusting personally in the one sacrifice offered by Jesus that atoned for the sins of the whole world people are counted as righteous in the sight of God.[302] What follows is that we are reconciled to God, our alienation is overcome and we enter a new dimension of life. Paul uses the image of baptism to convey the meaning of what has taken place:

> "We have been buried with (Christ) by baptism into death, so that, just as Christ was raised from the dead by the glory of the Father, so we too might walk in newness of life".[303]

Baptism is an act of initiation into this new life. It is highly symbolic in the way that it was carried out in the apostolic and post-apostolic periods. Usually it happened by total immersion, in which the new believer was submerged in water (often running water to symbolise the carrying away of sin) and then brought out of the water, whilst the words of administration, "I baptise you in the name of Jesus", or "in the name of the Father, Son and Holy Spirit", were pronounced over the candidate. It was also customary to remove one's everyday clothes and put on a special robe.

In this rite we can see the three-fold transference from the old world to the new by death (entering the water), burial (going under the water) and resurrection (emerging from the water). The removal of the impediments of the old way of life is signified by the change of clothes. Possibly, if the baptism happened in a river, the transference from one world to another is indicated by entering the water from one bank and leaving it by the other. This imagery is further reflected in Paul's letter to the believers in Colossae:

> "You who were estranged and hostile in mind, doing evil deeds, he has now reconciled in the body of (Christ's) flesh through death".[304]

---

[302] Romans 3:21-31.
[303] Romans 6:4.
[304] Colossians 1:21-22.

"In (Christ) you also were circumcised...When you were *buried* with him in baptism, you were also *raised* with him through faith in the power of God, who raised him from the dead".[305]

"If you have been *raised* with Christ, seek the things that are above... Set your minds on things that are above, not on things that are on earth. For you have *died*, and your life is hidden with Christ in God".[306]

The symbolism of the change of garments, seems to be implied in the following injunction:

"Put to death, therefore, whatever in you is earthly... Seeing that you have *stripped off the old self...Clothe yourselves* with compassion, kindness, humility, meekness and patience... Above all, *clothe yourselves* with love".[307]

The second pathway to a new life is the gift of God's Spirit for those united with Christ in his death and resurrection. This new presence of the Spirit is also related intimately to the transition from one world to the other:

"Through Christ Jesus the law of the Spirit of life set me free from the law of sin and death... (We) do not live according to the sinful nature but according to the Spirit. Those who live according to the sinful nature have their minds set on what that nature desires, but those who live in accordance with the Spirit have their minds set on what the Spirit desires...The mind controlled by the Spirit is life and peace; the sinful mind is hostile to God...If you live according to the sinful nature, you will die; but if by the Spirit you put to death the misdeeds of the body you will live."[308]

---

[305] Colossians 2:11-12. The italicised words are intended to emphasise the images of death (by crucifixion) and resurrection and the new set of clothes of entering the new world.
[306] Colossians 3:1-2.
[307] Colossians 3:5, 12, 14. (emphasis added)
[308] Romans 8:2, 4-7, 13 (NIV).

The language Paul uses here coincides with that he has already used in speaking of baptism as dying and rising with Christ. The new life is life in the Spirit, which empowers believers to rid themselves of the desires, prompted by the unreconstructed, sinful nature still enmeshed in the thought processes of the old world, that used to dominate their minds and emotions.

In his letter to the churches of Galatia, Paul spells out in detail the complete contrast between the two worlds: one controlled by "the law of sin and death" and the other by "the law of the Spirit of life." In a nutshell, in passing from one world to the other we come alive:

> "Live by the Spirit...and do not gratify the desires of the flesh (sinful nature)...*Those who belong to Christ Jesus have crucified the flesh (sinful nature) with its passions and desires.* If we live by the Spirit, let us also be guided by the Spirit."[309]

Paul gives a list of examples of the desires of the flesh. He then contrasts these with a further list of the fruit of the Spirit.[310] The reality that distinguishes the two arises from the origin of each. In the first case, it is fallen human nature that stimulates an appetite for passionate yearnings that can only be satisfied by thoughts and deeds which further destroy our humanity. In the second case, it is the work of God's Spirit that, through a new birth, produces those virtues that correspond to the kind of humans God intends us to be.

Between two worlds

Believers in Jesus are united to him, who has given his life to set them on a

---

[309] Galatians 5:16, 18, 24-25; emphasis added.
[310] Galatians 5: 19-23.

new path, and his Spirit to enable them to keep to that way of living. At the same time, they continue, whilst living on this earth, to be in daily contact with the old way of life with its myriad temptations and pressures to stray from the new commitments they have entered into. It is not surprising, therefore, that the apostolic letters to the young Christian communities remind them to guard against the kind of world that they have undertaken to leave. They are strongly urged not to be drawn back into the kind of life that once dominated their thinking and actions.

Paul, in his letter to "the saints who are (in Ephesus[311])", reminds the believers in Jesus of the destructive powers that once held sway over their lives:

> "You were dead through the trespasses and sins in which you once lived, following the course of this world, following the...spirit that is now at work among those who are disobedient. All of us once lived among them...following the desires of flesh and senses". [312]

> "You must no longer live as the Gentiles live, in the futility of their minds. They are darkened in their understanding, alienated from the life of God because of their ignorance and hardness of heart. They have...abandoned themselves to licentiousness, greedy to practise every kind of impurity".[313]

Towards the end of his letter to the church in Rome, having written at length about the transformations that Jesus has brought, once for all, through his sacrificial offering, Paul goes on to exhort the believers to maintain their new life through their living sacrifice presented to God:

> "Present your bodies as a living sacrifice, holy and acceptable to God, which is your spiritual worship. Do not be conformed

---

[311] The most reliable manuscripts omit "in Ephesus".
[312] Ephesians 2:1-3.
[313] Ephesians 4:17-19.

to the (pattern of this) world, but be transformed by the renewing of your minds, so that you may discern what is the will of God – what is good and acceptable and perfect."[314]

"The pattern of this world" is in stark contrast to God's kingdom of righteousness and justice. Paul spells out some of the elements of this divergence in two passages that warn of the appalling consequence for those who are still sucked into this world's system of belief and behaviour:

> "The wicked will not inherit the kingdom of God. Do not be deceived: neither the sexually immoral nor idolaters nor adulterers nor male prostitutes nor homosexual offenders nor thieves nor the greedy nor drunkards nor slanderers nor swindlers will *inherit the kingdom of God*. And that is what some of you were."[315]

> "Among you there must not even be a hint of sexual immorality, or of any kind of impurity, or of greed, because these are improper for God's holy people...For of this you can be sure: no immoral, impure or greedy person – such a person is an idolater – has any *inheritance in the kingdom of Christ and of God*."[316]

> "Now the works of the flesh are obvious...I am warning you, as I warned you before: those who do such things will not *inherit the kingdom of God*".[317]

In each case, the list is extensive in its depiction of the offences that exclude people from the blessings of participating in God's new world. In each case, sexual immorality of every category heads the list, perhaps because of its power to distort the experience of pleasure and the damaging consequences that it inflicts on others. However, the injustices that are caused by people's

---

[314] Romans 12:1-2.
[315] 1 Corinthians 6:9-11 (NIV) (emphasis added).
[316] Ephesians 5:3-5 (NIV) (emphasis added).
[317] Galatians 5:19, 21 (emphasis added).

unbridled lust for financial gain is also made central to the ill-effects of a corrupt life. It is called idolatry, which in Biblical language is the fount of all evil-doing. Idolatry means false worship, i.e. orienting one's life upon deceit and fraud. It fails miserably to deliver the hoped for abundance of life.

Another symbol that is used frequently for the old world in the pages of the apostolic letters is that of darkness; naturally its antithesis is light:

> "For once you were darkness, but now in the Lord you are light – for the fruit of the light is found in all that is good and right and true...Take no part in the unfruitful works of darkness, but instead expose them. For it is shameful even to mention what such people do secretly; but everything exposed by the light becomes visible..."[318]

> "But you, beloved, are not in darkness...; you are all children of light and children of the day; we are not of the night or of darkness... Those who are drunk get drunk at night. But since we belong to the day, let us be sober."[319]

Darkness is a figure of speech that points to what is obscure, so cannot easily be discerned and identified. It is the absence of light; it hides the dishonest deeds which bring shame on the people who commit them.

A vision of the new world

So far I have explored something of what the early Christians depicted about the reality of the new world. They experienced it in stark contrast to the way the old world operates. The distinction between the two has to be highlighted, in order that the core essence and characteristics of both may be illuminated. However, shining a spotlight on the divergences and conflicts between the two does not do complete justice to what is expected of those who have passed from one to the other. The high moral standard

---

[318] Ephesians 5:8-9, 11-13.
[319] 1 Thessalonians 5:4-6. For other references to darkness and light, see, 2 Corinthians 6:14; Colossians 1:13-14; 1 Peter 2:9; 1 John 2:9.

specified for those who inherit God's new world, those he has reconciled to himself, surpasses the level of moral conduct hoped for within the old world.

The apostolic writers used the language of purity, holiness and sanctification to describe life in the new world:

> "Let us cleanse ourselves from every defilement of body and spirit, making holiness perfect in the fear of God".[320]

> "It is God's will that you should be sanctified...For God did not call us to be impure, but to live a holy life".[321]

> "Make every effort to live in peace with all...and to be holy, without holiness no-one will see the Lord".[322]

> "As he who called you is holy, be holy yourselves in all your conduct; for it is written, 'You shall be holy, for I am holy'".[323]

These injunctions all stem from the perfectly pure nature of God:

> "God is light and in him there is no darkness at all".

So, it is incumbent on all who wish to have fellowship with God that "they walk in the light".[324]

Now, this calling to absolute moral purity does not consist predominantly in the negative commitment to abstain from all that corrupts, disfigures and dehumanises human beings and hinders them from being what God intended them to be. Rather, it speaks of a positive dedication to being models of God's character:

---

[320] 2 Corinthians 7:1.
[321] 1 Thessalonians 4:3, 7 (NIV).
[322] Hebrews 12:14 (NIV)
[323] 1 Peter 1:15-16.
[324] 1 John 1:5, 7.

"As God's chosen ones, holy and beloved, clothe yourselves with compassion, kindness, humility, meekness and patience. Bear with one another and, if anyone has a complaint against another, forgive each other; just as the Lord has forgiven you, so you must also forgive".[325]

"The wisdom from above is first pure, then peaceable, gentle, willing to yield, full of mercy and good fruits, without a trace of partiality or hypocrisy...A harvest of righteousness is sown in peace for those who make peace".[326]

On two occasions in the letters, Jesus' teaching in the Sermon on the Mount is clearly echoed for the sake of believers who would not have either heard him in the flesh or have had a record of what he taught. Paul, writing to Christians in Rome, fills out in some detail what is "the good, acceptable and perfect will of God":

"Love one another with mutual affection; outdo one another in showing honour...contribute to the needs of the saints; extend hospitality to strangers...Bless those who persecute you; bless and do not curse them... Live in harmony with one another; do not be haughty, but associate with the lowly...Do not repay anyone evil for evil. If it is possible, so far as it depends on you, live peaceably with all. Beloved never avenge yourselves...If your enemies are hungry, feed them; if they are thirsty, give them something to drink...Overcome evil with good".[327]

Peter, writing to scattered Christian communities in Asia Minor, exhorts them to

"Have unity of spirit, love for one another, a tender heart and a humble mind. Do not repay evil for evil or abuse for abuse; but, on the contrary, repay with a blessing."[328]

---

[325] Colossians 3:12-13.
[326] James 3:17-18.
[327] Romans 12:10, 13, 14, 16-21.
[328] 1 Peter 3:8-11.

In both cases, the Christians were undergoing persecution, sometimes of a very degrading kind. The way they are to react is to manifest an extremely high pattern of goodwill and generosity towards those who despise, detest and abuse them.

Finally, the way of conforming to the reality of the new world is in keeping with what will occur one day, when the old world will be abolished and the new will be fully accomplished. God's action in the future, from a present-day perspective, will be explored in the next chapter.

CHAPTER 9
A New Heaven and a New Earth: the Home of Righteousness

"These words are trustworthy and true, for the Lord, the God of the spirits of the prophets, has sent his angel to show his servants what must soon take place"[329].

A comprehensive vision of the future

The present interaction between two worlds, inspired and propelled by substantially different core beliefs, will one day come to its conclusion. The old world will be abolished and the new will be inaugurated finally and completely. Until that time, the way of living out the presence of the new world is in accordance with what will be manifest at that time. So, for now, we wait in expectation of a glorious future:

> "In accordance with his promise, we wait for new heavens and a new earth, where righteousness is at home. Therefore, beloved, while you are waiting for these things, strive to be found by him at peace, without spot or blemish...Since you are forewarned, beware that you are not carried away with the error of the lawless and lose your own stability. But grow in the grace and knowledge of our Lord and Saviour Jesus Christ".[330]

---

[329] Revelation 22:6.
[330] 2 Peter 3:13-14, 17-18.

"Then I saw a new heaven and a new earth; for the first heaven and first earth had passed away, and the sea was no more. And I saw the holy city, the new Jerusalem, coming down out of heaven from God, prepared as a bride adorned for her husband. See the home of God is among mortals. He will dwell with them...He will wipe away every tear from their eyes. Death will be no more; mourning and crying and pain will be no more for the first things have passed away. And the one who was seated on the throne said, I am making all things new".[331]

The climax and transformation of God's present creation will mark the final separation of the two worlds. One will pass over into a new creation; the other will fall apart:

"The heavens will be dissolved, and the elements will melt with fire".[332]

The whole of human history is destined for a final cataclysmic event. Given the restricted knowledge of the workings of the universe and the way planet earth functions, first century populations would not have been able to give a detailed account of how all present reality will eventually be wound up. Even today, after the accumulated knowledge provided by scientific research is accessible, looking to the future is often a matter of speculation; how the complexities of natural processes will eventually pan out is not a matter of assured scientific demonstration.[333]

There may be a number of conjectures, but because we are talking about a reality which does not yet exist, attempts to extrapolate from the present to the future are only hypotheses. A large part of the problem is that so many

---

[331] Revelation 21: 1-5.
[332] 2 Peter 3:12.
[333] This fact is demonstrated in a recent book, that examines something of the psychology of anxiety in the face of possible conjectures on end times ('doomsday'); see, Mark O'Connell, Notes from an Apocalypse: A Personal Journey to the End of the World and Back (London: Granta, 2020).

possible events of the future can be imagined, but not predicted: for example, a pandemic much more deadly than COVID-19; the release of mega-destructive nuclear weapons; the collapse of nature due to environmental catastrophes; a collision between the earth and a gigantic meteor. Whatever may be the force(s) that bring to a final end the lived experience of human beings in this world, Christians are content to believe, on the authority of God's word and limited, existing scientific knowledge able to calculate the future, it will cease to exist. Only those who are confident that God's revealed word is true, know that a new material reality will take its place.

This vision of what is destined to transpire at the culmination of the present universe is unique to the Jewish and Christian faiths. It is first predicted in two passage of the Hebrew Scriptures (the Old Testament), towards the end of the prophecy of Isaiah:

> "I am about to create new heavens and a new earth, the former things shall not be remembered, or come to mind".[334]

> "As the new heavens and the new earth which I will make shall remain before me, says the Lord, so shall your descendants and your name remain".[335]

Contrary to much speculation within the Christian church down the ages, life after death will incorporate a real physical existence. The idea of the immortality of the 'soul' detached from the body, under the influence of an ancient Greek world view, is incompatible with the Biblical view of the integrated self (body, mind, psyche, spirit). The reality of human life is constituted by the whole person; it cannot be reduced to just one aspect of human experience on earth. Given the implications of the Christian affirmation that Jesus Christ was raised from the dead, not as a ghost, but as a fully transformed individual. Being human incorporates every aspect of

---

[334] Isaiah 65:17.
[335] Isaiah 66:22.

existence (physical, mental, emotional, and spiritual), on both sides of the grave:

> "The body is not an appendage to an eternal soul: a human being does not have, but is his or her body. Body and soul are two ways of referring to the essential person, one referring to the physical dimension, and the other to the intellectual, relational, personal dimension. Paul rejects the idea of existing as a disembodied spirit: *his clear expectation is the resurrection of the body and the life to come as a whole human being in the new creation*".[336]

> "The Hebrew scripture's word nephesh "basically means breath," and the term is often used to designate "a living being;" the word, along with the New Testament equivalent, psyche, can mean "life", and even "person" or "self." The term is broader in biblical usage than is commonly supposed, and it can be taken to stand for the unity of personality, since Hebraic thought conceives of the human being as a unity, rather than as a duality of body and soul".[337]

If the Judaeo-Christian view of the indivisible wholeness of the human being is true, and that life continues to exist beyond death, then it follows that this future life must possess a material existence. A person, beyond the end of this present existence, cannot simply continue to live on as a free-floating immaterial spirit. As would be expected, the Christian Scriptures can only refer to this fresh, restored reality by using pictures taken from present experience.

---

[336] T. A. Noble, 'Anthropology' in Martin Davie (et al.), New Dictionary of Theology: Historical and Systematic (London: Inter-Varsity Press, 2016/2), 40; emphasis added.
[337] Robert McAfee Brown, 'Soul/Body' in Donald W. Musser and Joseph L. Price (eds.), A New Handbook of Christian Theology (Cambridge: The Lutterworth Press, 1992), 456-457. The key text comes in the second account of creation: "then the Lord God formed man from the dust of the ground, and breathed into his nostrils the breath of life; and the man became a living being" (Genesis 2:7).

Three images of resurrection

In two of his letters, both to the church in Corinth, Paul uses images that convey something of how the transformation takes place. Firstly, in speaking about the resurrection of the dead, he uses the analogy of a seed that, when planted in good earth, ceases to exist exactly as it used to be. He is speaking about the kind of body that will exist after our present bodies die and disappear:

> "With what kind of body do they come? ... What you sow does not come to life unless it dies...You do not sow the body that is to be, but a bare seed...God gives it a body as he has chosen".[338]

He then goes on to say that there are different kinds of flesh (in the resurrection),

> "One flesh for human beings, another for animals, another for birds and another for fish".[339]

This pronouncement seems to suggest that in the new world beyond death human beings will not be alone, but will be accompanied by familiar living creatures.

Paul concludes his discourse on the resurrection with further declarations of what will be:

> "What is sown is perishable, what is raised is imperishable. It is sown in dishonour it is raised in glory. It is sown in weakness, it is raised in power. It is sown a physical body, it is raised a spiritual body... What I am saying...is this: flesh and blood cannot inherit the kingdom of God, nor does the perishable

---

[338] 1 Corinthians 15:35-38.
[339] 1 Corinthians 15:39.

inherit the imperishable...We will all be changed...at the last trumpet...The dead will be raised imperishable, and we will be changed".[340]

Secondly and thirdly, Paul uses the images of a dwelling and clothing. He begins by reminding the Christians that "though our outer nature is wasting away," i.e. that as humans grow older so our physical bodies deteriorate, until eventually they can no longer support our present existence. Nevertheless, "our inner nature is being renewed day by day." At present we only experience what can be seen. All that we have lived through, however, is only temporary. What is prepared for us, which cannot yet be seen, is eternal.[341]

Paul, then, elaborates a bit more on how the change takes place, moving from the temporary to the eternal:

"If the earthly tent we live in is destroyed, we have a building from God, a house not made with hands, eternal in the heavens. For in this tent we groan, longing to be clothed with our heavenly dwelling...(so) when we have taken it off we will not be found naked. For while we are still in this tent, we groan under our burden, because we wish not to be unclothed but to be further clothed, so that what is mortal may be swallowed up by life".[342]

These images are close to the reality that will one day transpire, when those who die in the Lord, will experience a new life within a different dimension of existence: mortality/immortality; momentary/permanent; temporary/eternal. It is not surprising, therefore, that he concludes his discussion with the confident assertion that

"We would rather be away from the body and at home with

---

[340] 1 Corinthians 15:42-44, 50-52.
[341] 2 Corinthians 4:16-18
[342] 2Corinthians 5:1-4.

the Lord".[343]

Pictures of the new world

The end of John's vision, given to him on the island of Patmos (off the coast of modern Turkey) and written down in the Book of Revelation, gives insight into the kind of physical circumstances that will accompany this new life in the Lord. John sets down the images he received of the events that will happen at the end of present time, in order to encourage groups of Christians of his time, who were experiencing severe persecution, to persevere in the faith. The Book is addressed initially to seven churches on the mainland of Asia Minor.[344]

Interpreting the symbolic language

There is no doubt that Revelation is one of the most difficult books of the whole Bible to comprehend in a way that does justice to its meaning. It is full of sweeping pictures of God's judgements that will come upon both the earth and the heavens. They will set right the devastating consequences of the present world's corrupt authorities, whose unscrupulous governance, under the influence of extra-terrestrial evil powers, has oppressed the hapless subjects of their domains.

The book is full of symbols, designed to explain in pictorial form, the meaning of the message that John was transmitting to the seven churches, and beyond them to the Christian community at large. A major part of the problem for us of interpreting correctly the symbolic language in which much of the book is cast is that we do not have the benefit of having lived in the first century A.D. G. B. Caird, in his commentary on Revelation,[345] puts the matter this way:

> "The great advantage that the Christians of Asia had over us was that John was their personal friend. He might write things

---

[343] 2 Corinthians 5:8.
[344] Revelation 1:4.
[345] The Revelation of St John the Divine (London: A and C Black, 1966), 7.

that were strange to them, but they must have had a pretty shrewd idea how his mind worked".

Nevertheless,

"If they wanted to ask questions about the nature of John's experience, the structure of his book, or the meaning of his warning message, they had to look for their answers exactly where we must look, in the book itself".

After all, John was exiled on an island off the mainland. We may speculatively presume that he would not have been allowed to receive special guests, who could have questioned him on the various meanings of his message.

For the purposes of this study of two worlds, we do not need to follow the many varied ways in which the whole book of Revelation has been understood. Our concern is to refer to the imagery that is depicted in the last two chapters of John's vision that was communicated to him by the Spirit of Jesus. We do not have to suppose that John intended to cast what he saw as an enigma that could only be unlocked by a sophisticated code, available exclusively to an elite in the churches. As Caird remarks,

"John was not compiling a week-end problem book. Whatever else he may have intended, he cannot have set out to mystify".[346]

The book was intended for the whole church, for ordinary believers, who were challenged to open their ears and "listen to what the Spirit is saying to the churches." So, when looking at the final scene depicted in the last two chapters, we will take as a guiding principal of interpretation the literal meaning of much of what is said. The principle works, unless there are good reasons for accepting that the language should be understood in

---

[346] The Revelation of St John the Divine, 3.

figurative terms. In the latter case, it is clear that, for example, to speak of Jesus as the Lamb or his bride as the new Jerusalem, or to accept the measurements of the city as fact, are assumed to be figures of speech.

With this in mind, let us see what may legitimately be gleaned about the nature of the new heaven and the new earth. The two chapters, that bring to a climax the whole range of prophecies contained in, "the revelation of Jesus Christ, which God gave him to show his servants what must soon take place,"[347] are full of imagery. They have stretched the imagination of all subsequent readers, including, one supposes, the original recipients.

Such a task is not straightforward. There are many allusions throughout the chapters to other parts of the Scriptures. The author was well-versed in the writings of the Old Testament. He sees the references as representations from the past which can guide the present Christian communities to understand the realities "of what is, and what is to take place after this".[348] At the same time, the visions are infused with the Jesus-centred fulfilment of all God's plans and promises. John, who wrote what he saw, "testified to the word of God and to the testimony of Jesus Christ". [349] He signs off the whole prophecy with two direct references to Jesus:

> "The one who testifies to these things says, 'Surely I am coming soon'. Amen. Come, Lord Jesus"!

> "The grace of the Lord Jesus be with all the saints. Amen".[350]

The final instalment of God's creative action

The final episode in the extended drama of God's judgement on a thoroughly recalcitrant earth, concluding with the fall and destruction of

---
[347] Revelation 1:1.
[348] Revelation 1:19.
[349] Revelation 1:2.
[350] Revelation 22: 20-21.

Babylon (alias Rome),[351] is the announcement of a new heaven and a new earth. A new city, Jerusalem, representing the dwelling and immediate presence of God with his redeemed peoples, is set out in terms of great magnificence. Two events are recorded simultaneously. Firstly, his people will experience the proximity of God right in their midst, without any sense of shame or guilt. They will be free from all the suffering caused by the old world's campaigns of victimisation. They are the ones who have remained faithful in their allegiance to Jesus, despite what the enemies of God can throw at them. The pain of living concurrently in two different worlds is now over, for ever:

> "Death will be no more; mourning and crying and pain will be no more, for the first things have passed away".[352]

This new reality is an absolute certainty, for "these words are trustworthy and true".[353]

The second event is the marriage feast of the Lamb (Jesus). The lamb's bride is referred to as the "holy city Jerusalem." This is an image that is impossible for humans to visualise, for a city is not a proper object for a marriage. It has to be interpreted as "the great multitude that no one can count, from every nation, from all tribes and peoples and languages," which was seen earlier "standing before the throne and before the Lamb".[354] In other words, the church of Jesus Christ.[355]

Three times it is revealed that a certain class of people will be excluded from the holy presence of God in the holy city. They are characterised as people who have chosen to live by the beliefs and standards of the old world:

> "As for the cowardly, the faithless, the polluted, the murderers,

---

[351] Revelation 19:1-20:3.
[352] Revelation 21:4.
[353] Revelation 21:5.
[354] Revelation 7:9.
[355] See, Ephesians 5:25-32.

the fornicators, the sorcerers, the idolaters and all liars, their place will be in the lake that burns with fire and sulphur, which is the second death".[356]

"Nothing unclean will enter it (the city), nor anyone who practises abomination or falsehood".[357]

"Outside are the dogs and sorcerers and fornicators and murderers and idolaters, and everyone who loves and practises falsehood".[358]

The first of the passages lists some of the key examples of behaviour that is condemned by the standards of God's holiness: the "faithless" are those who refused to believe the truth; the "polluted" are those who corrupt themselves and/or violate others; the "fornicators" refers to those who are sexually immoral in any form; the "sorcerers" are those who practice any of the black arts; the "idolaters" allude to those who worship anything belonging to the material world.

The second passage is slightly more general, in denouncing a collection of practices under the headings of uncleanness (impurity), abomination (disgrace) and falsehood (deceit). All three passages refer to the energising power of dishonesty and deception. The liar is the person who knowingly and willingly falsifies the truth, i.e. anyone who turns what is real into something made-up and non-existent.

These three verses which accompany a vision of what is true, pure and wholesome, simply state the common practice of those caught up in the fantasies of the old world, self-generated by fictional pretences and concoctions. How often does one meet in this life people of complete integrity, whose unfailing sincerity and honesty is beyond all doubt? The probable answer is, very rarely. They would be people who never dissimulate

---

[356] Revelation 21:8.
[357] Revelation 21:27.
[358] Revelation 22:15.

in reflecting upon their own self-image, pretending to be what they know they are not. They would have renounced the temptation to distort or conceal something about themselves which they do not wish others to know.

Dishonesty and deception take many forms. Commonly, it may appear in the shape of character-assassination, when one person or, in the case of racist or sexist comments, a group of people are judged on the basis of a false type-cast estimation of their personality, background, or assumed racial or gender profile. Another example of insincerity is the temptation to exaggerate, when people are inclined habitually to condemn others with remarks like, "you/he/she always behaves in a certain way or is known for a particular disposition or tendency". One may well ask, "On what grounds are such negative judgements made? What concrete and verifiable evidence is adduced to accuse others of what may, at the least, be the result of pure prejudice or distortion"?

When the new world is fully realised, all dishonesty and deception will be removed. Everything will be clear, open and beyond all possibility of disagreement. All our hidden thoughts, motives, desires, plans and calculations will be revealed. We will see ourselves finally as we really are. No justifications, evasions or pretences will be accepted. At the day of judgement each one will be reviewed according to what is written in their particular 'book of life'.[359]

There is, however, another 'book of life', it is called the 'Lamb's book of life'.[360] All those whose names are written in this book will be welcomed into the new Jerusalem and will enjoy all the blessings of the new heaven and the new earth. Whose names will be found in this book? There are a number of hints throughout the prophecy about those whose names will be written down.

---

[359] Revelation 3:5; 20:12, 15.
[360] Revelation 21:27.

A Tale of Two Worlds

If we begin with the first mention of the 'book of life',[361] it refers to all those whose "who have not soiled their clothes", but have received the white robes of purity, because they have conquered.

Since the Conquerors are later said to "have washed their robes and made them white in the life-blood of the Lamb",[362] we may conclude that the stain is anything which qualifies or dilutes the church's faith in the saving grace of God. The book of life is the register of the citizens of the heavenly city. If the people are citizens of the heavenly, it is not because they have earned their place, but because Christ has loved them and "freed them from their sins by his own blood".[363] "Before all human faith or striving there lies the divine choice and divine initiative...A man cannot earn the right to have his name on the citizen roll, but he can forfeit it".[364]

One may assume that the act of conquering – mentioned in the case of each of the seven churches to which John writes in chapters 2 and 3 – means that those whom Jesus "has made to be a kingdom, priests serving God and Father",[365] have resisted all the various temptations and pressures to turn back from their first commitment to God's new order through Jesus. And so, those who maintain their robes cleansed from all stains and keep faith with God's word, despite all that the kingdom of Satan can throw against them,[366] will share in the bounties of the holy city. They will be those who do right and remain holy,[367] because they have been made righteous and holy by the blood of the Lamb.

Thus, in these ways, the story of the two worlds comes to an end. There will be an eternal separation. Only one city will remain:

---

[361] Revelation 3:5.
[362] Revelation 7:14.
[363] Revelation 1:5.
[364] Revelation 3:5. The quote is from The Revelation of St John, 48 and 49.
[365] Revelation 1:6.
[366] Revelation 22:14, 9, 18-19.
[367] Revelation 22: 11.

"Anyone whose name was not found in the book of life was thrown into the lake of fire".[368]

"John has allowed for the possibility that...human disobedience may in the end prove impregnable to the assaults of love. For such people the presence of God could be nothing but a horror from which they, like the earth they made their home, must flee, leaving not a trace behind".[369]

The lake of fire is also called the "second death." It must refer to a permanent exclusion from the eternal life that God promises to all who turn to Him in repentance and believe that, through the sacrifice of Jesus, the only Son of God, their life of blindness to His nature and mission is overcome.[370] Death is not just an event, but a state of being. Paul speaks of it as the act of "setting the mind on the flesh". It is being "hostile to God; not submitting to God's law". Those who are living in this state "cannot please God".[371]

In other words, the second death is reserved for all who have in this present existence adhered to a godless way of life encouraged and promoted as normal in the old world. That is the place where they profess to feel most comfortable. They would feel totally out of place in the new world, whose reality they have rejected. The pain of the second death is that what they have lost is irretrievable. Their constant and unchanging choice of hostility towards God is perpetuated after the first death. God's judgement is to confirm them in their choice of conducting their lives separated from God's offer of eternal life through faith in Jesus.[372]

---

[368] Revelation 20:15.
[369] The Revelation of St John, 260.
[370] John 3:16-21.
[371] Romans 8:6-7; see also, 1 John 3:14.
[372] Romans 1:24, 26, 28.

PART III

WHERE WILL IT ALL END?

CHAPTER 10
News Items and Observations

"The central doctrine of transgenderism is the belief that human will determines reality, as we create ourselves...These mystical doctrines of transgender ideology exemplify modern self-worship...Self-creation is not freedom, for it only changes our master. Since we are not gods, our efforts to create ourselves are hindered by the natural laws of our existence...Self-worship does not overcome the given nature of our embodied human existence"[373]

Introduction

The first two parts of the book have offered a framework of information and argument that sets the scene for the conclusions to be drawn in the final part. The main purpose of the whole study is to respond, from a Christian perspective, to the way in which the Christian faith is currently being treated in the Western world. Profound social changes in the last sixty years have wrenched Western nations from their Christian moorings.[374] To use a seafaring metaphor, much of Western culture seems to be caught up in the following situation:

---

[373] Nathaniel Blake, 'U.K. Court Decision Affirms Transgenderism is a Religion of Complete Self-Worship', The Federalist, 9 October, 2019.
[374] I explore, in some depth, the reasons why this happened and the tragic and destructive consequences that it has produced for contemporary societies that have embraced a post-Christian narrative; see, The Future of Reason, chapter 1: 'An Enigma and an Idea'.

'If recent history can be likened to a sea voyage, post-modernity represents mutiny – the determination to wrest the steering mechanism from the self-appointed ('enlightened') owners of the ship. Once having 'deconstructed' the (authority) of the captain and won over the crew, the mutineers go on a pleasure trip which may take them anywhere or nowhere – there is no map, no compass and the natural fixed-points of sun, stars, wind and currents are unreliable. No matter! The idea of destination, or of home-coming is an absurd illusion. Like the porpoises and whales (probably more intelligent than humans) the boat's passengers can give themselves up to endless play. When the engine runs out of fuel, we can sink the ship and take to the life-boats. Each group of passengers can then decide for itself which destination it wishes to take, none are right and none are wrong.'[375]

I have set the debate within the context of two conflicting 'worlds'. The first is the actual world represented by a struggle between ideas and practices launched by the Enlightenment and modernity and countered by a 'deconstructionist' agenda - the latter being identified with post-modernity. The second is the existence of another world, already present, which represents the future of what will be according to God's promises. This world is outlined in the New Testament section of the Bible.

The first world is guided by an amorphous secular humanism (modern and post-modern), which comprehensively rejects the claim that the Christian faith uncovers truth in all its manifestations. The second world refers to the Christian account and interpretation of the whole of reality, first set out in the core teachings of Jesus and his first disciples. The two sets of belief may coincide at certain points. This is due to two concrete factors. Firstly, human beings have to come to terms with the world as it has been created. Science, which bases its undertaking on the existence of constant natural laws that reflect the way it has been designed, to a certain extent helps them to do

---

[375] The Future of Reason, 21.

that. Secondly, humans still have to live, up to a point, by a vision of human life inspired by Christian belief.[376] The notion of human rights, for example, is a powerful illustration of this outworking. Nevertheless, as the present climate of increased hostility to all things Christian demonstrates, the tension between the two worlds is becoming ever more evident in political life, laws and their interpretation, social attitudes, life-styles and ethical decision-making.

Rather than simply making assertions about the present state of the world, exemplified generally in Western moral belief and behaviour, more credence to the whole argument is achieved by giving concrete examples of two main themes used as illustrations of how the old world is now living out its destiny. Grounds given for abortion and beliefs about sexuality, increasingly at odds with what Christian faith considers to be true and wholesome about human nature, are the two themes.

Other instances of current destructive practices could be cited that would serve the same purpose of portraying the widening gulf between what the Western world tolerates, or even promotes, and a Christian perspective on what is good and right. One could mention, for example, 'recreational' drug-taking, gambling, the arms-trade, the destruction of animal habitats, indifference to the plight of homeless people, the exploitation and trafficking of vulnerable women and children, the oppression of minority groups by totalitarian regimes, and so on. Abortion and sexuality have been

---

[376] Tom Holland, in his book, Dominion: The Making of the Western Mind, gives numerous examples from the history of the Western world, up to the present time, of the transforming influence of the Christian faith on the customs, traditions, ethical values and intellectual life of Western society. He contrasts this with the Greco-Roman world into which the Christian faith was born. In summary (from the Front-piece), the book "demonstrates just how novel and uncanny Christian teachings were when they first appeared in the world; and why the West, and all that today it takes for granted, is similarly strange in consequence. Even the increasing numbers in the West who have now abandoned the faith of their forebears and dismiss all religion as pointless superstition remain recognisably its heirs. Christianity's enduring impact is not confined to churches. It can be seen everywhere in the West: in science, in secularism, in gay rights, even in atheism. It is – to coin a phrase- the greatest story ever told".

chosen because they touch the very inner being of human identity in a way that no other issue matches. For this reason they are probably the most controversial matters facing humanity as a whole. To tackle them, therefore, identifies the nature and extent of the rift between the two worlds, the primary focus of this study.

The news items and observations selected are intended to reflect the reality of what is happening in real life. They are taken from various news outlets, representing different political, ethical and ideological perspectives that have happened or are continuing to happen. They have been culled from about 100 different sources. They illustrate well the polemical nature of the subject-matter of this book.

Abortion

In 2007, Amnesty International, long a most venerable voice for human rights, announced that it would promote abortion rights. Human Rights Watch and other organizations have also taken up the cause, as have many Western governments. The right to life, though, is the most basic of natural human rights. It takes precedence over self-determination. That pre-born children are persons is disputed but not disputable. Science textbooks attest that the embryo, once formed, is a unified distinct being that has begun to develop on its own impetus. In a recent article in The Atlantic,[377] Emma Green describes abortion rights activists as being "on high alert for what they describe as efforts to 'humanize fetuses,' revealing that abortion rights rely on a denial of the humanity of the pre-born person. However, this humanity is acknowledged in human rights' declarations. The United Nations Declaration on the Rights of the Child (1959), for example, holds that every child 'needs special safeguards and care, including legal

---

[377] Emma Green, 'When your Pregnancy is Political,' The Atlantic, 7 July 2019.

protection, *before* as well as after birth."[378]

"What follows is staggering. According to reliable figures,[379] abortion takes the lives of twelve million people every year - at least 12 times that of the Rwandan genocide. Since abortion was first legalized by the Soviet Union in 1920, it has taken the lives of over a billion persons. Abortion even dwarfs 'democide' – a term coined...to define the murder of people by governments like those of Hitler, Stalin and Mao – which took two hundred and sixty two million lives in the twentieth century...The paradox of abortion is that the largest human rights violation in the world is supported by the very community whose mission is to secure human rights".[380]

"Nearly a quarter of babies are aborted in England and Wales...new statistics reveal. Excluding still births and miscarriages, 23.8 per cent of pregnancies were cut short by abortions in 2018. While there were 657,076 live births, 205,000 unborn babies were killed...The number has risen dramatically since the 1967 Abortion Act came into force. In 1969, the first full year for which data was available, 6.4 per cent of pregnancies ended in abortion. This represents a 270 per cent increase over the last 50 years".[381]

"In many Asian cultures, sons are strongly valued to carry on the family name, inherit property, or to provide parents with care and financial support in sickness and old age. Daughters on the other hand, are often seen as a burden, due to the practice of dowry...and due to the traditional custom that daughters leave their birth parents behind after marriage to go on to live with and care for their husband's parents.

---

[378] This particular phrase (emphasis added) recognises that the child exists before as well as after birth. It was included in the Preamble to The Convention on the Rights of the Child, published in November 1989; see, https://www.humanium.org/en/convention/text/. There is more evidence given in Appendix A on what International Protocols stipulate and imply with regard to safeguarding the inherent dignity of the pre-born child.
[379] See, Thomas W. Jacobson and William Robert Johnston (eds.), Abortion: Worldwide Report (West Chester, Ohio: Global Life Campaign, 2018). During the COVID-19 pandemic, abortion was the leading cause of human deaths, far outweighing those caused by the virus.
[380] Daniel Philpott, Public Discourse, 10 July 2019.
[381] The Christian Institute, 14 August 2019.

Since the introduction of ultrasound technology...has made it easy and affordable for parents to know the sex of their child prior to birth, millions of girls have gone 'missing' due to the practice of sex-selective abortion. In India alone...approximately 15.8 million girls have been eliminated.[382] Nearly 550,000 girls go 'missing' at birth every year".[383]

"Members of the media were mostly interested in my finding that 96% of the 5,777 biologists who responded to me affirmed the view that a human life begins at fertilization. It was the reporting of the view – that human zygotes, embryos and fetuses are biological humans – that created such a strong backlash. It was not unexpected, as the finding provides fodder for conservative opponents of Roe v. Wade, the 1973 case in which the US Supreme Court had suggested there was no consensus on 'the difficult question of when life begins' and that 'the judiciary, at this point in the development of man's knowledge, (was) not in a position to speculate as to the answer.'"[384]"The Department of Health and Human services (HHS) again issued guidance...(that) clarifies that all the infants at the point of birth are legal persons...This protection has been part of existing law for decades yet has been either ignored or not enforced, allowing children born after abortion to be set aside to die from neglect, or actually killed".[385]

"Survivors like Melissa Ohden in Kansas City...know how critical these medical procedures are. At Melissa's seventh month of gestation, her mother elected to have an abortion. Miraculously, Melissa survived. She was delivered alive, set aside, and ignored. But this was not the end of her story. Melissa is with us today because a few nurses did just what we all would hope – they saw a vulnerable life and intervened to save her".[386]

---

[382] Sex Selective Abortion in India (Front Royal, VA: Population Research Institute, 2019).
[383] Jonathan Abbamonte, 'Ending daughter elimination in the developing world, Washington Examiner, 11 July 2019.
[384] Steve Jacobs, 'I Asked Thousands of Biologists When Life Begins. The Answer Wasn't Popular', Quillette, October 16, 2019.
[385] Susan Berry, 'HHS Agency Requires Abortion Survivors to be Treated, Breitbart, 15 July 2019.
[386] Russell D. Moore, 'A Law to Protect Abortion Survivors Shouldn't be Necessary, but it is', National Review, 14 February, 2020.

"A late-term abortionist is offering women an opportunity to hold their babies 'after delivery' or take a picture home as a 'remembrance' after ending their unborn child's life...: 'Once the process of healing has begun, you may want to consider a token of the precious time with you and your baby after delivery. Several post-abortion services (are) available:...holding your baby...; photographs...; funeral arrangements referral;...spiritual and ceremonial accommodations; remembrance certificate...Choosing...funeral arrangements would be a significant acknowledgement of the humanity of an aborted child'".[387]

"As hospital systems, clinics, and communities prepare to meet anticipated increases in demand for the care of people with COVID-19, strategies to mitigate spread of the virus and to maximize health-care resources are evolving. Some health systems...are implementing plans to cancel elective and non-urgent procedures to expand hospitals' capacity to provide critical care.

While most abortion care is delivered in outpatient settings, in some cases care may be delivered in hospital-based settings or surgical facilities. To the extent that hospital systems or ambulatory surgical facilities are categorizing procedures that can be delayed during the COVID-19 pandemic, abortion should not be categorized as such a procedure. Abortion is an essential component of comprehensive health care. It is also a time-sensitive service for which a delay of several weeks, or in some cases days, may increase the risks or potentially make it completely inaccessible. The consequences of being unable to obtain an abortion profoundly impact a person's life, health,

---

[387] Doug Mainwaring, 'Late-term abortionist offers parents the chance to cuddle with their dead babies before disposal', LifeSite News, 29 August 2019.

and well-being"[388]

Sexual Orientation

"Twin and family studies have shown that same-sex sexual behavior is partly genetically influenced, but previous searches for specific genes involved have been underpowered. We performed a genome-wide association study (GWAS) on 477,522 individuals, revealing five loci significantly associated with same-sex sexual behavior. In aggregate, all tested genetic variants accounted for 8 to 25% of variation in same-sex sexual behavior, only partially overlapped between males and females, and do not allow meaningful prediction of an individual's sexual behavior. Comparing these GWAS results with those for the proportion of same-sex to total number of sexual partners among non-heterosexuals suggests that there is no single continuum from opposite-sex to same-sex sexual behavior. Overall, our findings provide insights into the genetics underlying same-sex sexual behavior and underscore the complexity of sexuality."[389]

"The...APA[390] clearly states in its 2014 handbook on sexuality that sexual feelings sometimes change. So why are these people robbing your children - adults are next - of their simple right to be who they truly are? And why is this research study important? The answer to both questions is that

---

[388] 'Joint Statement on Abortion Access During the COVID-19 Outbreak,'The American College of Obstetricians and Gynecologists and the American Board of Obstetrics & Gynecology, 18 March, 2020. It is worth commenting that the real intention of this statement is to use the COVID-19 crisis as a smokescreen to launch a much more radical abortion programme on to a public rightly pre-occupied with a virulent pandemic. Just as medical professionals are courageously risking their own lives to save the lives of others, the abortionists are keen to continue their promotion of death. The abortionist's response to the pandemic was to influence governments to allow home abortions, when assistance at a clinic for pre-medical counselling and examination would not be legally mandatory. The lobby is now engaged in persuading these governments to make the practice permanent, notwithstanding the increased physical and mental threats that this poses to the mothers.
[389] Andrea Ganna (et al.), 'Large-Scale GWAS reveals insights into the genetic architecture of same-sex behavior,' Science (Abstract), 30 August, 2019.
[390] American Psychological Association.

everyone has the right to be the person they believe themselves to be, and no one has the right to force their philosophy, political beliefs, or faith onto anyone else. This new study will make it a bit harder to force the gay agenda onto everyone in the world, and it will make it a bit harder for gay activists to demean and bully people with whom they do not agree.

Virulent bigotry is easy to see. A real bigot, whether intentional or not, will not allow any other view to be discussed on any issue unless the other person is vilified and demeaned, regardless of the evidence. A true discourse of opposite viewpoints will not be allowed...It is very hard to listen to other viewpoints when your identity is only and forever based on your own definition of identity. We feel threatened when our core beliefs are challenged, even when there is significant contrary evidence...

The activists who are subverting free speech experience major cognitive dissonance when seriously challenged with evidence on homosexual non-genetic causation. Who can blame them, since for decades they have been bullied and abused for their beliefs? ...

However, LGBT activists' philosophy and behavior take freedom too far when they displace their own rage for being bullied onto the lives of others who accept scientific and anecdotal evidence that homosexuality is not inborn and is not immutable. No one is saying one cannot be gay...But LGBT activists are attempting to force people into gay ideology who have unwanted same-sex attraction. Do these activists have the legal or moral right to impose their beliefs onto children, adolescents and adults?"[391]

"The goal of the LGBT movement for many years now here in America has been exactly the same (to smash completely hetero-normativity)[392]. People who thought gay marriage was the end goal didn't realize that redefining marriage so that it would no longer mean the union of a man and a woman was only the beginning. The program aims to remove any and all notions

---

[391] David Pickup, 'What? I thought I was born gay,' Mercatornet, 3 September, 2019.
[392] See, Helen Barnes, Video, located on youtubehttps://www.youtube.com/watch?v=1112bsF2xOvg.

that heterosexuality is the default position for nearly 97% of human beings. Radical takes on sex and gender identity are another tool in the toolbox to achieve this goal: if there are no men or women, no boys or girls, etc. but only people who "identify" one way or the other then there is no longer any way to "privilege" (in their way of thinking) the heterosexual binary".[393]

Sex-orientation therapy

"In light of the latest attack on sexual orientation change efforts (SOCE), namely, Amazon's banning of books on the subject, we do well to separate fact from fiction. Are these change efforts really so dangerous? Should they be banned and even criminalized? According to the critics, 'conversion therapy' is dangerous and harmful because it tries to change something that cannot be changed...

As expressed in California's SB 1172, which was signed into law in 2012, when SOCE was criminalized for minors, 'Sexual orientation change efforts pose critical health risks to lesbian, gay, and bisexual people, including confusion, depression, guilt, helplessness, hopelessness, shame, social withdrawal, suicidality, substance abuse, stress, disappointment, self-blame, decreased self-esteem and authenticity to others, increased self-hatred, hostility and blame toward parents, feelings of anger and betrayal, loss of friends and potential romantic partners, problems in sexual and emotional intimacy, sexual dysfunction, high-risk sexual behaviors, a feeling of being dehumanized and untrue to self, a loss of faith, and a sense of having wasted time and resources. This is documented by the American Psychological Association task force on Appropriate Therapeutic Responses to Sexual Orientation in its 2009 Report....' Is this true? Certainly not. According to Christopher Doyle, himself a former homosexual and today, a licensed therapist, 'Despite the claims of harm cited in SB 1172, the American Psychological Association task force did not actually provide

---

[393] Rod Dreher, 'Heteronormativity Smashers,' The American Conservative, October 19, 2019.

evidence to back up the 28 health risks listed above. In fact, none of these health risks have been documented in the scientific peer-reviewed literature outside of a few published and unpublished anecdotal reports from adults. But there is not one single outcome-based study in the scientific literature of minors undergoing SOCE therapy to back up these claims...'

A new study[394] is challenging the American Psychological Association's contention that therapies for unwanted same-sex attraction are harmful. It finds that sexual orientation change efforts (SOCE), often derisively called 'conversion therapy,' improves the mental health of participants. We should also remember that the very term 'conversion therapy,'...is derogatory more than descriptive. It was coined by critics to describe professional efforts to help people with unwanted same-sex attractions...

More importantly, professionals involved in SOCE engage in talk therapy, speaking with their clients and helping them get to the root of their inner-conflicts and struggles. What on earth is so bad about this? What is it so frightening about it? Why is it, then, that books promoting SOCE are singled out? Why is it that professional therapy that addresses LGBT concerns is being banned and criminalized? Even the idea that homosexuality is immutable, a sacred plank of gay activism, is being challenged on many new fronts. Yes, the data is out there, but LGBT activists and their allies want to suppress it. Let the truth be told...This was nothing less than gay activism at its totalitarian worst. There is nothing enlightened, inclusive, or tolerant about it. Let the truth be told."

After Amazon knuckled under pressure from LGBT activists to ban books offering help to those dealing with unwanted same-sex attraction, former gays launched a petition demanding the online retailer reverse its decision...Those who have left homosexuality and now live chaste single lives or who have gone on to marry and form a family with a member of the opposite sex see a different motive behind Amazon's action. It is an

---

[394] 'Effects of Therapy on Religious Men Who Have Unwanted Same-Sex Attraction,' Linacre Quarterly, 23 July, 2019

attempt to silence all the voices of those who have found new life and freedom not through "conversion therapy," but through conversion to Jesus Christ, a distinction that seems lost on LGBT activists.

We exist. Do not erase our community,' said Daren Mehl, founder of Voice of the Voiceless, an organization that seeks to defend the rights of former homosexuals and those with unwanted same-sex attraction, and which launched the petition...Desires change. Sexual orientation changes. It is not immutable. We are outraged that a smear campaign by one individual (who stated that he never read these books) could convince Amazon to censor all books, audio-books, and Kindle material related to our experiences and viewpoints. For every major issue there are two sides to each story. For one side to be bullied and censored on every platform is counter to the values we have long held in common with Amazon'."[395]

Transgenderism
Its origin

"I've been asked to get to the origins of this movement... There are three things that I think have been changing since the mid-20th century. The first is in medicine, the second is what I like to call an ontology of desire, and the third is what I and others call the politicization of everything.

Let's start with medicine. When sex-change surgeries became surgically possible in the post-war period, it was understood to be something of a euphemism. Of course, a person couldn't literally change from one sex to the other, it would be more accurate to call it genital surgery, but people were trying to be euphemistic. These procedures were highly controversial, in part because they weren't always that successful. Paul McHugh (was) the psychiatrist who had to put an end to the surgeries in the 1970s at Johns Hopkins University, which he described as "collaborating with madness"...

---

[395] Michael L. Brown, 'The Truth about so-called 'conversion-therapy,' LifeSiteNews, 9 July, 2019.

People who wanted to change their sex back then were called transsexuals...

In my friend Douglas Murray's new book, *The Madness of Crowds*, he explains that the struggle for defining things turned into this hardware versus software issue. So, inter-sex for instance, is very much a hardware issue. You can't exactly get concerned about somebody who has a hardware issue because that's not their fault. Of course, the reality with homosexuality is that it's most likely some kind of combination of the two...

This brings me to my second point, which was what I'm calling the ontology of desire. That's basically when in the 1990s, the definition of Trans began to change. Transsexualism, specifically as a sexual fetish, as autogynephilia, had been known as a perversion. This was politically incorrect, so they changed it to paraphilia, which (also) became politically incorrect and is now known as an identity. The broader term "gender dysphoria" (formerly gender identity disorder) is actually still listed in the Diagnostic Statistical Manual of Mental Disorders, so it's still a disorder in the DSM...

Transgenderism was widened, adopted, and celebrated in the academy, in large part thanks to people like Judith Butler, who thought that gender was a performance. This is where it gets really interesting in the contradictions. On the one hand, this is Murray's point, transgenderism is a hardware issue for Trans people, but for everyone else gender is a software issue. So, if you think about it, the only people who are born women are Trans women, which is rather an astonishing claim.

This is where the "boy's brain in a girl's body" stuff comes in, which turns out to be more of a metaphor. A more accurate metaphor might be that of a soul — a gendered soul, the fundamental essence of a person. It goes back a very long way to the Gnostic heresies in Ancient times. The idea is that matter is less important and that it's all about your spirit or your essence. The exploitation of language evolved so quickly that basically everybody calling a trans-woman "she" — initially that was meant to be a courtesy to accommodate people not to make somebody who has had a hard life have a harder life — is now meant to signal our absolute uncontested belief in their femaleness. However, (it doesn't imply they have really changed sex), because trans-women are men...

The third point is the massive cultural and political tidal wave...In the 1990s people might have been forgiven for thinking, "This will never catch on. This is so outrageous. This is absurd." They would obviously be right, but...the Internet and all these other things came into play. Society had just gotten used to defining whole sections of the population by their desires with regard to homosexuality, trying to correct genuine injustices that gay people faced... They over-corrected and they became obsessed with identity...We started to lose sight of all these different intricacies with regard to sexuality.

Then, Trans piggy-backed onto gay rights, which had piggy-backed onto civil rights. A whole system of buzzwords popped up, like "transphobia," "transmisogyny," and "conversion therapy," and all these buzz words made people think, 'Gosh I don't want to be on the wrong side of history'...The point about civil rights is very important...In America, rightly, people are very sensitive about civil rights and their embarrassing history in that area. They don't want to repeat that, and I think that's a good impulse and we should respect that impulse...

Which brings me onto the final point: What has any of this got to do with sexualizing children? I want to suggest two things. The first is that it's created a massive cultural blind spot. Psychologists have always understood transsexualism to relate, or potentially relate, to adult sexuality...It's been masked by an ideology, and because of the politics of it all, there's a great fear for many people. It's a legitimate fear because they might get fired, or worse, for signalling some terrible 'phobia'.

This becomes very obvious in the subject of drag. Drag, which means "dressed as girl," comes from the Elizabethan period when women were forbidden from performing publicly, so men assumed the role of women. For some drag queens — I have spoken to one, James Davis, whose stage name is Elaine Lancaster — it really is about performance...Although he was saying that for him it's about performance, he recognizes that when he's in bars and other public places, people come up to him at the end, and it's all about sex for them. As an adult, who knows that and understands that, he can deal with it,...but why would we put children in that situation? Why would we invite salacious interest in children by dressing them up in drag? We shouldn't do that, and I'm referring here to a whole new phenomenon called "drag kids."

The argument we're supposed to accept rather unthinkingly is that, "Oh you're just being bigoted, and you're just prejudiced, because this is about self-expression." And I'm thinking well no...The analogy I would invite you to think about here is to imagine a little girl in a bikini. She's 13 years old, in her parent's private pool. Is it a big problem that she's wearing a bikini? No, it's not a big problem. She's in her parents' private pool. But if the same girl, in the same bikini, still 13 years old, is walking down a catwalk in a room full of adults, would we all feel uncomfortable? Yes, we all would feel uncomfortable. It's a completely different thing, and it's the same when it comes to drag.

This is not hypothetical. I invite you to look up the case of Desmond is Amazing, who should really be called "Desmond needs saving", because this poor little boy is dressed up in drag, gyrating in gay clubs in Brooklyn, and few have said anything because to do so would be "homophobic." Well, no, sorry...It is not, and never should be, acceptable to sexualize children. Our friends at the Human Rights Campaign would prefer that none of us knew these intricacies, that people like me didn't exist to remind you of them, that people like James Davis (the drag queen) didn't exist...They would prefer that the only people who opposed the sexualization of children were like the horrible, frightening right-wing boogeyman, the Heritage Foundation. Everyone who's too scared to talk about this will just have to get over that because there's too much at stake...And to be honest, the worst thing they can do is say that you're the boogeyman, and you just say, 'Boo'".[396]

'There is only one gender...'

"For aeons, we believed human beings came in two sexes, with the occasional Hermes crossed with Aphrodite. Today, however, we have come to learn from some sociologists, philosophers, and psychologists, and even some medical associations and surgeons, that there is no such thing as sex or sex differences; there is only "gender," or what you think your sex is. All that once was sex has now melted into gender. A name (gender) referring to a belief has replaced the name (sex) and its biological referents.

For those who are old enough to think that "gender" applies only to nouns, think again. Among today's cognoscenti, gender is whatever you may think (imagine, feel, believe) you are. It's "how you identify" — even if your identity is not grounded in any objective measure. No longer, therefore, need sex determine one's identity on birth certificates, census forms, driver's licenses, etc. Instead, you're free to determine your identity independent of any attachment to a biological sex marker. Your "gender" is whatever you believe and say it is.

It's not being biologically a man or a woman that determines your gender; it's your sense of being one that counts. But how can we have a sense of being a man or woman without supposing there are things apart from our senses that we call a 'man' or a 'woman?' And what would this man or woman something be if not a human being with a sex-based genetic structure? So, while 'each person's internal and individual experience' may be of 'gender' — or their sense of being a woman or a man — they nevertheless suffer from a form of delusion today called 'gender dysphoria' if their gender identity is out of sync with their sex. Based on its definition of gender identity, what is being 'sensed' is one's 'internal and individual

---

[396] Madeleine Kearns, 'The Origins of the Transgender Movement', National Review, 14 October 2019.

experience of gender' — that is, just another sensation. Thus, the definition references nothing outside, or apart from, one's mind".[397]

The Meaning of Gender

"From the 14th century, gender has referred to the essence of what male and female are, issuing from the Proto-Indo-European root gen- or gene. It fundamentally references the creation, birth, and begetting of new human beings, as in, to generate or engender. This root is also interestingly associated with the Latin gonos, from which we get our English word gonad. Of course, these are the uniquely determinative, wholly binary parts of our anatomy that cannot do what they do without their cooperative union with the body of the other gender. Gender refers to that which is inherently heterosexual.

Thus, gender's grammatical root—gene/gen—is also associated with such words as genesis, generation (both in terms of being generated as well as the historical time-frame when one was generated) and yes, of course, genitals, those two unavoidably binary parts of the human anatomy that help our gonads and associated cooperative parts do what gonads do: generate. Finally, gender also derives from the Latin genus meaning race, kin, family, kind, order, and species, that generative line from which another comes and thus belongs to.

If anything is the furthest thing from being a mere social construct, gender is. So the words 'sex' and 'gender' are indeed two objective sides of the same coin. Anyone who says differently is just making stuff up. This is precisely what the gender theorists are doing. Next we must address gender theory's "creative" relationship with science.

It cannot be stated strongly enough. There is no, not one, not even a wisp

---

[397] Terry Heinrichs, 'Transgenderism: Thinking Makes it so? The American Spectator, 15 October 2019.

of a scientific discovery that requires we now understand sex and gender as two different things. It is based purely in ideology stemming from a wish for how these people think reality ought to be. It is 100 percent sophistry, 0 percent science.

Of course, the primary distinction between sex and gender in general use as well as academia has largely been linguistic, merely to make it clear when male and female are meant and not the act of coitus, i.e., 'Sex involves the two genders.' As such, the use of the word 'gender' has always been, until very recently, extremely rare."[398]

"Facts not ideology determine reality"

"The American College of Paediatricians urges healthcare professionals, educators and legislators to reject all policies that condition children to accept as normal a life of chemical and surgical impersonation of the opposite sex. Facts – not ideology – determine reality.

1. Human sexuality is an objective biological binary trait: "XY" and "XX" are genetic markers of male and female, respectively – not genetic markers of a disorder.

2. No one is born with a gender. Everyone is born with a biological sex. Gender (an awareness and sense of oneself as male or female) is a sociological and psychological concept; not an objective biological one.

3. A person's belief that he or she is something they are not is, at best, a sign of confused thinking. When an otherwise healthy biological boy believes he is a girl, or an otherwise healthy biological girl believes she is a boy, an objective psychological problem exists that lies in the mind not the body, and it should be treated as such.

---

[398] Glenn T. Stanton, 'Why Sex and Gender are not Two Different Things', The Federalist, 15 October, 2019.

4. Puberty is not a disease and puberty-blocking hormones can be dangerous. Reversible or not, puberty- blocking hormones induce a state of disease – the absence of puberty – and inhibit growth and fertility in a previously biologically healthy child.

5. According to the DSM-5, as many as 98% of gender confused boys and 88% of gender confused girls eventually accept their biological sex after naturally passing through puberty.

6. Pre-pubertal children diagnosed with gender dysphoria may be given puberty blockers as young as eleven, and will require cross-sex hormones in later adolescence to continue impersonating the opposite sex. These children will never be able to conceive any genetically related children even via artificial reproductive technology. In addition, cross-sex hormones (testosterone and oestrogen) are associated with dangerous health risks including but not limited to cardiac disease, high blood pressure, blood clots, stroke, diabetes, and cancer.

7. Rates of suicide are nearly twenty times greater among adults who use cross-sex hormones and undergo sex reassignment surgery, even in Sweden which is among the most LGBTQ – affirming countries. What compassionate and reasonable person would condemn young children to this fate?

8. Conditioning children into believing a lifetime of chemical and surgical impersonation of the opposite sex is normal and healthful is child abuse. Endorsing gender discordance as normal via public education and legal policies will confuse children and parents, leading more children to present to "gender clinics" where they will be given puberty-blocking drugs. This, in turn, virtually ensures they will "choose" a lifetime of carcinogenic and otherwise toxic cross-sex hormones, and likely consider unnecessary surgical mutilation of their healthy body parts as young adults.

The bottom line is this: Our opponents advocate a new scientifically baseless standard of care for children with a psychological condition (GD) that would otherwise resolve after puberty for the vast majority of patients concerned. Specifically, they advise: affirmation of children's thoughts which are contrary to physical reality; the chemical castration of these children prior to puberty with GnRH agonists (puberty blockers which cause infertility, stunted growth, low bone density, and an unknown impact upon their brain development), and, finally, the permanent sterilization of these children prior to age 18 via cross-sex hormones.

There is an obvious self-fulfilling nature to encouraging young GD children to impersonate the opposite sex and then institute pubertal suppression. If a boy who questions whether or not he is a boy (who is meant to grow into a man) is treated as a girl, then has his natural pubertal progression to manhood suppressed, have we not set in motion an inevitable outcome? All of his same sex peers develop into young men, his opposite sex friends develop into young women, but he remains a pre-pubertal boy. He will be left psychosocially isolated and alone. He will be left with the psychological impression that something is wrong. He will be less able to identify with his same sex peers and being male, and thus be more likely to self-identify as "non-male" or female. Moreover, neuroscience reveals that the pre-frontal cortex of the brain which is responsible for judgment and risk assessment is not mature until the mid-twenties.

Never has it been more scientifically clear that children and adolescents are incapable of making informed decisions regarding permanent, irreversible and life-altering medical interventions. For this reason, the College maintains it is abusive to promote this ideology, first and foremost for the well-being of the gender dysphoric children themselves, and secondly, for all of their non-gender-discordant peers, many of whom will subsequently question their own gender identity, and face violations of their right to bodily privacy and safety.[399]

Puberty Blockers and Cross-sex hormones

"The role of the GP in caring for gender-questioning and transgender patients' is a new 12-page policy guide issued by The Royal College of General Practitioners (RCGP) to warn about the issues around transitioning children.

In a...'position statement', the RCGP says there is a lack of 'robust evidence' about the long-term effects of 'puberty blockers' that stop the body maturing, and 'cross-sex hormones'. The RCGP also urges the NHS to record what it calls every patient's 'biological sex' – in addition to their chosen gender identity – to avoid potentially calamitous medical mistakes...This group of medical experts has issued warnings about the lack of research and evidence when it comes to significantly interfering with a child's natural biological development...

Currently the General Medical Council advises doctors to 'promptly refer patients requesting treatment' to gender identity clinics. Whereas the RCGP warns there is 'a significant lack of robust, comprehensive evidence around the outcomes, side effects and unintended consequences of such treatments for people with gender dysphoria, particularly children and young people'. There are question marks over 'long-term safety [of puberty blockers] in transgender adolescents', while the effects of cross-sex hormones 'can be irreversible.'"[400]

---

[399] Michelle A. Cretella, M.D. (President of the American College of Pediatricians), Quentin Van Meter, M.D. (Vice President of the American College of Pediatricians), Pediatric Endocrinologist, Paul McHugh, M.D. (University Distinguished Service Professor of Psychiatry at Johns Hopkins Medical School and the former psychiatrist in chief at Johns Hopkins Hospital), 'Gender Ideology Harms Children', Report of the American College of Pediatricians, September 2017. For more information, please visit...the College website concerning sexuality and gender issues. A PDF version of this page can be downloaded here: 'Gender Ideology Harms Children'.
[400] 'The role of the GP in caring for gender-questioning and transgender patients', The Royal College of General Practitioners, 10 July, 2019.

Self-creation is not freedom

"Consider the case of David Mackereth, an English doctor whose Christian faith has been officially declared impermissible. Mackereth was fired from his job for refusing to 'refer to a man six foot tall with a beard' as 'she.' A judge upheld his firing, declaring that 'belief in Genesis 1:27, lack of belief in transgenderism, and conscientious objection to transgenderism in our judgement are incompatible with human dignity and conflict with the fundamental rights of others, specifically here, transgender individuals.' This ruling is part of a new religious establishment, complete with penal laws.

The judge's language is...revealing, insofar as it... is an affirmation of faith to declare that a tall, bearded man is, in some mystical sense, a woman. The claim that a male can be (or become) a woman is religious, not scientific. Thus, the judge not only condemned the biblical belief that God created us male and female, but also denounced 'lack of belief in transgenderism' for any reason, religious or secular. The doctrine of transgenderism will not tolerate rival faiths, and so this newly established creed aims to punish all nonconformists, be they Christian or atheist, Jew or Hindu. The central doctrine of transgenderism is the belief that human will determines reality, as we create ourselves. A man who identifies as a woman is therefore a woman and has always been. Social, chemical, and surgical alterations are merely the outward affirmation and outworking of this inward truth, and the imperfections of physical transition do not negate the metaphysical truth of gender identity. These mystical doctrines of transgender ideology exemplify modern self-worship... But discontentment lurks amid the triumphant claims that identity determines reality. Self-creation is not freedom, for it only changes our master. Desire appears as the most authentic aspect of the self, and so it, rather than reason or revelation, rules human efforts to create our own truth and meaning. Furthermore, since we are not gods, our efforts to create ourselves are hindered by the natural laws of our existence...Self-worship does not overcome the given nature of our embodied human existence... Thus, self-worship turns to self-loathing misanthropy. A tall, bearded man may hate the doctor who denies that he is actually a woman, but this is not because the doctor is vicious or deceitful. Rather, he hates the doctor because the doctor tells the unwelcome truth about embodied existence... The judge in Mackereth's case got it backwards. The teaching of Genesis 1:27 that God made humans, male and female, in the image of himself is the firm foundation for human dignity and human rights. The real threat comes not from a Christian doctor's refusal to pretend a man is a woman, but from a mystical ideology that worships the self.[401]

Conclusion

The news items and observations that I have quoted in this chapter are but a small sample of what could be said around the three main themes – abortion, sexual orientation and transgenderism - that I have focussed on throughout the book. They are intended to highlight the contrast between wisdom and folly, between sanity and stupidity, between rationality and mindlessness. They constitute, if you like, a rationale for the use of 'common sense'.[402] There is, of course, much more ground that could have been covered.[403]

In the context of this book's purpose, to demonstrate the clear divide between a Christian world-view and that proposed by a secular humanist mentality, and the reasons why the latter has come to dominate so-called 'progressive' thinking in the Western world, the examples given show the extent to which the last-mentioned end up by defying principles of common-sense.

---

[401] Nathaniel Blake, 'U.K. Court Decision ...'
[402] Common sense is a disputed topic in the fields of philosophy and psychiatry. However, its daily use can be discerned in a human being's capacity for making rational decisions, based on sound arguments and coherent judgements. In general terms it means that human beings generally do not behave in ways that experience shows have destructive consequences for people's well-being. One obvious example would be the use of sturdy, specially designed boots for climbing, rather than flimsy foot-wear that cannot cope with the terrain.
[403] I have collected 100 references on the topics from a variety of sources and perspectives. Clearly, not all could be used.

Abortion

In the case of abortion, for example, if it is certain (from a scientific viewpoint) that human life begins in a mother's womb when fertilisation happens, then logically the deliberate choice to end that life amounts to homicide, since, once begun, human life develops as a seamless whole until death, whether inside or outside the womb. The only possible rational reason for undergoing an abortion, one for which there is a just cause, based on the principle of the lesser of two evils, is to preserve the physical life of the mother. No other reason, even that of mental distress caused to the mother keeping the baby, often advanced by pro-choice activists, amounts to a convincing case. When presented with a pregnancy the mother feels she cannot cope with alone, the existence of groups, well-qualified and equipped to encourage and support women in their hour of need to continue with the pregnancy, is the most compassionate way of dealing with a sudden traumatic event. From many accounts given by the women concerned who, as a first response to their circumstances, approach abortion clinics to be rid of the encumbrance, this is not the advice and help that they receive.

There is simply no inherent right to take another human being's life, however demanding it may be to carry the baby to birth, and beyond. The only choice, in the most exceptional of cases, is between ending the baby's or the mother's life. In the latter case, a high degree of probability that a continued pregnancy would cause the mother's death would have to be validated by independent medical practitioners. If that is lacking, common-sense would declare that the option to kill without a valid cause would contradict the measured judgement of most people that human life is intrinsically sacred, and therefore to be protected.

Sexual orientation

In the case of sexual orientation, common-sense would indicate that if 98%

of any given population is aligned to a heterosexual identity, then the remaining 2% who find their identity to be orientated towards people of the same sex represents an anomalous, if not abnormal, situation. If it is also shown by present biological sciences that this statistically highly unusual occurrence is not genetically inherited, in the same way that skin colour and sex definitely is, then common-sense would suggest that the causes of the anomaly be explored with a view to discovering other likely explanations. Sexual orientation cannot be compared to racial origin or to the wholly innate reality that all human beings are born either female or male.

Likewise, common-sense would dictate that those who identify themselves as homosexual, but long to feel comfortable in forming heterosexual relationships, should have the right to seek the right kind of counselling that would help them to move from one identity to the other. As long as they take the initiative to receive advice and guidance provided by properly trained and validated analysts, no-one has the right to deny them this opportunity.

A number of the reasons, given by professional psychiatric and psychotherapeutic bodies, for denying this right can be shown to lack the demonstrable evidence required to prove that, in all such cases of counselling, irreparable harm is being caused. The most quoted reason given is that homosexuality is inborn and cannot be changed. Neither of these assertions is existentially true. Rather they spring from an ideological dogma, designed to convince the public that homosexual attraction is perfectly normal, not an aberration of human nature.

Transgenderism

In the case of transgenderism, a powerful new creed has taken hold of the minds and wills of important sectors of civil society in the West. It can be summed up in the affirmation "we believe that a trans-woman (trans-man) is a woman (man); full stop." Were it not for the intense emotional climate that the attempt to revolutionise discussion around the whole issue of sexuality has created, such a creed would be construed as a delusionary invention. Sadly, if an attempt is undertaken to transition from one's biological sex to a simulation of the opposite sex, it usually leads to distressing consequences.

Normally, as in the case of literature, we are able to distinguish between an historical biography, which attempts to sift carefully all the available evidence about some episode of the past (to be as factual as possible to what really happened) and an historical novel, which may be inspired by an event, but which creatively invents people and happenings for which there is no firm record (fiction).[404] In the case of transgender doctrine, however, the distinction between reality and fantasy has been obliterated. There is a kind of reality which exists, when a person is convinced they exist 'in the wrong body', but it is only in the mind of the individual. There is no factual connection between the subjective belief and the objective world.

When this happens with other beliefs that do not match any possible reality, as would be the insistent pronouncement, for example, "that I am Napoleon", "Einstein" or any other famous person from the past, we treat such an assertion as indicating a psychological disorder. When highly intelligent professional people affirm categorically that a transgender man is a man, and always has been, but is shown mistakenly on her birth certificate to be female, and therefore is masquerading as such until the transitioning procedure has been completed, it is common-sense to wonder whether such people are just confused or behaving irrationally.

If a person who is clearly male in all his physical attributes, nevertheless demands the right to be addressed as 'she', for 'I am a woman', others have a greater right to refer to the person as 'he' because that is the truth. In our

---

[404] Alexandre Dumas' historical novel, The Three Musketeers, written in the context of seventeenth century France with a number of real historical allusions and profiles of actual personages, but also with an imaginary plot invented by the author, would be an example of a literary invention. R.D. Blackmore's novel, Lorna Doone, also set in the 17th century, would be another example. According to the preface, the author neither "dares, nor desires, to claim for it the dignity or cumber it with the difficulty of an historical novel."

confused world, it so happens that in a number of high profile cases, people have been dismissed from their jobs for supposedly 'degendering' another colleague, patient or pupil. In other words, they are fired for telling the truth. Even in such a disordered society, as that created by advocates of transgenderism, one cannot help feeling utterly amazed at such follies as these.

Chapter 11
The end of folly and re-gaining good sense?

"Be careful how you live, not as unwise people but as wise, making the most of the time, because the days are evil. Do not be foolish, but understand what the will of the Lord is" (Ephesians 5:15-17)

The existence of two worlds

We are now approaching the end of this review of the content, reasons for and consequences of the radical separation between two worlds lived simultaneously on this one earth. By the beginning of the third decade of the twenty-first century the distinction between these two worlds has become ever more apparent. They can be distinguished as an old and new world, not in the geographical sense that explorers at the end of the fifteenth century, travelling West from the European continent, thought they had 'discovered' a 'new' world on the other side of the Atlantic. The worlds that this book has been exploring comprise two markedly different explanations of what constitutes the fundamental meaning of being human, and how people may best fulfil the purpose of their existence.

The parting of two ways

There is a profound rift between the two worlds. It flows from two conflicting convictions: either human life is shaped by the existence and presence of a personal God, who has stamped his blueprint and project on human beings, all of whom bear his image, or it is wholly contingent on what humans, who have rejected this belief about God, decide is the meaning of life. This division between the two has been masked for nearly seventeen hundred years by the ascendency of the first belief, which has left a long imprint on the societies and cultures of the Western world. Now, in the last sixty years, the second belief has gradually replaced the first. It has gained the upper-hand in forming the basic opinions of societies in headlong retreat from the God-centred convictions of the Judaeo-Christian faith.

The recent shift of influence from one set of beliefs to the other is becoming increasingly obvious. One of its main consequences concerns the grounding of moral convictions and the resulting effects produced on the character of human life in community. The shift to a divergent moral code has had considerable legal repercussions, producing changes which give expression to conflicting beliefs.

Three of the most conspicuous illustrations of the transformation come in areas closest to human self-understanding: the humanity and personhood of pre-born infants, the significance of sexual attraction, identity and behaviour, and gender self-affirmation. Since homosexual conduct has been decriminalised, a variety of sexual orientations has been recognised in existing equality laws: marriage has been extended to same-sex partners, self-professed gay, lesbian, bi-sexual and transsexual people have been accorded rights as protected minorities, alongside women, the disabled and those belonging to diverse racial and ethnic groups. On the question of rights, however, these have been achieved through the mistake of believing that homosexual and transsexual groups exhibit the same characteristics as the latter groups. They do not. Nevertheless, in spite of this error, a moral consensus about the normality of these issues appears to have been permanently accepted by societies as a whole.

This sequence of events, over the last sixty years, is a matter of fact. The Christian community does not express its sorrow and pain at this regrettable turn of affairs as a grievance, because of its loss of influence over social and moral affairs. Rather, it points to another fact: once the fundamental belief system that governs and guides political decision-making has decisively turned away from Christian convictions, certain adverse results become inevitable.

The long saturation of civil society by the Christian faith has not, however, completely dried up. One major instance of its abiding impact comes in the constant appeal made to the assumed validity of human rights, based on the presumed equality of every single human being, irrespective of their background, character, physical or mental capacities. Historically-speaking, these have been founded on the belief that the sacred nature of humans is inviolable, just because each one is made in the image of God, who is the personification of goodness.[405]

The way they are now often interpreted may deviate from the fundamental purpose for which they have previously been recognised. Some of them, such as freedoms of speech, assembly, and religious belief and activity are being gradually whittled away, even in hitherto Christian societies. Nevertheless, the power of the appeal to 'our' or 'my' rights is still evident in law-making and law-enforcement. They have come to replace former moral absolutes. Rights in the current, secular humanist world are, perhaps, the only ones left standing.

Current ambiguity towards Christian moral standards

What about the state of Christian moral values in the public domain? There was a time, when whole societies in the Western world adhered to the moral

---

[405] "For eighteen long centuries, the Christian conviction that all human life was sacred had been underpinned by one doctrine more than any other: that man and woman were created in God's image. The divine was to be found as much in the pauper, the convict or the prostitute as it was in the gentleman with his private income and book-lined study," Dominion, 425. "In Locke's account, the shape of human, the way in which the extension of the predicate human is determined, is not in the end separable from the religious reasons that Locke cites in support of basic equality...Someone in denial of or indifferent to the existence of God is not going to be able to come up with anything like the sort of basis for equality that Locke came up with", Jeremy Waldron, 'God, Locke and Equality' in Paul E. Sigmund (ed.), The Selected Political Writings of John Locke (New York: Norton, 2005), 314-318; see also, Being Human, 66-68.

codes proclaimed by the Christian Church and incorporated into the laws of the land. This is no longer the case. As we have seen in the instances of abortion, sexuality and the family, most Western societies have drifted a long way from Christian moral standards. These latter conform to the way that human beings are designed by their Creator, to fulfil in the best possible way their physical, intellectual, moral and spiritual natures.

Over the last sixty years many of the Christian-inspired ethical ideals have been overturned. The most notable examples have been the legalisation of abortion and the authorisation of civil partnerships and same-sex marriages. At the same time, an insidious assault to discredit Christian values has been waged in the media (both commercial and social), and by some campaigning groups. Now, for the first time, it is legally mandatory to promote the 'new morality' in the education of children from primary school age onwards. Once parents had the ultimate authority and responsibility for educating their own children in matters of human relationships and sexuality, according to their own beliefs. This parental right is still enshrined in international law.[406] However, in a number of instances, such as teen-age contraception advice, abortions, sexual relationships and gender dysphoria, parents are not indispensably involved at all. The right is not observed.

In order to illustrate another area of major ethical concern, where Christian and secular beliefs diverge to a certain extent, we could mention the intense lobbying being undertaken in the sphere of climate-change and care of the environment. There is agreement that this is a highly critical issue that has to be pursued, before irreparable damage has been done to the whole ecosystem. Two notable heroes of this movement, at two ends of the age spectrum, have become household names across the globe, Sir David Attenborough and Greta Thornberg. Their courage, energy and inspiration are to be applauded. And yet, the main reason for their involvement, as it is

---

[406] For example, in the European Convention on Human Rights, Protocol, Article 2, 'Right to Education': "No person shall be denied the right to education. In the exercise of any functions which it assumes in relation to education and to teaching, *the State shall respect the right of parents to ensure such education and teaching in conformity with their own religious and philosophical convictions;* (emphasis added).

for the vast majority of those from Western nations participating in this cause, does not fit well with the basis on which Christians are also engaged. For them the underlying motif seems to be survival. The motif seems to be to reverse the degradation caused to the climate and natural world by human greed and lethargy, before the whole planet becomes uninhabitable.

Perhaps, there still lurks, in the memory of some of the people most concerned about the destructive way the physical world is being treated, the realisation that the world does not belong to us. There is another who is the owner, the one who created the earth and constantly sustains it. We humans are not freeholders, but leaseholders, accountable to the Being who created us to take care of the environment. We are entrusted with the task of being conscientious stewards of an amazing gift. This is the major motive for Christians to be involved in the care of creation.

This digression recognises that fundamental values still permeate, to a certain extent, the conscience of those who have intellectually rejected the fact that their origin springs from the Christian Faith. However, in the realm of the concerns explored in this study, this is no longer the case. Another set of core beliefs has taken the place of Christian ones. The old world lives by a vision in marked contrast to that of the new world. In the phrase often used by secular philosophers, human existence has become emancipated from the tutelage of an imposed religion. Humans have finally gained an autonomy from the dictates of others, to decide for themselves what to believe and how to act. They can now follow their own inclinations, at least in their private lives, without the risk of falling foul of adverse legal rulings. To be able to make decisions about one's own life, without the interference of outside agencies, is considered to be at the heart of human freedom.[407] However, freedom is much more complex than such a superficial understanding would indicate. Freedom should be defined, not so much by the removal of constraints on personal desires, but by a conscious reflection

---

[407] There is much more to understanding freedom than the few sentences penned here, see J. Andrew Kirk, The Meaning of Freedom: A Study of Secular, Muslim and Christian Views (Carlisle: Paternoster Press, 1998).

on the purpose of freedom; not so much what are we free from, but what is freedom for.

It is not surprising that, in the clash between two distinct world-views, contemporary societies wish to embrace a conviction that allows people to run their own lives, without having to submit themselves to what they probably consider to be outlandish dogmas. They are free to nurture their inner desires and abandon themselves to what their longings dictate at any given moment. Is this not the reality of where the majority of people living in the Western world situate themselves today?

So, where does this leave Christians who now live in a world that vociferously denounces their prescriptions for living well? It is unlikely that they will be able to persuade people, who take the kind of stance I have been outlining, to leave behind their folly and to follow the way of ethical purity, as revealed in the New Testament. Christians now represent a small minority in a pluralistic social milieu. Their ability to influence decision-making processes in the political arena is limited. Sadly, some of their leaders, who one might assume would make a strong case for proclaiming the assets of the long tradition of Christian moral teaching, have largely yielded to the 'spirit of the times'. So, how should Christians respond to the new circumstances? I suggest that Christians are called increasingly to act now as a prophetic voice for their respective nations. I will explain what I mean by this in the rest of this chapter.

The prophetic mission of Christian communities

As the Bible understands this vocation, prophecy entails two specific activities. Firstly, there is the task of transmitting a message to the world that makes clear what is God's perfect will for the human race. A summary of this is found in the words of the prophet Micah:

> "'The Lord has told you...what is good; and what does the

Lord require of you but to do justice, and to love kindness and to walk humbly with your God" [408].

This is a prescription for those who acknowledged that God knows best what kind of life human beings will benefit from most. If they are willing to cultivate friendship with God, they will enjoy the blessings he delights to lavish on them. Secondly, there is the task of naming the consequences that will fall inevitably upon those who choose not to follow God's direction for a life of well-being.

So, in the present context in Western societies, where the first task is little heeded, Christians' main responsibility is to fulfil the second undertaking. It is a simple message, 'Take heed of where your God-denying choices are more than likely to lead you'. Such a proposal will seem harsh and presumptuous on the part of many hearers. However, those who sadly shut their ears and continue their pursuits, without weighing the consequences that ensue when the message is not listened to, are the ones who will suffer. Moreover, it is likely that, as an outcome of their false beliefs and wrong actions, they will also cause others to suffer.

Jesus drew the picture of two sets of people living alongside each other: those who are wise and those who are foolish. The first built their houses (lives) on a solid rock foundation. The second built theirs on unstable, shifting sand. When the storm came, the first house remained standing; the second crumbled and disintegrated. He was referring to those who accepted his message and those who rejected it. The tragedy is that the latter preferred to abide by their own wisdom, not that which comes from God.[409] As a result, they became homeless. Homelessness is a metaphor for the way many people experience their lives. Believing that there is only silence behind the vast universe of which planet earth is a microscopic part, they find themselves without shelter. All they can hear is an echo of their own longings shouted out to a vast cosmos that, according to their own perception, neither hears nor cares.

---

[408] Micah 6:8
[409] James 3:17-18

Our contemporary Western culture abhors what it calls a judgemental attitude towards the foolish choices that people make, although many are quick to condemn hypocritically those who make such judgements. Some people seem to gain much satisfaction in uncovering and denouncing what appears to be a self-righteous, narrow-minded attitude to others' life choices.[410] If this latter is the motive for taking on a prophetic task, it should be rejected. Rather, the motive should spring from a genuine sadness, care and compassion for all who willingly, but without due consideration, choose paths that end up in sorrow and self-destruction.[411]

The destructive impulse

At this point, I will make a slight digression, in order to show how the human instinct for self-destruction, as a contrast to the life and pleasure-seeking impulse, has been elaborated by the father of psychoanalysis, Sigmund Freud.[412] Freud himself summarises the conclusions he has come to in *Civilisation and its Discontents*:

> 'I can no longer understand how we can have overlooked the ubiquity of non-erotic aggressivity and destructiveness and can have failed to give it its due place in our interpretation of life...In all that follows I adopt the standpoint, therefore, that the inclination to aggression is an original, self-subsisting instinctual disposition in man, and I return to my view that it constitutes the greatest impediment to civilization...*This aggressive instinct is the derivative and the main representative of the death instinct which we have found alongside of Eros and which shares*

---

[410] A whole arsenal of words is now commonly used: bigoted, prejudiced, intolerant, dogmatic, opinionated, old-fashioned, outmoded, antiquated.
[411] Anne Bronte's novel, The Tenant of Wildfell Hall (London: Collins, 1954) (first published in 1848) depicts the heroine, Helen Huntingdon, attempting to fulfil an act of care and compassion towards her destructively dissolute husband, Arthur. Unfortunately, she was unsuccessful. Arthur proved to be incapable of curbing his controlling, libertarian obsessions. The result ended in his painful death at a young age, the result of a tragic accident from which he was physically and mentally too weak to recover.
[412] Space does not allow a full treatment of Freud's theory which he set out originally in his work, Beyond the Pleasure Principle (1920) and thereafter in The Future of an Illusion (1927) and Civilisation and its Discontents (1929). I dedicate several pages to an extended summary of his thinking on these topics in Being Human, 254-59, 273-274.

world-dominion with it. And it is this battle of the giants that our nursemaids try to appease with their lullaby about Heaven.'[413]

After a life time of considering how the instincts and drives that originate within the human psyche control the way that humans behave, he came, according to Stephen Thornton, to this final conclusion:

'Freud postulated that human beings are driven from birth by the desire to acquire and enhance bodily pleasure. Sexual energy (libido), redefined as any form of bodily pleasure, is the single most important motivating force in adult life. It is expressed as a self-preserving and pleasure principle. At the same time, humans, universally, demonstrate the trait of an irrational urge to destroy the sources of all forms of sexual energy in the annihilation of the self. From where does this aggressive, self-destructive and cruel instinct arise?'[414]

Freud throws down a challenge, which he himself was unable to unravel, to all subsequent generations. For him the ability to solve the problem of an innate aggression that exerts an equal and opposite effect to that of the pleasure principle – *Thanatos* (death) against *Eros* (love, life and gratification) – was an indispensable task, if civilisation was to be saved from disintegration.

There is evidence that in the abortion business the destruction of human beings leads to an emotionally incapacitating stress, caused by remorse, shame and grief. Likewise, in the free-expression of sexual inclinations, self-indulgence leads to the deformation of human nature.[415]

---

[413] See, Peter Gay, The Freud Reader (New York: Norton, 1995), 754, 755, 756 (emphasis added).
[414] Stephen P. Thornton, 'Sigmund Freud', www.iep.utm.edu/freud.
[415] Sexually Transmitted Diseases (STDs) are but one instance that demonstrates this reality. Perhaps, in Freud's language, eros (wrongly exploited) leads to thanatos.

Abortion: folly and good sense

In the case of abortion, the death instinct is absolutely clear. It can be monitored whilst a living human foetus, as it is extracted from a woman's womb, is dismembered. The visual images of the procedure show the violence that is enacted on a defenceless living being. As would be expected, pro-abortionists do everything within their power to ensure that this visual material does not come into the public domain. Moreover, they cover over the horror of the practice by pretending that the operation is not carried out against a pre-born human; rather, it represents nothing more than the removal of an unwanted 'blob' of tissue! The whole event, seeing (literally) that the abortion act is carried out to secure the extinction of the developing child, is a clear act of wanton aggression.

During the life time of Freud abortion was not yet legalised in Western nations. Had it been, it would not have been a surprise if he had categorised it as an act of assault that contributes to a belittling of the much vaunted Western civilisation; an act, quite impossible to reconcile with the upholding of professed Western moral values. Instead of defending abortion as a matter of being pro-choice, it would be truer to reality to categorise it as being pro-death. It is a clear example of Freud's discovery of the Thanatos principle at work in human beings.

I have already argued that all the reasons given for legitimising such a brutal action are unfounded, except when, on rare occasions, the mother's physical life is seriously threatened by the continuation of the pregnancy. In such cases, a decision may have to be taken as to which is the lesser of two evils: the loss of the mother's life or that of the child. They are equally precious.

There are, of course, alternatives open to those seeking an abortion. It is not obvious, judging by the high percentage of pregnancies that end in abortions, that abortion clinics do their utmost to deter women from going through with the procedure. Experience shows that, when they receive counselling and support to keep their babies, many change their minds about having an abortion, carry on the pregnancy, and are gratified by the advice they received.[416]

Sexuality: folly and good sense
Institutional acceptance of homosexuality

In the case of sexuality, there has been an expanding and intensifying campaign, now for over fifty years, to shatter the notion that monogamous heterosexuality is the gold-standard for maintaining healthy sexual relationships. There was a time when it was taken for granted by the vast majority in every society that homosexual attraction, self-identity and practice was an unnatural and abnormal deviation from a beneficial and wholesome sexual life-style. However, homosexual relations were suddenly declared to be normal, regular and well-adjusted sexual commitments on the part of a small minority of most populations. This has occurred, in spite of the fact that concrete empirical evidence for its inherent naturalness is missing.

Those in favour of such a declaration, misguidedly taken on board by prestigious medical professions and associations, simply made the assumption that what was already happening was perfectly acceptable, justifiable and proper. What followed was an immense reversal of the previous belief that homosexual attraction constituted a defect in some peoples' psychological nature, caused credibly by unfortunate and harmful intra-family relationships at a young age.

Professional bodies, in the field of psychiatry and allied disciplines, pronounced inadmissible any further research that was attempting to discover the likely psychological and emotional pressures that had produced

---

[416] In a recent case in the UK, a doctor who proscribed pills (progesterone) to pregnant women, who had taken the first of two tablets that would have affected the loss of their baby, but afterwards changed their mind and rejected the second one, that reversed the procedure, was suspended by the General Medical Council from his professional work. After an investigation, in which not one of the women was prepared to testify against him, but all were totally satisfied with his handling of their problem, he was completely exonerated from any wrong-doing. Those who were helped to bring their pregnancy to a positive end were all delighted by the choice they made that led to their new born child.

homosexual inclinations. Henceforth, it was asserted to be a perfectly proper way of expressing one's sexual nature. Consequently, it was eliminated from the register of psychological pathologies. So, what at the time (during the decade of the 1960s) was an ongoing scientific research project that was exploring some interesting and potentially fruitful theories about sexual identity was abruptly decommissioned.

Since that time, the view gradually took hold in the Western world that, far from being considered a psychological disorder, homosexual disposition was an entirely common-place orientation wholly on a par with that of heterosexuality, even though it occurred in only around 2-3% of a given population. One of the consequences has been that legitimate grounds for following what further scientific research might have discovered in its investigation of the likely origin of the trait has been cut short.[417]

The forceful and successful doctrinaire offensive to ban discussion of a scientific programme, open to being either verified or falsified according to the very nature of the scientific enterprise, is counter-intuitive and counter-productive. Science is rightly hostile to any suggestion that untested, dogmatic beliefs should be allowed to trump normal, rigorous scientific procedures. But that is precisely what has happened in this case.

The dogmatic presumption came to be upheld by the scientifically dubious assertion that homosexuality occurs as a genetically given force of nature; in simpler language, certain people are just born that way. The implication of the dogma is that such people can never change, even if they desire to do so. In recent years, however, such a doctrine has been somewhat modified by more up to date discoveries that throw further light on the reality of this sexual orientation. Firstly, as the result of research into children's development as sexual beings, an evolving scale of attraction either to the opposite or same sex has been explored. The main conclusion has been that during early pubescence the attraction can take a number of forms that fluctuate as the young person matures physically, mentally and emotionally.

---

[417] It is a prominent example of ideological, political intervention limiting scientific freedom to pursue justifiable research projects.

The outcome of such a process is that by the time they have left their teens a large majority of young people have settled into normal heterosexual relations. A tiny minority, nevertheless, profess ongoing same sex romantic attachments.

Secondly, as already discussed, wide-ranging, carefully modelled and controlled surveys have shown that homosexual orientation is not innate, caused by factors that arise as far back as pregnancy itself. In simple terms, there is no gay gene that explains completely the subsequent preference for gay relations. Same-sex preference is not inherent and can change.

Counselling for those experiencing unwanted homosexual attraction

This seems to be as far as specialists in the subject of sexuality have advanced. This being so, it seems inconceivable and medically unprofessional to attempt to forbid those professing same-sex attraction, but who feel distressed in doing so, from the right to seek expert counselling by qualified practitioners with a view to modifying their deeply-disturbed feelings.

In most cases of psychological anguish (for any cause), the medical profession is a caring and compassionate resource, which one may approach with full confidence that it will endeavour to use its knowledge to overcome, as far as is possible, the anxiety being experienced. Why, then, is homosexually-prompted suffering treated so unsympathetically? Why do professional psychotherapeutic bodies threaten to disaffiliate properly qualified counsellors from its membership, because they offer therapy to those who voluntarily request it? Why, moreover, do they also seek to persuade governments to ban such therapy by law? The only credible answer seems to be that the old myth about unchangeable orientation is still being promoted by pro-homosexual activists. In which case, why would transition in the opposite direction, from a heterosexual to homosexual identity, not also be discouraged and hindered? Evidently, source for the goose is not also source for the gander!

The problem for those who are suffering strong feelings of disorder, as a result of their homosexual disposition, and wish to find wholeness by reverting to a heterosexual alignment is compounded by a deliberate campaign. Pressure groups are misleading the general public about what is involved in 're-integrative therapy' and 'sexual orientation change efforts', by using the discredited misnomer 'conversion therapy'.

It is interesting to note, for example, that the Canadian government, in introducing a bill[418] to outlaw every conceivable counselling practice offered to young people under the age of eighteen, confused by their unwelcome sexual expression, invited only people who claimed to have been alarmed by their experience of such counselling to be present at its announcement. In order to be fair, why did it not invite an equal number of people who claimed to have been helped, through supportive therapeutic intervention, to discover the favourable nature for them of a heterosexual tendency? It is logical to conclude that the Canadian government, in this case, is itself waging a prejudiced and partisan offensive of its own, only willing to listen to evidence against the practice of orientation-change produced by groups representing one side of the debate. This is clearly an exercise in autocratic, coercive politics that should dismay all those seeking to uphold policies democratically generated.

In this campaign, to criminalise falsely-titled 'conversion therapy', there exists a massive, underlying dose of hypocrisy that is now becoming more evident since the exponential growth of sex-change practices for gender-confused young people is being highlighted. Thus, for adults who intentionally seek relief from unwanted same-sex attraction all possible help is now gradually being forbidden by law, thus denying their right to choose freely the treatment that, contrary to misleading propaganda, can produce the healing looked for.

---

[418] Bill C 8, tabled by the Justice Minister on 9th March, 2020.

However, for young people, not yet mature enough to decide rationally for themselves, to seek relief from what they momentarily consider to be unwanted attraction to their birth sex, 'conversion therapy' is becoming ever more available. Their freedom of choice, even against their parent's wise counsel not to succumb to the illusory promises of the transgender lobby, is being upheld; whilst that of the other group is being denied. The inconsistency is obvious. How is it rationally possible to defend the squaring of this particular circle? When will the Canadian government pass a law forbidding all transgender procedures for under-18s?

Transgenderism: folly and good sense

In the case of transgender beliefs and practices, the loss of sanity is even more remarkable than that occurring in the above two cases. By a consensus of human experience over millennia in every culture, and the unequivocal witness of the evidence presented by scientifically corroborated facts, human beings are designated either male or female for life by their physiological constitution. Nevertheless, a raft of people, otherwise deemed to be intelligent, make the preposterous claim that gender can be changed either by a variety of drug-related and surgical interventions or simply on an individual's personal testimony that he or she has changed gender.[419] Either of these allegations, or both together, is reckoned to be sufficient confirmation to support the transition.

The motivation for making irreversible alterations to normal, healthy, physical developments of a young person is the absurd belief that the change can be made on the grounds of an individual's strange conviction that his or her birth-sex doesn't conform to an alleged self-identity. Moreover, it staggers belief that many medical professionals, who have been trained in scientifically sophisticated procedures designed to heal

---

[419] A certificate to this effect is now available that, by law, confirms the deluded notion. Meanwhile, the person concerned remains physiologically the sex they were born with. Since when has it been acceptable for a law to be passed that denies a physical fact?

malfunctioning bodies and minds, can so easily overturn their long medical preparation by endorsing a young person's desire to transition from one gender to the other.

In this study I have investigated the claim that people can actually be (not just claim to be) the opposite sex to the one they were born. The sad answer is that all they can achieve is a simulation of being what they wish. The real substance is denied them. Attempts to dissimulate by adopting language conventions, such as demanding that others address them by the gender pronoun they are imitating, only confuses the issue even more. The threat of dismissal from one's job as a teacher or medical professional, for refusing to comply with a pupil's or patient's request to be called by his or her preferred pronoun, is tantamount to sanctioning the telling of a lie. It is hard to believe that anyone can think that such an act promotes good education or healthy living.

The adverse consequences of promoting the myth of transgenderism and pressing for its reality to be acknowledged in law hits adolescent girls and adult women the hardest. The classic case, spoken about most, is the closing down of specially protected spaces for women, defined by their biological-sex, in toilets, bathrooms and changing rooms, single-sex hospital wards, refuges for women suffering domestic violence, rape-crisis centres and prisons. Each of these situations are threatened by men claiming to be women, who demand free access to spaces properly designated for real women alone. The physical and psychological damage to women in these contexts is obvious to women.

Another case embraces all sports hitherto reserved exclusively for either men or women. Men, now claiming to be women, are demanding the right to be able to participate alongside women in all sports, even though they are intended for and have been restricted to women alone. The physical superiority of a male athlete is transparent, giving them an overwhelming advantage over female competitors, thus eliminating at one stroke women's sports. Moreover, one never hears of women claiming to be men demanding the right to participate in sports designated only for men. In order to avoid contradiction and inconsistency, if the rule is deemed valid in one direction, it should also be valid in the other. However, if a trans-man is a man, why is it inconceivable that (she) would wish to compete alongside real men? The answer is clear: it is biological reality!

It is not surprising that women, who have fought long and hard to be recognised as having the same rights as men, are greatly disturbed by the implication that womanhood no longer counts as a protected characteristic either in social engagement or in law. The fact of the matter is evident: if the binary nature of sex is no longer to be accepted, then the notion of male and female no longer exists. There would be no clear, objective definition of man and woman. If that is the logic of transgender thinking, then transgenderism itself disappears in a puff of smoke; there is nothing to 'transgender' from or to. [420] Transgender ideology counts as a major example of discrimination on the basis of sex (sexism). Sex as a protected characteristic is intended to protect girls and women from unfair physical, social, cultural and economic discrimination in every aspect of society.

On June 15, 2020, the USA Supreme Court gave a judgement by a two-thirds majority (6-3) that fundamentally has redefined the original meaning of sex-discrimination, as outlined in Title VII of the Civil Rights Act of 1964, which forbade discrimination against people on the basis of their race, colour or sex. The Court's new ruling is based on a widening of the meaning of sex from the original intention of the 1964 Act, to include homosexual orientation and transgender identity. To give reasons here why this reinterpretation of the meaning contemplated by the law's original design is historically and legally seriously flawed would require too much

---

[420] "Inherent in the notion of 'gender identity' is that there already exists a specific subjective experience of being a man and a woman. However, there cannot be significant intrinsic experiential differences between male and female human beings when we cannot know what those differences are...Medicine may be in danger of reinforcing social norms and reifying a concept that is impossible to define over and above material biological reality", 'Sex, gender and gender identity,' 7. What is happening in the milieu created by the transgender myth is actually the endorsement of outdated sex and gender stereotypes. In the attempt to validate young patients' self-expression, clinicians may inadvertently be reinforcing obsolete ideas about how men and women should be characterised.

space.[421]

What is crucial in the present debate is to note the way in which a legal process has ended up, not by properly explaining and upholding the law, but by creating a new law. In this way, the much vaulted separation of jurisdictions within the US Constitution – executive, legislative and judicial – has been shattered. This has come about, when aggressive campaigns have failed to achieve their ends through the democratic, law-making, congressional or parliamentary procedures. In this case, the US Congress has several times refused to recognise that sexual orientation and transgender identity should be included under the classification of sex.[422]

Sex-assigned at birth?

The insistence that trans-men are men and trans-women are women, or that a trans-man who gives birth to a child should be acknowledged as the father, not the mother, on the birth certificate is an attempt to substitute play-acting for objective fact. The grand dame of pantomime may be played by a male, because the audience is quite aware that convention requires the switch. Outside the theatre door, however, he reverts to his normal sex. The same is not true, however, of those who change their name to one recognisably belonging to the opposite sex, and wish to change their designated sex on their original birth-certificates and passports. Nor is it true of governments, when they put a question on census forms: sex - male, female or other? Finally, in this catalogue of examples of disassociation from the real world we

---

[421] To find a good summary of the arguments, see, Tyler O'Neal Alito: Court's 'Preposterous' Trans Ruling Threatens Religion, Speech, Privacy, and Safety', PJ Media, June 15, 2020. (This gives a textual resume of one of the Court's dissenting justices, Alito); also, Ryan T. Anderson, The Supreme Court's Mistaken and Misguided Sex Discrimination Ruling', Public Discourse, June 20, 2020; Joy Pullman, 'SCOTUS's Transgender Ruling Firebombs the Constitution', The Federalist', June 16, 2020; Megan M. Arago and David Upham, 'The Blindness of Justice Gorsuch's Woke Textualism,' Public Discourse, June 22, 2020.
[422] Under the new regime in the US Congress (2021), where the Democrat Party had a narrow majority in both houses, these two groups have now been acknowledged as protected designations.

could add the use of the term 'sex assigned at birth'. This is understood to mean that those, claiming to be disturbed by their gender, were misallocated a sex by officialdom, not that they were born that sex.[423]

All these attempts to pretend that we can create reality just as we most desire it, is utter folly. It does nothing, in the long run, to comfort those who suffer from painful gender confusion. The proliferation of people who, when they come to their senses, seek to de-transition is proof that the original gender confusion has only been enhanced. The situation for young people who believe that they are inhabiting the wrong body and are affirmed in their belief by some parents, medical professionals and teachers is made even more stressful. They are often being advised and encouraged to undergo prescriptions that will permanently alter their otherwise normal, healthy physical and mental growth into mature adults of the sex with which they were born.

The perplexity they are undoubtedly experiencing has little to do with their

---

[423] An extreme example of the utter folly of transgender expectations concerns a boy, aged three, telling his mother: "I am a boy because you gave me a boy's name". At the age of twelve he was given puberty blockers. He says that she eventually wants a womb transplant, so that she can be a mother when she is older; see, Issy Lyons, The Daily Telegraph, October 10, 2019. The young boy, presumably, was led to believe that his male sex originated in the name his parents gave him. Nine years later he kept believing that actually being a female was a matter of undergoing certain physiological interventions at the right time, so that he could change from the sex he was born in to the sex he chose to be. Is it possible to imagine any notions more likely to bring unprecedented confusion into the young lad's sense of identity? Is it surprising that those who willingly propose and encourage gender-change routines are accused of child-abuse? On June 24, 2020, The Sunday Times published a survey on the public's attitude to the law on gender re-assignment.When asked, "Should the law allow trans-people to self-identify"? 94% of 12,624 respondents answered "No".

physical fitness; it rests in their minds.[424] That is where it should be treated, not by drastically altering their physical constitution. Such a procedure, carried out on adolescents who do not yet have the intellectual and emotional capacity to hand themselves over to an untested drug-related therapy, has rightly been called child-abuse by leading clinicians in the field of gender-dysphoria.[425]

Trans-activists have never considered seriously the long-term effects for those whose true sex is being violated by those attempting to engineer a sex-

---

[424] Philosophically speaking, transgenderism follows the thought of 'transcendental idealism'. This is a way of relating to an external world outside our minds, in which the objects of our knowledge are mere appearances in our mind. The view was most powerfully elaborated by Immanuel Kant in his Critique of Pure Reason. He developed the thesis that things in the external world cannot be known as they are in themselves, only as they present themselves to how we view them. This belief accounts for the divorce that exists in a transgender individual's mind between what the mind perceives about the real world and the real world itself. Hence, the transgender individual claims that what I perceive about myself (my identity) is real, even though it does not connect with external facts outside the mind. Following the theory of idealism, the coherence between what we sense through our thinking about objects and what actually exists cannot be accurately either confirmed or denied. However, what happens in cases of gender dysphoria is that people who justify to themselves what can be known knows this only in their minds, but have no idea whether it connects to any objective reality. This fallacious philosophy leads to an intense individualism, relativism and solipsism. It means that humans cannot know whether there are absolute truths that exist outside the way the mind may apprehend them, and whether, therefore, they bear any relevance to a real world:
"Where confidence in representation and correspondence (as a definitions of truth) has broken down, there is no way of telling whether people's beliefs, held within their head, reflect any reality external to the neuro-physiological functioning of brain cells. How some people interpret their experience is legitimised within their own inner world, as long as they can justify it to themselves. (However), there is no objective standard of measurement, no way of determining for sure whether a statement of belief actually denotes anything", The Future of Reason, p. 166.
[425] The Report of the American College of Pediatricians, September 2017, quoted in the previous chapter, gives ample and convincing evidence of the grave (and unmonitored) consequences for those who have embarked on the process of transitioning away from their true sex.

change that can never happen.[426] Their response to mounting criticisms of the myth of gender-exchange is to heap verbal abuse on the critics, denouncing them as being transphobic, bigoted, intolerant, malicious, promoters of hate and uncaring. Such forceful language will not do! In the first place, it is false. The use of the term phobia/phobic in this context is wholly inaccurate: a phobia in its proper meaning does not correspond to the way it is being thrown around as an all-inclusive term of abuse. In a careful study of the right understanding of a phobia, I come to the following conclusion of how it should be used:

'Fear becomes a phobia, when it results in acute anxiety that becomes an obsession that consumes a person's life. Then it is likely to lead to intense dislike, physical aversion and loathing (of the object causing the anxiety). When it becomes a nagging compulsion, it will probably end up in justifying acts of hatred of known people, including extreme verbal abuse (such as bullying), ostracism and physical violence.

Phobia should be reserved for...expressions of hostility and malice towards individuals or groups. It should not be used as a catch-all phrase aimed at all people who believe, on moral and practical grounds, that (certain kinds of) sexual activity (are) unnatural, abnormal and aberrant.'[427]

Their conviction is not born out of fear, even less of hate, but out of compassion for those living through unresolved and disturbing thoughts and experiences. The increasing use of phobia to designate people who

---

[426] Prior to the change of government in the USA in 2020, the US Department of Health and Human Services (HHS) has revisited its policies and now prohibits discrimination on the basis of biological sex, rather than 'gender identity'. It announced that "it is returning to the government's interpretation of sex discrimination according to the plain meaning of the word 'sex' as male or female as determined by biology". Gregory Baylor, Senior Counsel for the liberty group, 'Alliance Defending Freedom', commented that, "confirming the clear meaning of sex as grounded in human biology ensures that women will continue to have equal opportunities in sports, school and work, and it provides privacy rights for all Americans".
[427] The Abuse of Language, 197.

keep to the one true, objective definition of sex and gender in real life - every person is biologically either a male or a female for life – should be dropped. It is an abuse of the plain use of language, being used purely as a language of abuse.

As for the other words that are commonly applied to those who argue that transgender, strictly speaking, does not exist, they can all be used with equal force against transgender warriors who will not tolerate any other opinion than their own. They are the real bigots, who are dogmatically-opinionated. Although unintentional, their actions contradict the conviction that they really care for a young person suffering from identity confusion. If it is correct to label transgender procedures for under-age young people as abuse, then safe-guarding vulnerable children from abusive practices (that includes ideological indoctrination) becomes a paramount social responsibility.

Conclusion

If my central thesis, that the recent intense repudiation of Christian belief and moral values is confirmation of the existence of two conflicting worlds within the one human race, then the place of Christian witness in the public arena of contentious debate takes on a fresh dynamic. The Christian community can no longer assume that the Western world adheres to its world-view. This should not be taken as affirming that the long tradition of Christian thought and moral guidance has been completely wiped-out, as Tom Holland has recently shown.[428] However, an insidious offensive against Christian inspired precepts, that are designed to promote optimum individual and social well-being, is in full swing. The utilitarian motto of the campaign seems to be, 'maximise the pleasure principle and minimise the depressing consequences'.

It appears unlikely that Christian ethical values, even though they express

---

[428] Dominion: The Making of the Western Mind.

the order laid down in God's perfect pattern for the human species, will once again be adopted by a generation which believes that it knows better than God what most benefits human flourishing. It is contradictory to assume that these values belong to the past, because they are outdated, unfashionable and obsolete. In reality they will be validated in the future, because they conform to God's design for a new creation.

The history of humankind presents a repetitive account of the dismal failure of human beings to discern the only way of life that promotes their maximum moral, physical, mental and spiritual health. The defects were shown, millennia ago, in the history of the Israelites, hence the mission of the prophets sent by God to warn his people of the folly of their ways. It is plain in the Greek and Roman civilisations, and in every one that has followed. Tragically they have occurred also amongst elements of the Christian Church in their various interventions in the affairs of the state and in their authoritarian subjection of its members to spurious teaching and, sometimes, immoral practices.

Thus, in the light of much of its past history, the contemporary Christian community needs to be humble in claiming to fulfil what Jesus affirmed was its mission - to be "the salt of the earth" and "the light of the world."[429] As I have indicated, this community is called to follow the profile of the world to come, as set out by Jesus and his first disciples. Part of its mission is to be self-critical, acknowledging before God and the watching world its failures to live up to its high calling, and to ask for forgiveness and God's grace to follow more closely the way of Jesus. Another part of its mission is to warn the world, already passing away, of the inevitable consequences of the many ill-considered follies it commits in seeking to be free from the belief systems and moral dictates of the past.

I finish this study with a verse of a hymn penned by John Newton, the famous ex-owner and trafficker of slaves, who later, after becoming a Christian, joined William Wilberforce and others to achieve the abolition of

---

[429] Matthew 5: 13-14.

slavery throughout the British colonies. It sums up in an appropriate, poetic form the gist of my thesis:

> 'Saviour, if of Zion's[430] city
> I, thro' grace, a member am,
> let the world deride or pity,
> I will glory in thy name;
> fading is the worldling's pleasure,
> all his boasted pomp and show;
> solid joys and lasting treasure
> none but Zion's children know.'

In reality it is a prayer to live as though, as a Christian, one was already living humbly and unpretentiously in the world that is coming and, in part, is already here.

---

[430] The new Jerusalem, centre of the new heavens and new earth. The writer of the Letter to the Hebrews in the New Testament proclaimed, 'Here we have no lasting city, but we are looking for a city to come' (Hebrews 13:14).

APPENDIX A

Personhood and Human Rights of the Unborn Child in International Law[431]

Preface

The decriminalisation of abortion in certain restricted circumstances took place in a number of countries in the Western world around half a century ago. Surprisingly though it may seem, since abortion in these nations is now taken for granted, changing the law may well have been contrary to obligations they undertook to abide by international law[431]. Such an outcome, ever since the previous prohibition of abortion was overturned, though largely ignored by the nations concerned, has resulted in the deliberate killing of millions of human beings. If the consequence of having disregarded a major implication of the treaties they signed up to has in fact contributed towards such an outstanding calamity, there still could be some hope that the right to life of the unborn can be guaranteed in the future.

The basis of human rights in the modern world

Few people would disagree that the Universal Declaration of Human Rights

---

[431] In this summary of the articles that have been promulgated in international law documents on the extent of the right to life, I am indebted to a closely argued and comprehensively resourced article by Tom Finegan, 'The Right to Life in International Human Rights Law', published on-line by the Heritage Foundation, on behalf of the Richard and Helen Devos Centre for Religion and Civil Society, January 24, 2020. His article, therefore, should be consulted to give a more complete account of the reasoning behind the conclusions that have been drawn from an analysis of the documents referred to.

(UDHR)[432] is the gold standard for understanding what is entailed by speaking about and enacting the fundamental rights in law of every individual human being. It sets out in clear and unequivocal language the core elements of these rights.

In the Preamble, the UDHR speaks of "the inherent dignity and...the equal and inalienable rights of all members of the human family". It prefaces this conviction with the word 'recognition,' thus testifying to the reality that dignity and equal and inalienable rights belong to human beings simply by virtue of their being human. Further on, it is said that "the peoples of the United Nations have in the Charter reaffirmed their faith in fundamental human rights, in the dignity and worth of the human person and in the equal rights of men and women"[433]. It continues, "Member States have pledged themselves to achieve, in co-operation with the United Nations, the promotion of universal respect for the observance of human rights and fundamental freedoms".

The Declaration proceeds with the solemn words, "Now, therefore, the General Assembly, proclaims..." What follows is a list of thirty Articles. For the purposes of this summary of its position on human rights, the following Articles are the most germane. They are the ones that establish the basic concepts of dignity, liberty, equality and the right to life:

Article 1. "All human beings are born free and equal in dignity and rights...;

Article 3. "Everyone has the right to life, liberty and security of person;

Article 6. "Everyone has the right to recognition everywhere as a person before the law;

Article 7. "...All are entitled to equal protection against any discrimination in violation of this Declaration and against any incitement to such

---

[432] The UDHR was adopted by the UN Assembly on 10 December 1948. That date in December has been celebrated each year as World Human Rights Day.
[433] The Declaration was intended to set out in detail the content of basic human rights as referred to in the UN's Charter.

discrimination."

The language of the Declaration is lucid, precise and intelligible. There should be no reason, therefore, to dispute its meaning and intention. Human rights are rooted in human nature. Charles Malik, the Lebanese representative to the United Nations, and the rapporteur of the drafting committee of the UDHR, wrote about the significance of the words, 'inherent dignity' and 'inalienable rights' in the text:

> "You can recognise only what must have been there, and what is already there cannot, in the present context, be anything but what nature has placed there. Furthermore dignity is qualified as being 'inherent' to man and his rights as being 'inalienable'...It is difficult to find in the English language better qualifications to exhibit the law of nature than these two".[434]

For the purposes of this study, which centres on "the inalienable rights of the unborn child", the key words and phrases to note from the Declaration are, "all members of the human family", "the dignity and worth of the human person", "all human beings", "everyone as a person", "all are entitled to equal protection..." The reason for singling out these particular words is that some nations, that adopted the Declaration and later signed up to legal treaties that incorporated the Declaration's articles into international human rights' bills, nevertheless justified abortion. The main reason for discarding this aspect of their commitment to Article 3 of the UDHR is that pre-born humans are not to be recognised as 'fully' human. The arguments will be explained further on.

---

[434] Habib Malik (ed.), The Challenge of Human Rights: Charles Malik and the Universal Declaration (Oxford: The Charles Malik Foundation, 2000), 161-162.

Subsequent International Conventions and Covenants concerning Human Rights Law

On the question of human rights, the following Declarations have confirmed the basic principles of the UDHR. The Declaration of the Rights of the Child, adopted by the UN's General Assembly on the 20 November, 1959, specifically affirmed that

> "The child, by reason of his physical and mental immaturity, needs special safeguards and care, including appropriate legal protection, *before as well as after birth*".[435]

This paragraph was included, word for word, in the Preamble to The Convention on the Rights of the Child, also adopted by the General Assembly thirty years later (20 November 1989). The importance of the words in italics for the rights of the unborn child cannot be overemphasised. It is logical to assume that "the special safeguards and care, including legal protection," means that the pre-born infant's right to life must be legally protected by all the nations which have approved the two Documents. It also means that the human entity in utero is accorded the same status as the one who is born. They are both referred to as 'the child'. There is an unbroken continuity between the living human being before and after birth. The question immediately arises, how can the legalisation of abortion be reconciled with the appropriate legal protection due to the child before, as well as after birth? Surely it is imperative to assume that this protection before birth is only applicable if the infant is alive.

The phrase quoted is a clarification of what was assumed by the drafting committee of the UDHR not to need specifying, since "all human beings" of necessity covered the unborn child. To quote Charles Malik again:

---

[435] Emphasis added

"While the delegations of...three countries wished to omit the phrase 'from the moment of conception' in the interests of brevity, they considered the idea to be implied in the general terms of Article 3".[436]

The International Covenant on Civil and Political Rights (ICCPR) (1966) in its Article 6 (5) protects the right to life of the unborn child in cases where their mothers otherwise would have been sentenced to death:

"Sentence of death shall not be imposed for crimes committed by persons below eighteen years of age and shall not be carried out on pregnant women."

The International Covenant on Economic, Social and Cultural Rights (1966) in its Article 12(2) (a) recognises that the unborn child requires human rights protection:

"1. The States, Parties to the present Covenant, recognize the right of everyone to the enjoyment of the highest attainable standard of physical and mental health'.

2. The steps to be taken by the States, Parties to the present Covenant, to achieve the full realization of this right shall include those necessary for:

(a) The provision for the reduction of the stillbirth-rate and of infant mortality and for the healthy development of the child".

In interpreting the implications of these injunctions to member States, who were signatories to the two Conventions, it should be understood that the UN's Declaration on the Rights of the Child had already stated that the word 'child' includes those as yet unborn.

---

[436] United Nations, 'Summary of the Record of the 35th meeting on Human Rights, Drafting Committee on an International Bill of Rights', 2nd session, p.5.

Here there is incontrovertible evidence that these three Conventions and Covenants, solidly embedded in international law, recognised that the pre-born human being has an inalienable right to life. Moreover,

> "no argument was made against (any of these) proposals to the effect that the unborn child does not possess human rights as such, and no argument was made to the effect that there is a human right to abortion."[437]

The Vienna Convention on the Law of Treaties (VCLT) (1969), Articles 31 and 32 state that

> "1. A treaty shall be interpreted in good faith in accordance with the ordinary meaning to be given to the terms of the treaty in its context and in the light of its object and purpose.
>
> 2. Recourse may be had to supplementary means of interpretation, including the preparatory work of the treaty and the circumstances of its conclusion, in order to confirm the meaning resulting from the application of article 31, or to determine the meaning when the interpretation according to article 31:
>
> (a) Leaves the meaning ambiguous or obscure; or
>
> (b) Leads to a result which is manifestly absurd or unreasonable."

It can be reliably asserted that in none of the cases where the word 'child' is mentioned in any of these treaties is the word either 'ambiguous', 'obscure', or 'leads to a result manifestly absurd or unreasonable'. The conclusion to this discussion, therefore, based on the textual evidence of the three international Covenants is that the inalienable right to life of the unborn

---

[437] 'Summary of the Record...', 5.

child is protected in international law. As a result, abortion clearly contravenes such a right.

How come, then, that States that have duly signed these binding treaties, have also passed laws that contravene the provisions that safeguard the right to life of all unborn children? Reasons given to turn the provisions on their head and justify abortion, in some cases up to birth, will now be considered.

Human rights philosophy reinterpreted

If, as has been shown, International Declarations and Treatises declare that the unborn child belongs inherently among the members of the "whole human family," and if it is a reality that

> "honest and scientifically informed thinkers in favour of abortion rights know that the unborn entity is a human being, and that they usually...subscribe to at least some vestigial respect for the idea that it is intrinsically wrong to kill innocent persons,"[438]

a challenging dilemma for pro-abortionists has been created.

> "The obvious solution...is to deny that unborn human beings are moral persons (or, what is essentially the same thing, possess equal human dignity). *For the denial to be minimally plausible, of course, it must appeal to a criterion of moral personhood (or of possessing human dignity) the unborn fail to satisfy*".[439]

In point of fact, such a necessary intellectual move simply created another dilemma, although one that has never been recognised by pro-abortion pressure groups. In their opinion the move, which became indispensable in

---

[438] 'The Right to Life', 15.
[439] 'The Right to Life', 15 (emphasis added).

order to defend the notion of a 'right of abortion', could be justified by divorcing the notion of personhood from that of being human. In doing this, they divorced themselves from the whole long tradition of human rights philosophy and law, enshrined in the four UN documents that have been mentioned above. The reinterpreted definition of personhood that was adopted related to a human being's ability to operate at a level of self-consciousness.

This created two more dilemmas. Firstly, it introduced into the discussion an extrinsic criterion that human beings had to adhere to, whilst the preceding foundation for human rights was always linked indisputably to just being human. A human being, at any stage of gestation, was automatically considered to be a person, because of their intrinsic dignity and worth. Secondly, it was obliged to discover a means of ascertaining exactly when the capacity to act self-consciously actually kicked in.

The consequence of adopting this new criterion for distinguishing personhood from humanness meant that new-born babies were equally excluded from being what might be called a full-blown person, a factor that has been seized on by those in favour of infanticide in some circumstances.[440] Indeed, logically, justifying the right of abortion on the premise that the pre-born is not a person also establishes the right to end the life of anyone who has not yet achieved the status of being able to function self-consciously:

> "This rationale for legalised killing is tantamount to holding that a human being in a Persistent Vegetative State...is sub-personal and, therefore, does not possess equal human dignity".[441]

By extension this could also be applied to the case of young people, at a

---

[440] The kind of arguments adduced to defend infanticide on the basis of the new version of personhood can be followed in Alberto Giubilini and Francesca Minerva, 'After-Birth Abortion: Why Should the baby Live? Journal of Medical Ethics, Vol. 39, No. 5 (2013), 261-263.
[441] The Right to Life', 16.

later stage in their development, who exhibit profound mental incapacities. The problem is easy to detect. There is no wholly unambiguous way of deciding when a human being switches from being a non-person and gains the status of personhood. What might be considered by abortionists as a clever ploy, in order to affirm that abortion does not contravene an unconditional human right (presumably by States passing laws that allow it to happen), actually unravels the whole human rights discourse.

The logical consequences that follow are absolutely immense, even though they may be unintended (at least by some pro-abortion groups). If personhood is dependent on achieving a level of self-consciousness that passes the criterion for counting as a person, before which a human being could only be on the way to the finishing line, then some can be judged to be more worthy of esteem than others. There is a whiff in the air that societies, by a series of logical steps from the absolute right of abortion to conclusions about certain classes of severely disabled human beings, are heading towards the approval of eugenics as a practice.

This is not a fantasy. During the summer of 2020, the founder of the US abortionist establishment, Planned Parenthood, Margaret Sanger, was exposed as having a sympathy for the implementation of a eugenics programme, on the grounds that it would be better if certain breeds of people were not born. Planned Parenthood of Greater New York announced in July 2020 that

> "The removal of Margaret Sanger's name from our building is both a necessary and overdue step to reckon with our legacy and acknowledge Planned Parenthood's contributions to historical reproductive harm within communities of color."[442]

---

[442] Likewise, "A leading (British) abortion provider has changed its name to break ties with Marie Stopes, the controversial birth control pioneer who believed in the creation of a super race:

In recent times, some governments have passed laws that allow abortions to take place up to birth. One reason given is that the baby is shown to be carrying a physical defect, as minor as a cleft-lip or club-foot. It is easy to see where the revisionist account of personhood is likely to lead. The idea that society can introduce a gradation in the worthiness of people on the basis of an extrinsic criterion that has to be justified by society shows that this account is fundamentally incompatible with basic human equality. This equality can only be based on the one criterion that a living human being, before and after birth, whatever their capacities, is by definition a person.

Societies that have legislated for abortion have now, over seven decades after the UDHR was approved by the General Assembly of the UN, turned a full circle. Instead of the uncompromising commitment to the unequivocal equality and intrinsic dignity of all human beings, these societies now deem some human beings to possess mental, physical, psychological and moral qualities superior to others:

> "Any position that concedes that some are more persons than others, and that these others can have their basic interests deliberately destroyed on the condition that persons overall benefit ('the greater good') is a position that is implicitly utilitarian and cannot credibly affirm...Article 3 of the UDHR (that) "everyone has a right to life"[443].

The only argument for abortion that attempts any kind of fundamental moral rationalisation is based on this incoherent argument that humanness and personhood are two distinct features to be applied to different stages of a human's development. By this token, a mother is considered to be fully a

---

"Marie Stopes International, which provides contraception and abortions to women and girls in 37 countries, is now known as MSI Reproductive Choices. The charity said her views on eugenics were in "stark contrast" to its values. Stopes was a member of the Eugenics Society and advocated for the sterilisation of people considered unfit for parenthood", see, https://www.bbc.co.uk/news/uk-54970977, 17 November, 2020.
The change of name hardly disassociates the organisation from its founder, seeing that MSI still keeps her name.
[443] 'The Right to Life', 20.

person, whilst the baby she is carrying is judged to have not yet achieved that status. The consequence of such a false contention is that her rights trump those of the baby she wishes to be rid of.

The argument is based on a consequentialist theory of moral norms, which in this case states that the supreme ethical test is that of discerning how an undesirable result can be avoided. In reality, abortion is not defended on any universally recognised moral principle: it does not arise from the intrinsic, inherent dignity of the whole human family from conception till death, but from emotional considerations, rooted only in the individual self. This latter is an exceedingly poverty-stricken foundation for enacting coherently grounded laws, capable of being approved on the basis of morally consistent and responsible arguments that can become part of international covenants and treaties.

Eleanor Roosevelt (the chair-person of the UDHR drafting committee), in a telling riposte to another member's assertion that, as dignity is not a human right, it should not be included in any of the UDHR's Articles, replied, "human dignity explains why we have rights in the first place".[444] Tragically, the decriminalisation of abortion, not only annuls a crucial part of those international law documents that treat crucial aspects of human rights, it negates the very basis of human rights *per se*. It would seem, therefore, that those institutions, associations and societies committed to overturning laws, enacted by nations who signed these documents, by permitting the non-criminal activity of deliberately killing the most vulnerable and innocent of human persons, should be held to account for encouraging nations to flout international conventions they have signed up to.

---

[444] See, Mary Ann Glendon, A World Made New: Eleanor Roosevelt and the Universal Declaration of Human Rights (New York: Random House, 2001), 66-67.

APPENDIX B

Transgender identity and its ideological roots

Introduction

Behind the controversy surrounding the claim that people can change their gender by stating that they no longer identify with the sex 'assigned' to them at birth,[445] lies a set of philosophical, moral and political assumptions. Together these form an ideology that has become a powerful tool in the hands of those promoting the alleged reality that one's sex is not fixed for life, but is fluid and changeable.

Ideologies are intellectual movements that advocate specific political ends. In the twentieth century Communism, for example, was identified as an ideology based on a system of belief, grounded in the thinking of Marx, Engels and Lenin. It combined theories with political strategies for change.[446] The current defence of transgender identity (transgenderism) is clearly an ideology, in that it combines both intellectual theories and practices designed to bring about fundamental changes in contemporary societies. These beliefs and tactics are the subject of this brief study.[447]

---

[445] The word 'assigned,' used by transgender people of their birth sex, is a cunningly employed euphemism. It is, of course, incorrect. The proper word to use is 'recognised' or 'identified,' seeing that a person's birth sex is immutable. Physiologically speaking it cannot, on the whim of the individual concerned, ever be changed.
[446] The article in the Britannica gives a useful definition of its history and component parts, see https://www.britannica.com/topic/ideology-society.
[447] Two recently published books probe persuasively the theoretical assumptions and practical programmes of transgender ideology, see, Helen Pluckrose and James Lindsay, Cynical Theories: How Universities Made Everything about Race, Gender, and Identity – and Why This Harms Everybody (Rugby: Swift Press, 2020), Carl R. Trueman, The Rise and Triumph of the Modern Self: Cultural Amnesia, Expressive Individualism, and the Road to Sexual Revolution (Wheaton IL: Crossway, 2020).

The theoretical origins of transgenderism in post-modern philosophy

The philosophical under-girding of transgenderism was originally supplied by the intellectual movement known as post-modernity, conceived as a set of assumptions based on a particular reading of history. It was formulated mainly by a number of French academics in the 1970s and early 1980s, of whom the most well-known were Lyotard, Foucault, Derrida, and Baudrillard:

> "Post-modernity can best be described as a complex cultural and social movement...premised on a thoroughgoing critique of the normal assumptions associated with the Enlightenment".[448]

It comes as a strong critique of the presumptions of modernity, namely the power of rational thinking to discover truth about the world, the status of science as the norm for objective thinking, the universal nature of human beings, ethical principles of right and wrong as absolute demands on conscience, universal human rights and the inviolable nature of individuals. Modernity was castigated as a meta-narrative, i.e. an over-arching interpretation which explains the whole of reality. In its place, early post-modernity understood history to be composed of a discontinuous succession of fairly random events without any transcendental meaning or purpose. There is no one story, only many stories. It

> "exposes the pretensions of the modern discourse, and in particular the claims sometimes made on behalf of science that it has the power to deliver an increasingly problem-free world...(It) defends the legitimate aspirations of 'the other', namely those who are 'different' from me, giving them the right to shape their beliefs and lives in accordance with their own subjectivity...It allows for a heterodoxy which challenges the 'orthodoxy' of a late capitalist, globalised system, which

---

[448] The Future of Reason, 18.

manifestly coerces and oppresses vast segments of humanity... It is iconoclastic, irreverent, counter-cultural. It is highly compatible with a post-revolutionary...pluralist age...It challenges...modernity with its passionless rationalism and unremitting tedium".[449]

Above all, post-modernity affirms that objective reality does not exist. It is always exposed to subjective interpretations. There are no criteria in existence that can state definitively, this is the truth about the way things are. On the contrary, beliefs are a matter of social construction. By and large, they are imposed from above by those who have inherited or gained social and political power in a society. So, post-modernity in its original presentation is an exercise in the deconstruction of an ongoing, destructive power-play, engineered mainly by white, and highly educated, middle-class males against the legitimate interests of non-white, less well-educated, lower-class people:

"It is largely a reaction against something else...It knows what it does not like, but is confused about alternatives".[450]

The second stage of transgender ideology

The first wave of post-modern thought, then, aimed to deconstruct what well-educated, Western peoples tended to take for granted concerning the way an objective, real world could be known and handled. It sought to overthrow the convictions implanted by the impact of modernity, a system of belief founded on the following principles: rationality; the ability to know the truth; the universal and absolute nature of moral values; the inviolable dignity of every single human individual; the sure method of scientific methodology, based on verifiable and falsifiable evidence, to uncover the reality of the natural world. Post-modernity sought to overturn the

---

[449] The Future of Reason, 19.
[450] The Future of Reason, 19.

confidence that modern people had in their own identity, and in their understanding of how social and political life should be best organised. In other words, it was intended as a disruption of a particular interpretation of history, with the aim of emancipating thought from archaic traditions and setting it on an upward, progressive path towards a better life for all.

However, it remained largely an intellectual movement that did not engender any clear strategy for transforming what it considered a deluded interpretation of recent history, in order to promote a different way of conceiving social ends and means. In other words, it did not respond positively to Karl Marx's famous eleventh thesis on Feuerbach:

"The philosophers have only interpreted the world, in various ways; the point, however is to change it".

Pluckrose and Lindsay summarise post-modernity's initial failure to engage realistically with the kind of life they despised:

"Despite proving simultaneously modish and influential, this approach has its limits. Endless dismantling and disruption- or, as they call it, *deconstruction* - is not only destined to consume itself; it is also fated to consume everything interesting and thus render itself *boring*...That is Theory couldn't content itself with nihilistic despair. It needed something to do, something actionable. Because of its own morally and politically charged core, it had to apply itself to the problem it saw at the core of society: unjust access to power... But postmodernism did not die. From the ashes arose a new set of Theorists whose mission was to make some core tenets of postmodernism applicable and to *reconstruct* a better world".[451]

In a nutshell the new post-modernity became a forceful advocate of political engagement to secure lasting change in the legal recognition of

---

[451] Cynical Theories, 45-46 (emphasis is original).

presumed identity concerns felt by some minority groups. It also engaged in the political programme of advancing a cause that would eventually take route in the consciousness of cultures as a whole. Thus, for example, the rights in law of adult homosexual relationships was not considered to be acceptable enough to meet the claims of gay-leaning minority groups. The initial T (Transgender) was added to the acronym LGB (Lesbian, Gay, Bisexual), which previously was used as an emblem of the demand that homosexually-inclined people be acknowledged as a minority group that deserves a specially protected status. This action produced the desired effect. In light of attempts to discriminate against their legitimate claims to equal treatment in society, homosexuality and transgender were added to sex, race/ethnicity, religion, age and disability as protected characteristics of groups whose rights were deemed worthy of special safeguarding and promotion.

Alongside the political agitation to ensure new laws were passed to champion the entitlement of these new groups, a fresh vocabulary was created with the intention of educating the general population into the acceptance of a new interpretation of socially acceptable behaviour and the destigmatisation of outmoded conventions. Words like tolerance, equality, discrimination, diversity, rights, choice, progressive, offence, bigotry and hate began to be used, not so much in their hitherto accepted sense, but as a militant means to change people's mind-sets. In order for this to be accomplished novel meanings were injected into their employment.[452] As Pluckrose and Lindsay rightly say,

> "The intense scrutiny of language and development of ever stricter rules for terminology pertaining to identity often known as *political correctness* came to a head in the 1990s"[453]

---

[452] In my book, The Abuse of Language, I have described the way in which these words and others have been hijacked to fulfil specific ideological tasks in favour of the next philosophical shift being undertaken by a subsequent generation of post-modern idealists.
[453] Cynical Theories, 62 (emphasis is original).

The second wave of post-modern theory emphasised, then, the power of language either to promote or counter-act the 'accepted' way of interpreting and changing social norms. The protagonists set about instigating new speech codes: for example, tolerance mutated into intolerance for any non-acceptable views; equality became a slogan for preferred opinions, as in 'equal marriage'; discrimination became a buzz-word used for anything considered by campaigning groups to be unfair treatment; progressive meant ideas or actions a particular group approved of; diversity came to mean the acceptance of all opinions held by 'oppressed' minority groups (religious groups being excluded) and their favoured standing in such matters as job selection; homophobia and transphobia were invented to categorise negatively all those who denied, on the basis of well-researched evidence, that either homosexual preference or transgender existence were immutable, and so on.

Populations in the Western world are now continuously under scrutiny by the 'politically correct,' to ascertain whether, or not, they are using language according to the approved meaning of the new lexicon. The underlying cause of this struggle to change the normal meaning of language, or to invent new words, lies in the philosophical confusion engendered by post-modern thought. At its root exists the belief that the realities of an objective world, subsisting independently of human perceptions and internal impressions, cannot be discovered as undeniable facts of existence.

This is a frontal attack on the possibility of anything being known about the world, and human existence within it, as justifiably true. All talk about objective truth and its opposite, error, falsehood and fallacy, is interpreted as the means by which the powerful and privileged impose their view of life on 'marginalised' identity groups, denying them the entitlements to which they are due. This position is highly ironic, and wholly inconsistent, for the same group appeals to an objective truth that

> "some identities were privileged over others and that this injustice is objectively true...the second wave of (*applied*)

postmodernists focused on dismantling hierarchies and making truth claims about power, language and privilege... Theory underwent a *moral* mutation: it adopted a number of beliefs about the rights and wrongs of power and privilege".[454]

In other words, in order to promote their scheme, post-modernists could not escape from the need to appeal to objective facts and absolute statements of moral right and wrong. However, there remains a considerable gulf set between the 'modern' and 'post-modern' means of achieving presumed objective knowledge. In the latter case, a different form of knowledge was hailed as the only kind of information that anyone could be certain about. It springs from the shared experiences of members of identity groups, who have been the unjust victims of incorrect theory, social hostility and political inequity. To give one example, this fundamental change in human cognition accounts for the popular mantra in transgender circles that "a transwoman is a woman" and "menstruates". To summarise this 'brave new world',

> "knowledge is inadequate unless it includes the experiential knowledge of minority groups... The knowledge produced by dominant groups – including science and reason – is... merely the product of their cultural traditions and is not superior to the knowledge produced by other cultural traditions".[455]

The logical conclusion to this way of viewing theory is that legitimate disagreement is not an option. Not only that, but to oppose this kind of post-modern thinking is insincere and exhibits profound moral failure. It is the result of systemic bigotry. In reality, what is being witnessed in this discourse is pure dogma, not open to confirmation or refutation by normal rational criteria. Post-modern theory in this guise has enclosed itself in a solipsistic bubble of its own creating.

---

[454] Cynical Theories, 48 (emphasis is original).
[455] Cynical Theories, 196.

The third stage of transgender ideology

Pluckrose and Lindsay detect a third wave of post-modern philosophy, as it pertains to all forms of sexual identity, arising around the year 2010. It may be characterised by looking at the promotion of Queer (Q) theory. The original sexual revolution covered lesbianism (L), male homosexuality (G - 'gay') and bisexuality (LGB). To this was added transgenderism (T) at a later stage. Subsequently Q was added to the acronym and the plus sign + came at the end to indicate the plethora of different sexualities available for anyone with enough imagination to invent, and claim them as a recognizable right.

One understanding of Queer theory is that it

"Refers to the destabilization of categories and the disruption of norms or accepted truths associated with it".[456]

Thus, for example, 'woman' does not indicate a particular class of people but a performance that engenders a socially constructed reality. Historically speaking, so it is affirmed, gender, sex and sexuality have always complied with socially imposed norms. This paves the way for Queer theory to deny the binary division of the human sexes, based on their immutable biological certainty. This, perhaps curiously, leads further to a denial of the fixed categories, L, G, B and even T, for each one requires belief in what is called 'sexual essentialism'. That would imply that there are innate factors, biological and psychological impressions, stamped upon a minority of people from birth onwards – they are "born that way".

According to this theory, essentialism makes the mistake of rooting its argument in the true nature of things. Whilst, in the real world, sexuality is a fluid concept. It is not surprising, therefore, that 'well-established' feminists have been vociferous in challenging the notion of self-chosen gender, on the grounds that it completely evacuates womanhood of any consistent

---
[456] Cynical Theories, 54.

content, and thus implicitly denies women the specific rights that they have so long struggled for.

It is surprising, therefore, and inconsistent that LGB campaigning groups like Stonewall have willingly added T and Q to the acronym that has become the accepted emblem of their causes. If the advocates of T and Q theory were to be correct in their assumption that sexual self-identification is a fluid matter, so that it may change from time to time, then LGB orientation, by the same reasoning, is also flexible. Any person may come to the conclusion that their sexual orientation has mutated. By a logical extension of this way of thinking, change counselling, for those who freely wish to modify their homosexual attraction, should be a normal psychotherapeutic practice.

So, although advocates of Queer theory would probably deny some of the implicit conclusions that should be drawn from their beliefs, it would be logical to infer that, if sexuality is fluid, then it is changeable. If it is changeable, then people who once declared themselves to be homosexually inclined can, at a later stage in their understanding, transform their identity perception into being heterosexual (the reverse process has never been questioned by the LGB lobby). Likewise transgender people can recover their conformity to their biological sex. This should mean that the intense pressure currently being aimed at banning freely-chosen therapy, intent on modifying sexual identity, would have no basis in the theory being promoted by third-wave post-modernity.

The main problem with all notions of sexuality, based on the refusal to listen to properly validated evidence, is that civilised dialogue is thrown out of the window. Trevor Philips, the former director of the British Equalities Commission, has written a pungent article in The Times Newspaper,[457] referring to the increasing advance of certain sectors of society, not open to admitting that their theories might be open to challenge. Amongst other

---

[457] 'The March of Wokeism is an All-pervasive Oppression,' The Times Newspaper, November 7. 2020.

matters, he confronts the 'woke' self-image as stemming from the imposition by a small minority of their often narrow interpretations of equality, diversity, justice and tolerance:

> "the woke affect to care for the excluded...They present themselves as passionate campaigners for justice, yet they are ready to yield to the whims of the mob and dole out summary retribution to anyone deemed a heretic...They purport to seek greater diversity, yet require all women or all ethnic minorities to share their view or be branded quislings."

> "The drive for decency," he says, "is steadily being hijacked by extremists, bringing a dark edge of censoriousness to the quest for better workplace behaviour".

He asks the question whether "the identity of the individual using (certain kinds of) language makes a difference to its acceptability?" He goes on to speak of "a kind of speech apartheid, and a whole new chapter in censorship". As a black man himself, a person who has spent a life-time working for an end to racial injustices, he sees clearly how much damage is being done to the cause of real justice to the 'oppressed' minorities by a small coterie of self-righteous, virtue-seeking 'extremists' (his word). This is where the cultural war, initiated by the false philosophy of post-modernity, has reached its malignant, contemporary resting-place.

Perhaps the most threatening of all its manifestations is the current push to reclassify the meaning of so-called hate-speech in ways that will inevitably curtail further the already creeping restrictions on the freedom of speech, so eloquently stated in Article 19 of the UDHR, and subsequently upheld by further internationally promulgated Declarations and Covenants:

> "Everyone has the right to freedom of opinion and expression; this right includes freedom to hold opinions without interference and to seek, receive and impart information and ideas through any media and regardless of frontiers".

It follows, then, that the first question to ask of attempts to curtail free-speech (expressing the liberty "to hold opinions without interference") is how can these be justified on the basis of universal human rights? According to international human rights' law, they cannot.

The theoretical origins of transgenderism in redesigning the self

Whilst echoing the historical analysis presented above in drawing the conclusions of post-modern thought for the sexual revolution, Carl Trueman expounds a slightly different historical narrative.[458] He draws on the presuppositions of the Romantic movement of the 18th and 19th centuries, and their subsequent followers, as the key to understanding the present radical shift in affirming authentic knowledge about human life.

From the objective world, presupposed by the scientific enterprise, a number of writers, poets, artists, and philosophers inaugurated a turn to the inner, psychological life of feelings and intuitions. They proposed an inward quest for personal psychological comfort and well-being. As there was no intrinsic basis in nature, and even less in a non-material spiritual sphere, to glean a cogent meaning for human existence, the opaque depths of the inner life were cast as the route to real knowledge. He cites persons such as Rousseau, Wordsworth, Shelley, Blake and De Quincey as the chief protagonists of this profound shift inwards to the acquiring of 'true' knowledge. Charles Taylor in his magnum opus, *A Secular Age*, characterises the turn inwards as expressive individualism and the culture of authenticity:

> "The understanding of life which emerges with the Romantic expressivism of the late eighteenth century, is that each of us has his/her own way of realising our humanity, and that it is important to find and live out one's own..."[459]

---

[458] The Rise and Triumph of the Modern Self.
[459] A Secular Age, 475.

Trueman summarises what he calls "the intuitive moral structure of our modern social imaginary"[460] in these terms:

"(It) prioritizes victimhood, sees selfhood in psychological terms, regards traditional sexual codes as oppressive and life-denying, and places a premium on the individual's right to define his or her own existence".[461]

What has happened in Western culture over the last 250 years is a move from one view of the world to another completely different (from what has been called mimesis to poiesis):

"These two terms refer to two different ways of thinking about the world. A mimetic view regards the world as having a given order and a given meaning and thus sees human beings as required to discover that meaning and conform themselves to it. Poiesis, by way of contrast, sees the world as so much raw material out of which meaning and purpose can be created by the individual".[462]

The change of perspective is extremely profound. The main consequence of the shift is that humans are now destined to create their own meaning, purpose in life and identity from within their own internal imagination. The corollary is that any idea of what it means to be human given from outside one's own self-consciousness, especially if its source is rooted in a traditional belief system, is to be treated with deep suspicion. Truths about life, even if confirmed by careful scientific analysis, if they come from an external source are deemed to be social constructs invented by those whose aim is to intimidate and abuse credulous people.

Such is the explanation of the transgender consciousness. The inner,

---
[460] Imaginary is used as a term to explain a general consensus in society around the legitimacy of certain moral values and behaviours.
[461] The Rise and Triumph, 63.
[462] The Rise and Triumph, 39.

subjective world is the only source of knowledge and understanding that the individual can be certain about. Nothing from the objective reality of the given natural world, even less that of a message revealed from a Supreme Being supposed to have created the living world, can persuade purveyors of transgender convictions to change their minds. There is, however, a deep problem for a person who relies on their subjective experience to be the final word of truth for them personally. They are unable to connect with a world that exists outside themselves, when it counters their own cherished ideals.

The effect of this mindset on moral reasoning, discernment and action is quite devastating. Personal preferences are substituted for universal moral imperatives. What 'feels' right is right. No arguments are need to justify opinions. Moral assertions are given the status of moral norms. They are considered sufficient to reject contrary beliefs as always rooted in other people's personal prejudices. The result is that ethical discussion becomes an exercise in who can shout the loudest. It is transformed into a polemical battle in which the winner takes all. In fact it is an exercise in the manipulation of power in the interests of personal shibboleths, the very reality that third wave post-modernists abominate.

Conclusion

This brief summary of how and why transgender confusion has erupted so swiftly and confusingly in contemporary societies has revealed that its main cause lies in its fallacious intellectual theories. In order to be able to help people (especially adolescents), captured by misunderstanding and confusion, with gentleness and sympathetic care, it is necessary to arrive at its root cause.

Hopefully, after a time of growth in the upheaval and upset being currently caused by misinterpretations and mistreatments of the symptoms being experienced and shown, the lives of transgender-inclined people can be restored to a natural, common sense way of life. That is what the vast majority of any population, who care genuinely for their highest well-being, would want for disorientated individuals, influenced to believe something about themselves which is both false and destructive.

Bibliography

American College of Obstetricians and Gynecologists, The and American Board of Obstetrics & Gynecology, The, *Joint Statement on Abortion Access During the COVID-19 Outbreak,'* 18 March, 2020

Anderson, Ryan T. and Desanctis, Alexandra, *Tearing us Apart: How Abortion Harms Everything and Solves Nothing* (Regenery Publishing, 2022)

Anderson, Ryan T. and Verner, Adam, *Truth Overruled: The Future of Marriage and Religious Freedom* (Regenery Publishing, 2015)

Anderson, Ryan T. and George P. George, *What is Marriage? Man and Woman: A Defense* (Black Hills Audio Books, 2020)

Bayer Ronald, *Homosexuality and American Psychiatry: The Politics of Diagnosis* (Princeton: Princeton University Press, 1987)

Belusek, Darrin, *Marriage, Scripture and the Church; Theological Discernment on the Question of Same-Sex Union* (MI: Grand Rapids, Baker Academic, 2021)

Blair, K. L., & Hoskin, R. A., 'Transgender exclusion from the world of dating: Patterns of acceptance and rejection of hypothetical trans-dating partners as a function of sexual and gender identity,' *Journal of Social and Personal Relationships, 36* (7), 2074-2095 (2019)

Branstrom, Richard, John E. Pachankis, 'Reduction in Mental health Treatment Utilization Among Transgender Individuals after Gender-Affirming Surgeries: A Total Population Study', *American Journal of Psychiatry, Vol. 177, Issue 8,* published online, 1 August, 2020

Bronte, Anne, *The Tenant of Wildfell Hall* (London: Collins, 1954) (first published in 1848)

Bryan, Jonathan, *Eye Can Write: A memoir of a child's silent soul emerging* (London: Lagom, 2018)

Caird, G.B., *The Revelation of St John the Divine* (London: A and C Black, 1966)

Carson, D.A., *The Gospel according to John* (Leicester: IVP, 1991)

Carter, Warren, *John: Storyteller, Interpreter, Evangelist* (Peabody: Hendrickson Publishers, 2006)

Chaplin, Jonathan, 'A Time to Marry – Twice', *Ethics in Brief*, Vol. 18, No. 2, 2012

Churcher-Clarke, Anna and Spiliadis, Anastassis, 'The Value of Extended Clinical Assessment for Adolescents presenting with Gender Identity Difficulties' (Research Article) in *Clinical Child Psychology and Psychiatry* (February 6, 2019).

Convention on the Rights of the Child, The (published in November 1989); see, https://www.humanium.org/en/convention/text/

Cretella, Michelle A., Van Meter, Quentin, McHugh, Paul, 'Gender Ideology Harms Children', (Report of the American College of Pediatricians, September 2017)

Davie, Martin (et al.), *New Dictionary of Theology: Historical and Systematic* (London: Inter-Varsity Press, 2016/2)

Diamond, Lisa M. and Rosky, Clifford J., 'Scrutinizing Immutability: Research on Sexual

Diamond, Lisa M., Orientation and U.S. Legal Advocacy for Sexual Minorities,' *The Journal of Sex Research* 53(2016): 363-391

Diamond, Lisa, M, *Sexual Fluidity: Understanding Women's Love and Desire* (CambridgeMass.:Harvard University Press, 2008)

Dummitt, Christopher, 'I Basically Just Made It Up: Confessions of a Social Constructionist', *Quillette*, September 17, 2019

Erasmus, Desiderius, *Praise of Folly* (Harmondsworth, UK: Penguin, 1993/2)

European Convention on Human Rights, Protocol, Article 2, 'Right to Education'

Evans, Marcus, 'Freedom to think: the need for a thorough assessment and treatment of gender dysphoric children', *BJPsych Bulletin, doir:10.1192/bjb.2020.72*, 3

Favale, Abigail, *The Genesis of Gender: A Christian Theory* (San Francisco, CA: Ignatius Press, 2022)

Finegan, Tom, 'The Right to Life in International Human Rights Law', published on-line by the Heritage Foundation, January 24, 2020

Goddard, Andrew, 'Reframing the Same-sex Marriage Debate', *Ethics in Brief*, vol. 18, no. 4, 2013

Graham, Robert (et al.), 'The Health of Lesbian, Gay, Bisexual and Transgender People: Building A Foundation for Better Understanding' *Report from the US Institute of Medicine (IOM)* (Washington, DC: The National Academies Press, 2011)

Ganna, Andrea (et al.), 'Large-Scale GWAS reveals insights into the genetic architecture of same-sex behavior,' *Science* (Abstract), 30 August, 2019

Gay, Peter, *The Freud Reader* (New York: Norton, 1995)

Giubilini, Alberto and Minerva, Francesca, 'After-Birth Abortion: Why Should the baby Live? *Journal of Medical Ethics*, Vol. 39, No. 5 (2013)

Glendon, Mary Ann, *A World Made New: Eleanor Roosevelt and the Universal Declaration of Human Rights* (New York: Random House, 2001)

Grams, Rollin G., Marshall, I. Howard, Penner, Peter and Routledge, Robin (Eds.), *Bible and Mission: A Conversation between Biblical Studies and Missiology* (Schwarzenfeld, Germany: Neufeld Verlag, 2008)

Griffin Lucy, Clyde Katie, Byng Richard and Bewley Susan, 'Sex, gender and gender identity: a re-evaluation of the evidence', *BJPsych Bulletin*, 2020, doi: 10.1192/bjb.2020.73, 3.

Heinrichs, Terry, 'Transgenderism: Thinking Makes it so? *The American Spectator*, 15 October 2019.

Hursthouse, Rosalind, 'Virtue Theory and Abortion' in Hugh LaFollette (Ed.), *Ethics in Practice:Anthology* (Oxford: Blackwell Publishers, 2002/2)

Jacobson, Thomas W. and Johnston, William Robert (Eds.), *Abortion: Worldwide Report* (West Chester, Ohio: Global Life Campaign, 2018)

James,Sharon, *Lies we are Told, the Truth we must hold: World-views and their Consequences* (Fearn, UK: Christian Focus Publications, 2022)

James, Sharon, *Gender Ideology: What do Christians Need to Know?* (Fearn, UK: Christian Focus Publications, 2019)

Jones, Stanton and Yarhouse, Mark, 'A Longitudinal Study of Attempted Religiously Mediated Sexual Orientation Change." *Journal of Sex and Marital Therapy*, 37 (5), 2011, 404–27

Katz, Jonathan, *The Invention of Heterosexuality* (Chicago: University of Chicago Press, 2007/2)

Kearns, Madeleine, 'The Origins of the Transgender Movement', *National Review*, 14 October 2019

Kirk, J. Andrew, *The Meaning of Freedom: A Study of Secular, Muslim and Christian Views* (Carlisle: Paternoster Press, 1998)

_____*The Future of Reason, Science and Faith: Following Modernity and Post-Modernity* (Aldershot: Ashgate Publishing, 2007)

_____*Civilisations in Conflict: Islam, the West and Christian Faith* (Oxford: Regnum Books International, 2011)

_____ *The Church and the World: Understanding the Relevance of Mission* (Milton Keynes: Paternoster, 2014)

_____*Being Human: An Historical Inquiry Into Who Who We Are* (Eugene, OR: Wipf and Stock, 2019)

_____*The Abuse of Language and the Language of Abuse* (Tolworth, UK: Grosvenor House Publishing, 2019)

Lyotard, *The Postmodern Condition: A Report on Knowledge* (Manchester, UK: Manchester University Press, 1984)

MacLanahan, Sara, Tach, Laura and Schneider, Daniel, 'The Causal Effects of Father Absence,' *Annual Review of Sociology*, 39, (July 2013), 399-427

Malik, Habib (ed.), *The Challenge of Human Rights: Charles Malik and the Universal Declaration* (Oxford: The Charles Malik Foundation, 2000) Marquis, Don, 'An Argument that Abortion is Wrong' in LaFollette, Hugh, (ed.), *Ethics in Practice: An Anthology* (Oxford: Blackwell Publishers, 2002/2)

Mary Anne Warren, 'On the Moral and Legal Status of Abortion' in *Peter Singer (ed.), A Companion to Ethics* (Oxford: Blackwell Publishers, 1993)

Mayer, Lawrence S. and McHugh, Paul R., 'Sexuality and Gender: Findings from the Biological, Psychological and Social Sciences', *The New Atlantis*, Fall 2016

Mueller, Sven C., 'Mental health Treatment Utilization in Transgender Persons: What we Know and What We Don't Know (editorial), *American Journal of Psychiatry, Vol. 177, Issue 8,* published online, 1 August, 2020

Murray, Douglas, *The Madness of Crowds: Gender, Race and Identity* (London: Bloomsbury Continuum, 2019)

Musser, Donald W. and Price, Joseph L. (eds.), *A New Handbook of Christian Theology* (Cambridge: The Lutterworth Press, 1992)

Perry, Louise, *The Case Against the Sexual Revolution: A New Guide to Sex in the 21st Century* (Cambridge, Polity Press, 2022)

Pluckrose, Helen and Lindsay, James, *Cynical Theories: How Universities Made Everything about Race, Gender, and Identity – and Why This Harms Everybody* (Rugby: Swift Press, 2020)

Philip Rieff, *Sacred Order/Social Order* (Charlottesville: University of Virginia Press, 2006-2008)

Rivers, Julian, 'Redefining Marriage: the case for caution,' *Cambridge Papers*, Vol. 21, No. 3, September 2012

Rosick, Christopher, 'Motivational, Ethical and Epistemological Foundations in the Treatment of Unwanted Homoerotic Attraction,' *Journal of Mental and Family Therapy*, Vol. 29, 1, 13, January 2003

Royal College of General Practitioners,The, 'The role of the GP in caring for gender-questioning and transgender patients', 10 July, 2019.

Santero, Paul L., Whitehead, Neil E., and Ballesteros, Dolores, 'Effects of Therapy on Religious Men Who Have Unwanted Same-Sex Attraction', *The Linacre Quarterly XX(X)*, 2018, 1-17

Sartre, Jean-Paul, *Existentialism is a Humanism* (New Haven, CT: Yale University Press, 2007)

Sigmund, Paul E. (ed.), *The Selected Political Writings of John Locke* (New York: Norton, 2005)

Soh, Debra, *The End of Gender: Debunking the Myths about Sex and Identity in our Society* (New York: Simon and Schuster, 2020)

Sprigg, Peter, 'Evidence Shows Sexual Orientation Can Change: Debunking the Myth of "Immutability," ' *Family Research Council*, March 2019. Issue Analysis IS19C01

Stanton, Glenn T., 'Why Sex and Gender are not Two Different Things', *The Federalist*, 15 October, 2019

Stark, Rodney, *The Triumph of Christianity: How the Jesus Movement Became the World's Largest Movement* (New York: Harper Collins, 2012)

Todorov Tzvetan, *The Imperfect Garden: The Legacy of Humanism*

(Princeton, NJ: Princeton University Press, 2002)

Tom Holland, *Dominion: The Making of the Western Mind* (London: Little, Brown, 2019)

Trueman, Carl R., *The Rise and Triumph of the Modern Self: Cultural Amnesia, Expressive Individualism, and the Road to Sexual Revolution* (Wheaton IL: Crossway, 2020)

Vonholdt, Christi. R., 'The Deconstruction of Marriage and Family', *German Institute for Youth and Society*, March 2003

Watkins, Christopher, *Biblical Critical Theory: How the Bible's Unfolding Story Makes Sense of Modern Life and Culture* (Grand Rapids, MI: Zondervan, 2022)

Witte, *The Western Case for Monogamy over Polygamy* (Cambridge: CUP, 2015)

Wright, Tom, *History and Eschatology* (London: SPCK, 2019)

Index

Abortion, 240, 253, 268-278
and being human (personhood), 38-41, 50-52, 113-118, 275-278
and the COVID-19 pandemic, 32-35, 223-25
and the law, 29-32
and the use of language about the unborn, 113-117
decriminalisation, 31, 117
law and moral virtue, the, 53-55
survival of aborted babies, 222
Abortion Act, The (1967), 32, 35-36, 221
Amazon company, 227-228
American College of Pediatricians, 234
American Psychological Association, 227-228
Bieber, Irving, 68
Christian faith, 21-22
cleanliness and uncleanness, 170-171
gaining the world and forfeiting one's life, 172-173
the seed that dies, 173-174
the truth will make you free, 174-175
Christian heritage, 21
Christian moral codes, 24, 246-249
Church-State relationship, 22
Church, The, 165-167

a new community, 190-200
its beginning, 165-167
its prophetic mission, 259-252, 266
College for Sexual and Relationship Psychotherapy, The, 90
Common-sense, 239, 243
Constantine, 22
Convention on the Rights of the Child (1989), The, 271-272
Council for Psychotherapy (UK), 64
Cultural shift, 21
Diagnostic Statistical Manual of Mental Disorders, 229
Downs Syndrome, 31
Drag, 230-231
Dummitt, Christopher, 106-108, 138-139
Enlightenment, Age of, 83, 218
Environment, The, 23
Erasmus, Desiderius, 109 112, 139
Existentialism, 85
Family life, 58-59
Fertilisation and human life, 222
Foolishness, 110-111
Foucault, Michel, 106
Free-speech, 23
Freud, Anna, 69
Freud, Sigmund, 68, 252-253, 254

Gender, 233-234
  facts, 235-237
  meaning, 233
  nonconformity, 75
  theory, 105-108
General Medical Council, 237
Hate speech, 139-140, 288-289
'Health and Reproductive Rights', 30, 35, 116
Homophobia, 87
Human Fertilisation and Embryology Act, The (1990), 30
Human identity, 37, 39,
Humanism, secular, 21, 25, 84, 85, 119
Human rights, 21, 220, 268-270
Ideology, 279
Imago Dei, 40-41
Infanticide, 47-50
Infant Life (Preservation) Act, The (1929), 30
International Covenant on Civil and Political Rights (1966), 272
International Covenant on Economic, Cultural and Social Rights (1966), 272
Islam, 36
Jesus, the Christ, 25
  and the good news of God's kingdom. 158, 163
  baptism, 157-158
  conversation with Nicodemus, 160-161
  nature of his kingship, 184-186
  temptation, 159-160
  the gift of God's Holy Spirit, 188-189
  trial before Pilate, 163-164, 176-178
  Joseph of Arimathea, 164
Language, 24
LGBT+, 64, 71, 74, 75, 81, 85, 102, 104, 225, 227, 228
Newton, John, 266-267
Malik, Charles, 270
Manifesto of the Gay Liberation Front, (1971), 58-59
Mayer, Lawrence A and McHugh, Paul R, 69-70
McHugh, Paul, 228
Monogamy, life-long, 58
Mother's rights, The, 43-46, 116-118
Murray, Douglas, 119-121, 229
Offences against the person Act (1861), 29-30
Peter, apostle, 198
Philips, Trevor, 287
Planned Parenthood, 34, 276
Post-modernity, 153-156, 280-283
  second-stage, 281-285
  third stage, 286-289
Poverty, 23
Queer Theory, 286-287
Resurrection of Christian believers, 204-205
Right to life, The, 41-42, 269
Romantic Movement, 289

Roosevelt, Eleanor, 278
Royal College of General Practitioners, 237
Royal College of Psychiatrists, The, 63
Sanger, Margaret, 276
Sartre, Jean-Paul, 84-86
Saul of Tarsus (the apostle Paul), 189-199
Science and religious belief, 153
Scriptures, the Christian, 22, 26, 144-151, 144-157, 152-154
   explanation, 152-153
   inspiration, 144
   interpretation, 147-151
   nature,145-146
   purpose, 147
Self, The, 289-291
Sermon on the Mount, 167-171
   Beatitudes, The, 167-170
Sexuality,
   a gift from God, 57
   and biological definition, 79
   and brain-structure, 80
   and discrimination, 94
   and human rights, 121-123, 126-127
   and marriage, 91-94, 118-119
   and same-sex attraction, 66-70
   and science, 61-62, 123
   and sex-education, 95-104
   and the law, 260-261
   and verification of its truth, 59-60
   as a political project, 119-123

   from birth? 64-67, 255-257, 262-263
   its importance, 57-60
   its binary nature, 118-119
   mental health and stress, 70-75
Sexual orientation
   and scientific evidence, 62-63, 124-126, 225-227
   an explanation, 63-65
   change, 90-91, 123,126
   re-orientation therapy, 89, 226-228, 242, 257-259
   variability, 87-92
Stonewall riots (1969), 85
Stopes, Marie, 277
Taylor, Charles, 289
Toleration, 23
Transgenderism, 75-81, 104, 126-140, 217, 281, 283-286
   and detransitioning, 135
   and its ideological origin, 137-140. 228-233, 281, 289-292
   and possible causes, 135-136, 230-232
   and the development of children, 126-129
   and the law (a case-study), 239-240
   and therapeutic practice, 130-133, 242
   definition, 127
   irreversible damage, 238, 258-260
   reality and fantasy, 243-244, 259-261, 262-263

Transphobia, 139-140, 264-265
Trueman, Carl, 289
Truth, 120, 155, 175-176
   and evidence, 155-156
United Nations Declaration on the Rights of the Child (1959), 220. 271-172
Universal Declaration of Human Rights, 268-270
Vienna Convention on the Law of Treaties (1969), 273
West, the, 21, 22,24, 25, 36-39, 63, 82, 109-110, 139
World (s), 23,26, 57, 86, 178-186
   its destructive impulse, 251-252
   new, 58, 157-164, 188-200
   new heavens and a new earth, 201-213
   pictures of, 207-213
   two worlds in conflict, 187, 189-191, 218-219, 244-246, 265-266
World Health Organisation, 31, 76
World-views, 26, 83-87

About the Author

J. Andrew Kirk has spent most of his adult life in theological education. After a three year curacy in a North London parish, where he met his future wife, he lived and taught in Buenos Aires, Argentina. There with his growing family (3 children) for 12 years, he worked with a number of different theological institutions.

He was a founder member of the Latin American Theological Fraternity (1970) and the Kairos Community (1976). Whilst in Latin America he wrote on the use of the Bible in Liberation Theology and on the revolutionary nature of Jesus life and ministry.

Returning to the UK, he helped found the London Institute for Contemporary Christianity (a lay academy) and taught there for eight years. He also acted as Theologian Missioner for the Church Mission Society during the same period. Subsequently he was appointed as the Dean of Mission at the Selly Oak Colleges in Birmingham and later a Senior Lecturer at the University of Birmingham in the field of Mission Studies.

Since retirement in 2002, he has been involved with theological institutions in the UK, Prague, Amsterdam and Budapest. He has also been involved in leading study sessions in Romania, Sweden, Singapore, the Lebanon, Armenia, South Korea and New Zealand. He.has continued writing. His latest books are *Being Human: An Historical Inquiry into Who We Are*, *The Abuse of Language and the Language of Abuse* (both published in 2019), and *Truth to Tell: Basic Questions and Best Explanations* (published in 2021). He has had 21 books published over a period of 50 years (three in Spanish). Some of his books have been translated into Portuguese, German, Swedish and Korean.

He is married to Gillian. They have four grandchildren. When not staring at a screen, he busies himself in local ministry, gardening, walking, playing badminton, trying to finish crosswords and supporting Arsenal FC.